AN AMERICAN FOUR-IN-HAND
IN BRITAIN

LECTOR HOUSE PUBLIC DOMAIN WORKS

AN AMERICAN FOUR-IN-HAND IN BRITAIN

ANDREW CARNEGIE

ISBN: 978-93-89679-65-6

Published: 1899

LECTOR HOUSE LLP
E-MAIL: lectorpublishing@gmail.com

AN AMERICAN FOUR-IN-HAND IN BRITAIN

BY

ANDREW CARNEGIE

1899.

I DEDICATE THESE PAGES
TO
MY FAVORITE HEROINE,
MY MOTHER.

PREFACE.

The publication of this book renders necessary a few words of explanation. It was originally printed for private circulation among a few dear friends — those who were not as well as those who were of the coaching party — to be treasured as a souvenir of happy days. The house which has undertaken the responsibility of giving it a wider circulation believed that its publication might give pleasure to some who would not otherwise see it. It is not difficult to persuade one that his work which has met with the approval of his immediate circle may be worthy of a larger audience; and the author was the more easily induced to consent to its reprint because, the first edition being exhausted, he was no longer able to fill many requests for copies.

The original intent of the book must be the excuse for the highly personal nature of the narrative, which could scarcely be changed without an entire remodelling, a task for which the writer had neither time nor inclination; so, with the exception of a few suppressions and some additions which seemed necessary under its new conditions, its character has not been materially altered. Trusting that his readers may derive from a perusal of its pages a tithe of the pleasure which the Gay Charioteers experienced in performing the journey, and wishing that all may live to see their "ships come home" and then enjoy a similar excursion for themselves, he subscribes himself,

Very Sincerely,
THE AUTHOR

New York, May 1, 1883.

CONTENTS

AN AMERICAN FOUR-IN-HAND IN BRITAIN.

Long enough ago to permit us to sing, "For we are boys, merry, merry boys, Merry, merry boys together," and the world lay all before us where to choose, Dod, Vandy, Harry, and I walked through Southern England with knapsacks on our backs. What pranks we played! Those were the happy days when we heard the chimes at midnight and laughed Sir Prudence out of countenance. "Dost thou think, because thou art virtuous, there shall be no more cakes and ale?" Nay, verily, Sir Gray Beard, and ginger shall be hot i' the mouth too! Then indeed

> "The sounding cataract
> Haunted me like a passion; the tall rock,
> The mountain, and the deep and gloomy wood,
> Their colors and their forms, were then to me
> An appetite; a feeling and a love
> That had no need of a remoter charm,
> By thought supplied, or any interest
> Unborrowed from the eye."

It was during this pedestrian excursion that I announced that some day, when my "ships came home," I should drive a party of my dearest friends from Brighton to Inverness. Black's "Adventures of a Phaeton" came not long after this to prove that another Scot had divined how idyllic the journey could be made. It was something of an air-castle—of a dream—those far-off days, but see how it has come to pass!

Air-Castles.

The world, in my opinion, is all wrong on the subject of air-castles. People are forever complaining that their châteaux en Espagne are never realized. But the trouble is with them—they fail to recognize them when they come. "To-day," says Carlyle, "is a king in disguise," and most people are in possession of their air-castles, but lack the trick to see 't.

Look around you! see Vandy, for instance. When we were thus doing Merrie England on foot, he with a very modest letter of credit stowed away in a belt round his sacred person—for Vandy it was who always carried the bag (and a faithful treasurer and a careful one too—good boy, Vandy!); he was a poor student then, and you should have heard him philosophize and lord it over us two, who had been somewhat fortunate in rolling mills, and were devoted to business. "Great Cæsar! boys, if I ever get fifteen hundred dollars a year income!" (This was the fortune I was vaguely figured up to be worth under ordinary conditions.) "Great

Cæsar! boys"—and here the fist would come down on the hard deal table, spilling a few drops of beer—"fifteen hundred dollars a year! Catch me working any more like a slave, as you and Harry do!" Well, well, Vandy's air-castle was fifteen hundred dollars a year; yet see him now when thousands roll in upon him every month. Hard at it still—and see the goddess laughing in her sleeve at the good joke on Vandy. He has his air-castle, but doesn't recognize the structure.

There is Miss Fashion. How fascinating she was when she descanted on her air-castle—then a pretty cottage with white and red roses clustering beside the door and twining over it in a true-lover's knot, symbolizing the lover's ideal of mutual help and dependence—the white upon the red. No large establishment for her, nor many servants! One horse (I admit it was always to be a big one), and an elegant little vehicle; plenty of garden and enough of pin money. On this point there was never to be the slightest doubt, so that she could really get the best magazines and one new book every month—any one she chose. A young hard-working husband, without too much income, so that she might experience the pleasure of planning to make their little go far. Behold her now! her husband a millionaire, a brown-stone front, half a dozen horses, a country place, and a box at the opera! But, bless your heart! she is as unconscious of the arrival of her castle as she is that years creep upon her apace.

The Goddess Fortune, my friends, rarely fails to give to mortals all they pray for and more; but how she must stand amazed at the blindness of her idolators, who continue to offer up their prayers at her shrine, wholly unconscious that their first requests have been granted! It takes Fortune a little time to prepare the gifts for so many supplicants—the toys each one specially wants; and lo and behold! before they can be delivered (though she works with speed betimes) the unreasonable mortals have lost conceit of their prizes, and their coming is a mockery; they are crying for something else. If the Fates be malignant, as old religions teach, how they must enjoy the folly of man!

Imagine a good spirit taking Fortune to task for the misery and discontent of mortals, as she gazes with piteous eyes upon our disappointments, our troubles, and, saddest of all, our regrets, charging her with producing such unhappiness. "Why have you done this?" would be the inquiry. Listen to the sardonic chuckle of the Fate: "Hush! I've only given them what they asked (chuckle—chuckle—chuckle)! Not my fault! See that unhappy wretch, sleeplessly and feverishly tossing on his pillow, and in his waking hours absorbing all his lofty faculties in gambling at the Stock Exchange—wife, children, home, music, art, culture, all forgotten. He was once a bright, promising, ingenuous youth. He was born among trees and green fields, spent the morn of life in the country, sensitive and responsive to all nature's whisperings; lay in cool, leafy shades, wandered in forest glades, and paddled in the 'complaining brooks which make the meadow green.' Nay, not many years ago he returned at intervals to these scenes, and found their charm had still power over him—felt the truth of the poet's words, that

> "'To him who in the love of nature holds
> Communion with her visible forms, she speaks
> A various language; for his gayer hours

> She has a voice of gladness, and a smile
> And eloquence of beauty, and she glides
> Into his darker musings, with a mild
> And healing sympathy, that steals away
> Their sharpness, ere he is aware.'

"He asked for enough to live honorably upon among his fellows," continues the Fate, "and to keep his parents comfortable in their old age—a matter of a few hundreds a year—and I gave him this and thousands more. Ha, ha, ha! Silence! Look at him; he doesn't see the joke. Oh yes, you may try to tell it to him, if you like. He has no time to listen, nor ears to hear, nor eyes to see; no, nor soul to understand your language. He's 'short' on New Jersey Central or 'long' on Reading, and, bless you! he must strain every fibre if he would save himself from ruin.

"He could commune with you in your youth, you say; he had your language then. No doubt! no doubt! so did he then know his Latin and whisper his prayers at his mother's knee. The Latin has gone; his praying continues—nay has increased, for his fears and selfish wants have multiplied since he was an innocent, ignorant child, and he has much more to ask from God for his own ends, now that he is a wise man and is supposed to know much (chuckle—chuckle—chuckle).

"There is another mortal," we hear the Fate saying to the Good Fairy. "Look at her, decked out in all the vagaries of changeable Fashion; note her fixed-up look, her conventional air, her nervous, unmeaning, simpering smile—the same to-day, yesterday, and forever—something to all men, much to none. See her at home in her chamber! Why mopes she, looking so haggard, with features expressionless and inane? What worm gnaws at her heart and makes her life so petty? She, too, came into the world a bright and happy thing, and grew up fond of music and of birds, and with a passion for flowers and all of Nature's sweets; so careful, too, of mother and of father, the very embodiment of love to all around her. You should have seen her in her teens, a glorious ray from heaven—'making a sunshine in a shady place'—so natural, so hearty, with a carolling laugh like the falling of waters. In her most secret prayers she asked only for a kind lover with a fair competence, that they might live modestly, without ostentation. She was a good girl and I granted her wish and more," says Fate. "Her air-castle was small, but I sent her a magnificent one. She is courted, flattered, has every gift in my power to bestow; yet she pines in the midst of them. The fruits of her rare gardens have no flavor for her—Dead Sea fruits indeed, which fall to ashes on her lips. She has entered for the race of Fashion, and her soul is absorbed in its jealousies and disappointments. You may speak to her as of old; tell her there is something noble in that domain of human life where duties grow—something not only beyond but different from Fashion, higher than dress or show. She understands you not.

"Hand her a bunch of violets. Does she learn their lesson with their odor (which her dog scents as well as she)? Comes there to her the inner meaning, the scent of the new-mown hay that speaks of past hours of purity, of the fresh breeze that fanned her cheek in childhood's halcyon days, the love of all things of the green earth and the sense of the goodness of God which his flowers ever hold within their petals for those who know their language? 'They will decorate me to-night for the ball!' That is the be-all and the end-all of her ladyship's love for flowers.

"Show her a picture with more of heaven than earth in it, and glimpses of the light that never shone on sea or shore. If the artist be in fashion she will call it 'pretty,' when it is grand. Give her music. Is it the opera? Oh yes, she will attend. It is the fashion. But place within her reach the soul-moving oratorio (with more religion in it than in twenty sermons) or the suggestive symphony. No, a previous engagement prevents. Why, just think of it—*one can't talk there!* Yet this woman could once play with feeling and sing with expression, delighting her young companions. Of her one could truly say,

> "'Oh! to see or hear her singing! scarce I know which is divinest—
> For her looks sing too—she modulates her gestures on the tune;
> And her mouth stirs with the song, like song; and when the notes are finest,
> 'Tis the eyes that shoot out vocal light, and seem to swell them on.'

And now she has fallen to this!"

"Has she children?" inquires the Good Spirit.

"No," says Fate, "we are not altogether relentless. How could we give such a woman children and look you in the face? It is sometimes thought necessary even to go as far as this, but in such cases we commend the poor infants to the special care of the great Father, for mother they have none. But look! there is a man now who did so pray for a son and heir that we gave him one, and yonder goes the result. God in heaven! why are men so rash in their blindness as to pray for anything! Surely 'Thy will be done' were best."

I am as bad as Sterne in his "Sentimental Journey," and will never get on at this rate. I started to argue that the Fates were too kind instead of not kind enough; at least, my air-castles have ever been mere toys compared with the realities, for never did I dream, in my wildest days, that the intended drive through Britain would assume the princely proportions of a four-in-hand, crowded with a dozen of my dearest friends. A modest phaeton or wagonette with a pair of horses was the extent of my dream, but the Fairy sent me four, you see, and two friends for every one I had pleased myself with imagining as sure to take the journey with me.

Embarkation.

But now to a sober beginning of the story of the coach. It was in the leafy month of June—the very first day thereof, however—in the year of our Lord 1881, that the good ship Bothnia (Cunard Line, of course), Captain McMicken (a true Scot and bold British sailor), steamed from the future Metropolis of the World for the shores of Merrie England. She had many passengers, but among them were eleven who outranked all others, if their respective opinions of each other were to be accepted as the true standard of judgment. I had received for many months before the sweetest pleasure imaginable in startling first one and then another with requests to report at headquarters, Windsor Hotel, New York, May 31st, prepared to embark. It was on St. Valentine's Day that the Prima Donna received a missive which caused her young heart to flutter. What a pretty reply came! Here is a short extract:

"Three months to dream of it; three months to live in it; and my whole lifetime afterward to think it over. I am the happiest girl alive, only sometimes I can't believe it's all going to happen."

To Davenport, Iowa, went another invitation. In due time came a return missive from the proud City of the River:

"Will I go to Paradise for three months on a coach? Agent of Providence, I will!"

Isn't it glorious to make one's friends so happy?

* * * * *

Harbor of New York, June 1, 1881.
On board Steamer Bothnia.

Call the roll.

Queen Dowager, Head of the Clan (no Salic Law in our family); Miss J. J. (Prima Donna); Miss A. F. (Stewardess); Mr. and Mrs. McC. (Dainty Davie); Mr. and Mrs. K. (Paisley Troubadours); Mr. B. F. V. (Vandy); Mr. H. P., Jr. (Our Pard); Mr. G. F. McC. (General Manager); ten in all, making, together with the scribe, the All-coaching Eleven.

Ting-a-ling-a-ling! The tears are shed, the kisses ta'en. The helpless hulk breathes the breath of life. The pulsations of its mighty heart are felt, the last rope that binds us to land cast off; and now see the hundreds of handkerchiefs waving from the pier fading and fading away. But note among the wavers one slight graceful figure; Miss C. of our party, present in spirit if bodily absent on duty, much to the regret of us all. The wavings from deck to shore tell our friends

"how slow our souls sailed on,
How fast our ship."

On the Bothnia.

The Bothnia turned her face to the east, and out upon old ocean's gray and melancholy waste sailed the Gay Charioteers. As we steamed down the bay three steamers crowded with the most enterprising of Europe's people passed us, emigrants coming to find in the bounteous bosom of the Great Republic the blessings of equality, the just reward of honest labor. Ah, favored land! the best of the Old World seek your shores to swell to still grander proportions your assured greatness. That all come only for the material benefits you confer, I do not believe. Crowning these material considerations, I insist that the more intelligent of these people feel the spirit of true manhood stirring within them, and glory in the thought that they are to become part of a powerful people, of a government founded upon the born equality of man, free from military despotism and class distinctions. There is a trace of the serf in the man who lives contentedly in a land with ranks above him. One hundred and seventeen thousand came last month, and the cry is still they come! O ye self-constituted rulers of men in Europe, know you not that the knell of dynasties and of rank is sounding? Are you so deaf that you do not hear the thunders, so blind that you do not see the lightnings which now and then give warning of the storm that is to precede the reign of the people?

There is everything in the way one takes things. "Whatever is, is right," is a good maxim for travellers to adopt, but the Charioteers improved on that. The first resolution they passed was, "Whatever is, is lovely; all that does happen and all that doesn't shall be altogether lovely." We shall quarrel with nothing, admire everything and everybody. A surly beggar shall afford us sport, if any one can be surly under our smiles; and stale bread and poor fare shall only serve to remind us that we have banqueted at the Windsor. Even no dinner at all shall pass for a good joke. Rain shall be hailed as good for the growing corn; a cold day pass as invigorating, a warm one welcomed as suggestive of summer at home, and even a Scotch mist serve to remind us of the mysterious ways of Providence. In this mood the start was made. Could any one suggest a better for our purpose?

Now comes a splendid place to skip—the ocean voyage. Everybody writes that up upon the first trip, and every family knows all about it from the long descriptive letters of the absent one doing Europe.

When one has crossed the Atlantic twenty odd times there seems just about as much sense in boring one's readers with an account of the trip as if the journey were by rail from New York to Chicago. We had a fine, smooth run, and though some of us were a trifle distrait, most of us were supremely happy. A sea voyage compared with land travel is a good deal like matrimony compared with single blessedness, I take it: either decidedly better or decidedly worse. To him who finds himself comfortable at sea, the ocean is the grandest of treats. He never fails to feel himself a boy again while on the waves. There is an exultation about it. "He walks the monarch of the peopled deck," glories in the storm, rises with and revels in it. Heroic song comes to him. The ship becomes a live thing, and if the monster rears and plunges it is akin to bounding on his thoroughbred who knows its rider. Many men feel thus, and I am happily of them, but the ladies who are at their best at sea are few.

The travellers, however, bore the journey well, though one or two proved indifferent sailors. One morning I had to make several calls upon members below and administer my favorite remedy; but pale and dejected as the patients were, not one failed to smile a ghastly smile, and repeat after a fashion the cabalistic words—"Altogether lovely."

The Atlantic.

He who has never ridden out a hurricane on the Atlantic is to be pitied. It seems almost ridiculous to talk of storms when on such a monster as the Servia. Neptune now may "his dread trident shake" and only give us pleasure, for in these days we laugh at his pretensions. Even he is fast going the way of all kings, his wildest roar being about on a par with the last Bull of the Pope, to which we listen with wonder but without fear.

In no branch of human progress has greater advance been made within the past twenty years than in ocean navigation by steam; not so much in the matter of speed as in cost of transport. The Persia, once the best ship of the Cunard Line, required an expenditure of thirty-five dollars as against her successors' one dollar. The Servia will carry thirty-five tons across the ocean for what one ton cost in the Persia. A revolution indeed! and one which brings the products of American soil close to the British shores. Quite recently flour has been carried from Chicago to Liverpool for forty-eight cents (2s.) per barrel. The farmer of Illinois is as near the principal markets of Britain as the farmer in England who grows his crops one hundred miles from his market and transports by rail; and, in return for this, the pig-iron manufacturer of Britain is as near the New York market as is his competitor on the Hudson.

Some of the good people of Britain who are interested in land believe that the competition of America has reached its height. Deluded souls, it has only begun!

One cannot be a day at sea without meeting the American who regrets that the Stars and Stripes have been commercially driven from the ocean. This always reminds me of a fable of the lion and the turtle. The lion was proudly walking along the shore, the real king of his domain, the land. The turtle mocked him, saying, Oh, that's nothing, any one can walk on land. Let's see you try it in the water. The lion tried. Result: the turtle fed upon him for many days. America can only render herself ridiculous by entering the water. That is England's domain.

> "Her home is on the mountain wave,
> Her march is o'er the deep."

The American Navy.

We are talking just now about building some ships for a proposed American Navy, which is equivalent to saying that we are going to furnish ships to the enemy, if we are ever foolish enough to have one—for it takes two fools to wage war. Unless America resolves to change her whole policy as a republic, teaching mankind the victories of peace, far more renowned than those of war, and goes back to the ideas of monarchical governments, she should build no ships of war; but if she will leave her unique position among the nations, and step down to the level of quarrellers, let her beat the navies of Britain and France, for the ships of a weak naval power are the certain prey of the stronger in time of war. In peace they are useless.

In thinking of the real glories of America, my mind goes first to this—that she has no army worthy of the name, and scarcely a war ship of whose complete inefficiency in case of active service we are not permitted to indulge the most sanguine anticipations.

What has America to do following in the wake of brutal, pugilistic nations still under the influence of feudal institutions, who exhaust their revenues training men how best to butcher their fellows, and in building up huge ships for purposes of destruction! No, no, let monarchies play this game as long as the people tolerate it, but for the Republic "all her paths are peace," or the bright hopes which the masses of Europe repose in her are destined to a sad eclipse.

Travellers know the character and abilities of the men in charge of a Cunard ship, but have they ever considered for what pittances such men are obtained? Captain, $3,250 per annum; first officer, $1,000; second, third, and fourth officers, $600. For what sum, think you, can be had a man capable of controlling the ponderous machinery of the Servia? Chief engineer, $1,250. You have seen the firemen at work down below, perhaps. Do you know any work so hard as this? Price $30 per month. The first cost of a steel ship—and it is scarcely worth while in these days to think of any other kind—is about one-half on the Clyde what it is on the Delaware. Steel can be made, and is made, in Britain for about one half its cost here. Not in our day will it be wise for America to leave the land. It is a very fair division, as matters stand—the land for America, the sea for England.

* * * * *

Friday, June 10, 1881.

Ireland.

Land ahoy! There it was, the long dark low-lying cloud, which was no cloud, but the outline of one of the most unfortunate of lands—unhappy Ireland, cursed by the well-meaning attempt of England to grow Englishmen there. England's experience north of the Tweed should have taught her better.

Conquerors cannot rule as conquerors a people who have parliamentary institutions and publish newspapers; and neither of these can ever be taken away from Ireland. They always come to stay. You may succeed in keeping down slaves for a while, but then you must govern them as slaves, and the Irish people have advanced beyond this. Just in proportion as they do grow less like serfs and more like men, the impossibility of England's governing Ireland must grow likewise. I hear some Americans reproaching the Irish people for rioting and fighting so much; the real trouble is they don't fight half enough. Take my own heroic Scotland; let even Mr. Gladstone, one of ourselves and our best beloved, send an Englishman as Lord Advocate to Scotland, and let him dare pass a measure for Scotland in Parliament against the wishes of the Scotch members, and all the uprisings in Ireland would seem like farces to the thorough work Scotland would make of English interference. She would not stand it a minute. Neither should Ireland. If she has the elements of a great people within her borders, she will never submit. In less than a generation Ireland can be made as loyal a member of the British confederacy as Scotland is; and all that is necessary to produce this is that she should be dealt with as England has to deal with Scotland. Let the Emerald Isle, then, fight against the attempted dominion of England, as Scotland fought against it, and may the result be the same—that Ireland shall govern herself, as Scotland does, through her own representatives duly elected by the people. "To this complexion must it come at last," and the sooner the better for all parties concerned.

We reached Liverpool Saturday morning. How pleasant it is to step on shore in a strange land and be greeted by kind friends on the quay! Their welcome to England counted for so much.

Mr. and Mrs. P. had been fellow passengers. A special car was waiting to take them to London, but they decided not to go, and Mr. P. very kindly placed it at the disposal of Mr. J. and family (who were, fortunately for us, also fellow-passengers) and our party, so that we began our travelling upon the other side under unexpectedly favorable conditions.

To such of the party as were getting their first glimpse of the beautiful isle, the journey to London seemed an awakening from happy dreams. They had dreamed that England looked thus and thus, and now their dreams had come true. The scenery of the Midland route is very fine, much more attractive than that of the other line.

The party spent from Saturday until Thursday at the Westminster Hotel, in monster London, every one being free to do what most interested him or her. Groups of three or four were formed for this purpose by the law of natural selection, but the roll was called for breakfasts and dinners, so that we all met daily and were fully advised of each other's movements.

House of Commons.

The House of Commons claimed the first place with our party, all being anxious to see the Mother of Parliaments. It is not so easy a matter to do this as to see our Congress in session; but thanks to our friend Mr. R. C. and to others, we were fortunate in being able to do so frequently. Our ladies had the pleasure of being taken into the Ladies' Gallery by one of the rising statesmen of England, Sir Charles Dilke, a Cabinet Minister, and one who has had the boldness, and as I think the rare sagacity, to say that he prefers the republican to the monarchical system of government. The world is to hear of Sir Charles Dilke, if he live and health be granted him, and above all, if he remain steadfast to his honest opinions. So many public men in England "stoop to conquer," forgetting that whatever else they may conquer thereafter they never can conquer that *stoop*; that "drags down their life"!

We really heard John Bright speak—the one of all men living whom our party wished most to see and to hear. I had not forgotten hearing him speak in Dunfermline, when I was seven years of age, and well do I remember that when I got home I told mother he made one mistake; for when speaking of Mr. Smith (the Liberal candidate) he called him a *men*, instead of a *maan*. When introduced to Mr. Bright I was delighted to find that he had not forgotten Dunfermline, nor the acquaintances he had made there.

Temperance.

A grand character, that of the sturdy Quaker; once the best hated man in Britain, but one to whom both continents are now glad to confess their gratitude. He has been wiser than his generation, but has lived to see it grow up to him. Certainly no American can look down from the gallery upon that white head without beseeching heaven to shower its choicest blessings upon it. He spoke calmly upon the Permissive Liquor Bill, and gave the ministerial statement in regard to it. All he said was good common sense; we could do something by regulating the traffic and confining it to reasonable hours, but after all the great cure must come from the better education of the masses, who must be brought to feel that it is unworthy of their manhood to brutalize themselves with liquor. England has set herself at last to the most important of all work—the thorough education of her people; and we may confidently expect to see a great improvement in their habits in the next generation. My plan for mastering the monster evil of intemperance is that our temperance societies, instead of pledging men never to taste alcoholic beverages, should be really temperance agencies and require their members to use them only at meals—never to drink wines or spirits without eating. The man who takes *one* glass of wine, or beer, or spirits at dinner is clearly none the worse for it. I judge that if the medical fraternity were polled, a large majority would say he was the better for it, at least after a certain age. Why can't we recognize the fact that all races indulge in stimulants and will continue to do so? It is the regulation, not the eradication, of this appetite that is practical. The coming man is to consider it low to walk up to a bar and gulp down liquor. The race will come to this platform generations before they will accept that of Sir Wilfrid Lawson and his total abstinence ideas.

This was written before the Church of England movement in this direction was known to me. Much good must come of its efforts; but I confess I should like to see that church show that it is in earnest by removing the deep reproach cast upon it by recent statements, which pass uncontradicted. Listen to this startling announcement: This holy Church of England, mark you, is the largest owner of gin palaces in the world. The head of the church, the Archbishop of Canterbury, in passing from his palace at Lambeth to his abbey at Westminster, sees more than one hundred (I believe I understate the case) gin palaces which his church owns and has rented for such purposes; nay, it is shown that the church has always raised the rents of these houses, with which licenses go, as the sales of liquor have increased; so that her interest lies in extending the use of liquors as a beverage secretly upon one hand, while she poses before the world as laboring to restrict the curse with the other. Her right hand knows only too well what her left hand doeth. It does seem that the mere announcement of such a fact would work its own remedy—perhaps it will when its holy fathers are done with the vastly more important business of determining the size and shape of vestures, or the number of candles, or the posture of the priest most pleasing to God—but before the church can figure as much of an agency in the cause of temperance reform, it will have to wash its hands of its hundred gin palaces.

The article in *Harper's Magazine* upon Bedford Square, giving glowing accounts of this Arcadian colony, with its æsthetic homes, its Tabard Inn, and its club, made us all desire to visit it. We did so one afternoon, and received a very cordial welcome from Mrs. C. in the absence of her husband. She kindly showed us the grounds and explained all to us. Truth compels me to say we were sadly disappointed, but for this we had probably only ourselves to blame. It is so natural to imagine that exquisite wood-cuts and pretty illustrations set forth grander things than exist. The houses were much inferior to our preconceived ideas, and many had soft woods painted, and most of the cheap shams of ordinary structures. The absence of grand trees, shady dells, and ornamental grounds, and the exceedingly cheap and cheap-looking houses made all seem like a new settlement in the Far West rather than the latest development of culture. From this criticism Mr. C.'s own pretty little home is wholly exempt, and no doubt there are many other homes there equally admirable. I speak only of the general impression made upon our party by a very hasty visit. Bedford Park is no doubt an excellent idea, and destined to do much good, only it is different from what we had expected.

Stafford House.

Extremes meet. It was from houses such as I have spoken of that we went direct to Stafford House, to meet the Marquis of Stafford by appointment, and to be shown over that palace by him. What a change! If the former were not up to our expectations, this exceeded them. I don't suppose any one ever has expected to see such a staircase as enchants him upon entering Stafford House. This is the most magnificent residence any of us has ever seen. I will not trust myself to speak of its beauties, nor of the treasures it contains. One begins to understand to what the Marquis of Stafford is born. The Sutherland family have a million two hundred thousand acres of land in Britain; no other family in the world compares with them as landowners. It is positively startling to think of it. Almost the entire County of Sutherland is theirs. Stafford House is their London residence. They have Trentham Hall and Lillieshall in Mid-England, and glorious Dunrobin Castle in Scotland.

The Marquis sits in the House of Commons as member for Sutherland County; and what do you think! he is a painstaking director of the London and North-Western Railway, and I am informed pays strict attention to its affairs. The Duke of Devonshire is Chairman of the Barrow Steel Company. Lord Granville has iron works, and Earl Dudley is one of the principal iron manufacturers of England. It is all right, you see, my friends, to be a steel-rail manufacturer or an iron-master. How fortunate! But the line must be drawn somewhere, and we draw it at trade. The A. T. Stewarts and the Morrisons have no standing in society in England. They are in vulgar trade. Now if they brewed beer, for instance, they would be somebodies, and might confidently look forward to a baronetcy at least; for a great deal of beer a peerage is not beyond reach.

We heard a performance of the "Messiah" in Albert Hall, which the Prima Donna agreed with me was better in two important particulars than any similar performance we had heard in America. First in vigor of attack by the chorus; this was superb; from the first instant the full volume and quality of sound were perfect. The other point was that all-important one of enunciation. We have no chorus in New York which rivals what we heard, though we have an orchestra which is equal to any. The words were, of course, familiar, and we could scarcely judge whether we were correct in our impression, but we believed that even had they been strange to us we could nevertheless have understood every word. Since my return to New York I have heard this oratorio given by the Oratorio Society, and am delighted to note that Dr. Damrosch has greatly improved his chorus in this respect; but the English do pronounce perfectly in singing. This opinion was confirmed by the music subsequently heard in various places throughout our travels. In public as well as in private singing the purity of enunciation struck us as remarkable. If I ever set up for a music teacher I shall bequeath to my favorite pupil as the secret of success but one word, *"enunciation."*

Parliament.

Some of us went almost every day to Westminster, but dancing attendance upon Parliament is much like doing so upon Congress. The interesting debates are few and far between. The daily routine is uninteresting, and one sees how rapidly all houses of legislation are losing their hold upon public attention. A debate upon the propriety of allowing Manchester to dispose of her sewage to please herself, or of permitting Dunfermline to bring in a supply of water, seems such a waste of time. The Imperial Parliament of Great Britain is much in want of something to do when it condescends to occupy its time with trifling questions which the community interested can best settle; but even in matters of national importance debates are no longer what they were. The questions have already been threshed out in the Reviews—those coming forums of discussion—and all that can be said already said by writers upon both sides of the question who know its bearings much better than the leaders of party. When the *Fortnightly* or the *Nineteenth Century* gets through with a subject the Prime Minister only rises to sum up the result at which the Morleys and Rogerses, the Spencers and Huxleys, the Giffens and Howards have previously arrived.

The English are prone to contrast the men of America and England who are in political life, and the balance is no doubt greatly in their favor. But the reason lies upon the surface: America has solved the fundamental questions of government, and no changes are desired of sufficient moment to engage the minds of her ablest men. During the civil war, when new issues arose and had to be met, the men who stepped forward to guide the nation were of an entirely different class from those prominent in politics either before or since. Contrast the men of Buchanan's administration with those the war called to the front—Lincoln, Seward, Stanton, Sumner, Edmunds, Morton, or the generals of that time, with Grant, Sherman, Sheridan, Hancock. All of these men I have known well, except one or two of the least prominent. I have met some of the best known politicians in England. Compared morally or intellectually, I do not think there is much, if any, difference between them; while for original creative power I believe the Americans superior. That a band of men so remarkable as to cause surprise to other nations will promptly arise whenever there is real work to do, no one who knows the American people can doubt; but no man of real ability is going to spend his energies endeavoring to control appointments to the New York Custom House, any more than he will continue very long to waste his time discussing Manchester sewage. Much as my English friends dislike to believe it, I tell them that when there is really no great work to be done, when the conflict between feudal and democratic ideas ends, as it is fast coming to an end, and there is no vestige of privilege left from throne to knighthood, only vain, weak men will seek election to Parliament, and such will stand ready to do the bidding of the constituencies as our agents in Congress do. But this need not alarm our English friends; there will then be much less bribery before election and much less succumbing to social court influences after it. The brains of a country will be found where the real work is to do. The House of Lords registers the decrees of the House of Commons. The House of Commons is soon to register the decrees of the monthlies. Both these things may be pronounced good. In the next generation the debates of Parliament will affect the political currents of the age as little as the fulminations of the pulpit affect religious thought at present; and then a man who feels he has real power within him will think of entering Parliament about as soon as he would think of entering the House of Lords or the American Congress.

"The parliament of man, the federation of the world,"

comes on apace; but its form is to be largely impersonal. The press is the universal parliament. The leaders in that forum make your "statesman" dance as they pipe.

The same law is robbing the pulpit of real power. Who cares what the Reverend Mr. Froth preaches nowadays, when he ventures beyond the homilies? Three pages by Professor Robertson Smith in the "Encyclopædia Britannica" destroy more theology in an hour than all the preachers in the land can build up in a lifetime. If any man wants *bona fide* substantial power and influence in this world, he must handle the pen—that's flat. Truly, it is a nobler weapon than the sword, and a much nobler one than the tongue, both of which have nearly had their day.

We had a happy luncheon with our good friends the C.'s, one of our London days; and some of our party who had heard that there was not a great variety of edibles in England saw reason to revise their ideas. Another day we had a notable procession for miles through London streets and suburbs to the residence of our friend, Mr. B. Five hansoms in line driven pell-mell reminded me of our Tokio experiences with gin-rikshaws, two Bettos tandem in each.

The Stars and Stripes.

It was a pretty, graceful courtesy, my friend, to display from the upper window the "Stars and Stripes," in honor of the arrival of your American guests, and prettier still to have across your hall as a portière, under which all must bow as they entered, that flag which tells of a government founded upon the born equality of man. Thanks! Such things touch the heart as well as the patriotic chord which vibrates in the breast of every one so fortunate as to claim that glorious standard as the emblem of the land he fondly calls his own. Colonel Robert Ingersoll, that wonderful orator, says that when abroad, after a long interval, he saw in one of the seaports the Stars and Stripes fluttering in the breeze, "he felt the air had blossomed into joy." It was he too who told the South long ago that "there wasn't air enough upon the American continent to float two flags." Right there, Colonel!

Do you know why the American worships the starry banner with a more intense passion than even the Briton does his flag? I will tell you. It is because it is not the flag of a government which discriminates between her children, decreeing privilege to one and denying it to another, but the flag of the people which gives the same rights to all. The British flag was born too soon to be close to the masses. It came before their time, when they had little or no power. They were not consulted about it. Some conclave made it, as a pope is made, and handed it down to the nation. But the American flag bears in every fibre the warrant, "*We the People in Congress assembled.*" It is their own child, and how supremely it is beloved!

It is a significant fact that in no riot or local outbreak have soldiers of the United States, bearing the national flag, ever been assaulted. Militia troops have sometimes been stoned, but United States troops never. During the worst riot ever known in America, that in our own good city of Pittsburgh, Pennsylvania, twenty-eight United States soldiers, all there were in the barracks, marched through the thousands of excited men unmolested. I really believe that had any man in the crowd dared to touch that flag, General Dix's famous order would have been promptly enforced by his companions. Major-General Hancock recently told me that he had never known United States soldiers to be attacked by citizens. He was in command of the troops during the riots in the coal regions in Pennsylvania some years ago, and whenever a body of his regulars appeared they were respected and peace reigned.

General Dix's order was, "If any man attempts to pull down the flag shoot him on the spot." So say we all of us. And it will be the same in Britain some day, ay and in Ireland too, when an end has been made of privilege and there is not a government and a people, but only a government of the people, for the people, and by the people. The day is not so far off either as some of you think, mark me.

But good-bye, London, and all the thoughts which crowd upon one when in your mighty whirl. You monster London, we are all glad to escape you! But ere we "gang awa'" shall we not note our visit to one we are proud to call our friend, and of whom Scotland is proud, Dr. Samuel Smiles, a writer of books indeed—books which influence his own generation much, and the younger generation more. Burns's wish was that he,

> "For poor auld Scotland's sake,
> Some useful plan or book could make,
> Or sing a sang at least."

Well, the Doctor has made several books that are books, and I have heard him sing a song, too, for the days of Auld Lang Syne. May he live long, and long may his devoted wife be spared to watch over him!

* * * * *

Thursday Morning, June 16, 1881.

Brighton.

We are off for Brighton. Mr. and Miss B. accompany us. Mr. and Mrs. K. have run up to Paisley with the children, and Mr. and Mrs. G. have joined us in their place. The coach, horses, and servants went down during the night.

We had time to visit the unequalled aquarium and to do the parade before dinner. Miss F. and I stole off to make a much more interesting visit; we called upon William Black, whose acquaintance I had been fortunate enough to make in Rome, and whom I had told that I should some day imitate his "Adventures of a Phaeton." A week before we sailed from New York, I had dined with President Garfield at Secretary Blaine's in Washington. After dinner, conversation turned upon my proposed journey, and the President became much interested. "It is the 'Adventures of a Phaeton' on a grand scale," he remarked. "By the way, has Black ever written any other story quite so good as that? I do not think he has." In this there was a general concurrence. He then said: "But I am provoked with Black just now. A man who writes to entertain has no right to end a story as miserably as he has done that of 'MacLeod of Dare.' Fiction should give us the bright side of existence. *Real life has tragedies enough of its own.*"

A few weeks more and we were to have in his own case the most terrible proof of the words he had spoken so solemnly. I can never forget the sad, careworn expression of his face as he uttered them.

> "But come it soon or come it fast,
> It is but death that comes at last."

One might almost be willing to die if, as in Garfield's case, there should flash from his grave, at the touch of a mutual sorrow, to both divisions of the great English-speaking race, the knowledge that they are brothers. This discovery will bear good fruit in time.

> "Nothing in his life became him like the leaving it."

Garfield's life was not in vain. It tells its own story—this poor boy toiling upward to the proudest position on earth, the elected of fifty millions of freemen; a position compared with which that of king or kaiser is as nothing. Let other nations ask themselves where are *our* Lincolns and Garfields? Ah, they grow not except where all men are born equal! The cold shade of aristocracy nips them in the bud.

William Black.

Mr. Black came to see us off, but arrived at our starting-place a few minutes too late. A thousand pities! Had we only known that he intended to do us this honor, until high noon, ay, and till dewy eve, would we have waited. Just think of our start being graced by the author of "The Adventures of a Phaeton," and we privileged to give him three rousing cheers as our horn sounded! Though grieved to miss him, it was a consolation to know that he had come, and we felt that his spirit was with us and dwelt with us during the entire journey. Many a time the incidents of his charming story came back to us, but I am sorry to record, as a faithful chronicler, that we young people missed one of its most absorbing features—we had no lovers. At least, I am not apprized that any engagements were made upon the journey, although, for my part, I couldn't help falling in love just a tiny bit with the charming young ladies who delighted us with their company.

*　*　*　*　*

BRIGHTON, Friday Morning, June 17.

The Supreme Moment.

Let us call the roll once more at the door of the Grand Hotel, Brighton, that our history may be complete: Mr. and Mrs. B., London; Mr. and Mrs. T. G., Wolverhampton; Miss M. L., Dunfermline; Miss E. F., Liverpool; Mr. and Mrs. McC., Miss J. J., Miss A. F., Mr. B. F. V., Mr. H. P., Jr., Mr. G. F. McC., the Queen Dowager and the Scribe. These be the names of the new and delectable order of the Gay Charioteers, who mounted their coach at Brighton and began the long journey to the North Countrie on the day and date aforesaid. And here, O my good friends, let me say that until a man has stood at the door and seen his own four-in-hand drive up before him, the horses—four noble bays—champing the bits, their harness buckles glistening in the sun; the coach spick and span new and as glossy as a mirror, with the coachman on the box and the footman behind; and then, enchanted, has called to his friends, "Come, look, there it is, just as I had pictured it!" and has then seen them mount to their places with beaming faces—until, as I say, he has had that experience, don't tell me that he has known the most exquisite sensation in life, for I know he hasn't. It was Izaak Walton, I believe, who when asked what he considered the most thrilling sensation in life, answered that he supposed it was the tug of a thirty-pound salmon. Well, that was not a bad guess. I have taken the largest trout of the season on bonnie Loch Leven, have been drawn over Spirit Lake in Iowa in my skiff for half an hour by a monster pickerel, and have played with the speckled beauties in Dead River. It is glorious; making a hundred thousand is nothing to it; but there's a thrill beyond that, my dear old quaint Izaak. I remember in one of my sweet strolls "ayont the wood mill braes" with a great man, my Uncle Bailie M.—and I treasure the memory of these strolls as among the chief of my inheritance—this very question came up. I asked him what he thought the most thrilling thing in life. He mused awhile, as was the Bailie's wont, and I said, "I think I can tell you, Uncle." "What is it then, Andrea?" (Not And*rew* for the world.) "Well, Uncle, I think that when, in making a speech, one feels himself lifted, as it were, by some divine power into regions beyond himself, in which he seems to soar without effort, and swept by enthusiasm into the expression of some burning truth, which has lain brooding in his soul, throwing policy and prudence to the winds, he feels words whose eloquence surprises himself, burning hot, hissing through him like molten lava coursing the veins, he throws it forth, and panting for breath hears the quick, sharp, explosive roar of his fellow-men in thunder of assent, the precious moment which tells him that the audience is his own, but one soul in it and that his; I think this the supreme moment of life." "Go! Andrea, ye've hit it!" cried the Bailie, and didn't the dark eye sparkle! He had felt this often, had the Bailie; his nephew had only now and then been near enough to imagine the rest.

The happiness of giving happiness is far sweeter than the pleasure direct, and I recall no moments of my life in which the rarer pleasure seemed to suffuse my whole heart as when I stood at Brighton and saw my friends take their places that memorable morning. In this variable, fantastic climate of Britain the weather is ever a source of solicitude. What must it have been to me, when a good start was all important! I remember I awoke early in the morning and wondered whether it was sunny or rainy. If a clear day could have been purchased, it would have been obtained at almost any outlay. I could easily tell our fate by raising the window-blind, but I philosophically decided that it was best to lie still and take what heaven might choose to send us. I should know soon enough. If rain it was, I could not help it; if fair, it was glorious. But let me give one suggestion to those who in England are impious enough to ask heaven to change its plans: don't ask for dry weather; always resort to that last extremity when it is "a drizzle-drozzle" you wish. Your supplications are so much more likely to be answered, you know.

There never was a lovelier morning in England than that which greeted me when I pulled up the heavy Venetian blind and gazed on the rippling sea before me, with its hundreds of pretty little sails. I repeated to myself these favorite lines as I stood entranced:

> "The Bridegroom Sea is toying with the shore,
> His wedded bride; and in the fulness of his marriage joy
> He decorates her tawny brow with shells,
> Retires a space to see how fair she looks,
> Then proud runs up to kiss her."

That is what old ocean was doing that happy morning. I saw him at it, and I felt that if all created beings had one mouth I should like to kiss them too.

The Start.

All seated! The Queen Dowager next the coachman, and I at her side. The horn sounds, the crowd cheers, and we are off. A mile or two are traversed and there is a unanimous verdict upon one point—this suits us! Finer than we had dreamt! As we pass the pretty villas embossed in flowers and vines and all that makes England the home of happy homes, there comes the sound of increasing exclamations. How pretty! Oh, how beautiful! See, see, the roses! Oh the roses! Look at that lawn! How lovely! Enchanting! entrancing! superb! exquisite! Oh, I never saw anything like this in all my life! And then the hum of song—La-*la*-LA-LA, Ra-da-*da*-DUM! Yes, it is all true, all we dreamt or imagined, and beyond it. And so on we go through Brighton and up the hills to the famous Weald of Sussex.

While we make our first stop to water the horses at the wayside inn, and some of the men as well, for a glass of beer asserts its attractions, let me introduce you to two worthies whose names will occupy important places in our narrative, and dwell in our memories forever; men to whom we are indebted in a large measure for the success of the coaching experiment.

Ladies and gentlemen, this is Perry, Perry our coachman; and what he doesn't know about horses and how to handle them you needn't overtask yourselves trying to learn. And this is Joe—Joey, my lad—footman and coach manager. A good head and an eloquent tongue has Joe. Yes, and a kind heart. There is nothing he can do or think of doing for any of us—and he can do much—that he is not off and doing ere we ask him. "Skid, Joe!" "Right, Perry!" these talismanic words of our order we heard to-day for the first time. It will be many a long day before they cease to recall to the Charioteers some of the happiest recollections of life. Even as I write I am in English meadows far away and hear them tingling in my ears.

It was soon discovered that no mode of travel could be compared with coaching. By all other modes the views are obstructed by the hedges and walls; upon the top of the coach the eye wanders far and wide,

> "O'er deep waving fields and pastures green,
> With gentle slopes and groves between."

Everything of rural England is seen, and how exquisitely beautiful it all is, this quiet, peaceful, orderly land!

> "The ground's most gentle dimplement
> (As if God's finger touched, but did not press,
> In making England)—such an up and down
> Of verdure; nothing too much up and down,
> A ripple of land, such little hills the sky
> Can stoop to tenderly and the wheat-fields climb;
> Such nooks of valleys lined with orchises,
> Fed full of noises by invisible streams,
> I thought my father's land was worthy too of being Shakespeare's."

Rural England.

I think this extract from Mr. Winter's charming volume expresses the feelings one has amid such scenes better than anything I know of:

"If the beauty of England were merely superficial, it would produce a merely superficial effect. It would cause a passing pleasure, and would be forgotten. It certainly would not—as now in fact it does—inspire a deep, joyous, serene and grateful contentment, and linger in the mind, a gracious and beneficent remembrance. The conquering and lasting potency of it resides not alone in loveliness of expression, but in loveliness of character. Having first greatly blessed the British Islands with the natural advantages of position, climate, soil, and products, nature has wrought out their development and adornment as a necessary consequence of the spirit of their inhabitants. The picturesque variety and pastoral repose of the English landscape spring, in a considerable measure, from the imaginative taste and the affectionate gentleness of the English people. The state of the country, like its social constitution, flows from principles within (which are constantly suggested), and it steadily comforts and nourishes the mind with a sense of kindly feeling, moral rectitude, solidity, and permanence. Thus, in the peculiar beauty of England the ideal is made the actual, is expressed in things more than in words, and in things by which words are transcended. Milton's 'L'Allegro,' fine as it is, is not so fine as the scenery—the crystallized, embodied poetry—out of which it arose. All the delicious rural verse that has been written in England is only the excess and superflux of her own poetic opulence; it has rippled from the hearts of her poets just as the fragrance floats away from her hawthorn hedges. At every step of his progress the pilgrim through English scenes is impressed with this sovereign excellence of the accomplished fact, as contrasted with any words that can be said in its celebration."

The Scribe as a Singer.

The roads are a theme of continual wonder to those who have not before seen England. To say that from end to end of our journey they equalled those of New York Central Park would be to understate the fact. They are equal to the park roads on days when these are at their best, and are neither wet nor dusty. We bowl over them as balls do over billiard-tables. It is a glide rather than a roll, with no sensation of jolting. You could write or read on the coach almost as well as at home. I mean you could if there was any time to waste doing either, and you were not afraid of missing some beautiful picture which would dwell in your memory for years, or Aleck's last joke, or the Prima Donna's sweet song, Andrew's never-to-be-forgotten lilt, or the Queen Dowager's Scotch ballad pertaining to the district; or what might be even still more likely, if you didn't want to tell a story yourself, or even join in the roaring chorus as we roll along, for truly the exhilarating effect of the triumphant progress is such as to embolden one to do anything. I always liked Artemus Ward, perhaps because I found a point of similarity between him and myself. It was not he but his friend who "was saddest when he sang," as the old song has it. I noticed that my friends were strangely touched when I burst into song. I do not recall an instance when I was encored; but the apparent slight arose probably from a suspicion that if recalled I would have essayed the same song. This is unjust! I have another in reserve for such an occasion, if it ever happen. The words are different, although the tune may be somewhat similar. When I like a tune I stick to it, more or less, and when there are fine touches in several tunes I have been credited with an eclectic disposition. However this may be, there was never time upon our coach for anything which called our eyes and our attention from the rapid succession of pretty cottages, fine flowers, the birds and lowing herds, the grand lights and grander shadows of that uncertain fleecy sky, the luxuriance of the verdure, flowery dells and dewy meads, and the hundred surprising beauties that make England England.

These bind us captive and drive from the mind every thought of anything but the full and intense enjoyment of the present hour; and this comes without thought. Forgetful of the past, regardless of the future, from morn till night, it is one uninterrupted season of pure and unalloyed joyousness. Never were the words of the old Scotch song as timely as now:

> "The present moment is our ain,
> The neist we never see."

Having got the party fairly started, let me tell you something of our general arrangements for the campaign. The coach, horses, and servants are engaged at a stipulated sum per week, which includes their travelling expenses. We have nothing to do with their bills or arrangements, neither are we in any wise responsible for accidents to the property. Every one of the party is allowed a small hand-bag and a strap package; the former contains necessary articles for daily use, the latter waterproofs, shawls, shoes, etc. The Gay Charioteers march with supplies for one week. The trunks are forwarded every week to the point where we are to spend the succeeding Sunday, so that every Saturday evening we replenish our wardrobe, and at the Sunday dinner appear in full dress, making a difference between that and other days. This we found well worth observing, for our Sunday evenings were thereby made somewhat unusual affairs. In no case did any failure of this plan occur, nor were we ever put to the slightest inconvenience about clothing. Our hotel accommodations were secured by telegraph. The General Manager had engaged these for our first week's stage, previous to our start.

Luncheon.

The question of luncheon soon came to the front, for should we be favored with fine weather, much of the poetry and romance of the journey was sure to cluster round the midday halt. It was by a process of natural selection that she who had proved her genius for making salads on many occasions during the voyage should be unanimously appointed to fill the important position of stewardess, and given full and unlimited control of the hampers. Our stewardess only lived up to a well-deserved reputation by surprising us day after day with luncheons far excelling any dinner. Two coaching hampers, very complete affairs, were obtained in London. These the stewardess saw filled at the inn every morning with the best the country could afford, under her personal supervision, a labor of love. Our Pard's sweet tooth led him to many early excursions before breakfast in quest of sweets and flowers for us. Aleck was butler, and upon him we placed implicit reliance, and with excellent reason too, for the essential corkscrew and the use thereof—which may be rated as of prime necessity upon such a tour—and Aleck never failed us as superintendent of the bottles.

It was in obedience to the strictest tenets of our civil service reform association that the most important appointment of all was made with a unanimity which must ever be flattering to the distinguished gentleman who received the highly responsible appointment of General Manager. Just here let me say, for the peace of mind of any gentleman who may be tempted to try the coaching experiment upon a large scale, and for an extended tour: *Don't,* unless you have a dear friend with a clear head, an angelic disposition, a great big heart, and the tact essential for governing, who for your sake is willing to relieve you from the cares incident to such a tour—that is, if you expect to enjoy it as a recreation, and have something that will linger forever after in the memory as an adventure in wonderland. Should you however be one of those rare men who have a real liking for details, and so conceited as to think that you never get things done so well as when your own genius superintends them, being in this respect the antipode of a modest man like myself—who never does by any chance find any one who can so completely bungle matters as himself—it may of course be different. As for me, the very first inquiry I shall make of myself when I am about to take the road again—as pray heaven I may some day, and that ere long—will be this: Now who can I get for Prime Minister, one who will like to govern and allow me to laugh and frolic with the party without a care? The position of a king in a constitutional monarchy is the very ideal for a chief to emulate. It is delightful to feel so very certain that one "can do no wrong," even if infallibility be obtained, as Queen Victoria's is, because she is no longer allowed to do anything. Such was the case with the Scribe during the Coaching Tour. Happy man!

Grouping.

There must always be a tendency toward grouping in a large party: groups of four or five, and in extreme cases a group of two; and especially is this so when married people, cousins or dear friends, are of the company. To prevent anything like this, and insure our being one united party, I asked the gentlemen not to occupy the same seat twice in succession—a rule which gave the ladies a different companion at each meal, and a change upon the coach several times each day. This was understood to apply in a general way to our strolls, although in this case the General Manager, with rare discretion, winked at many infringements, which insured him grateful constituents of both sexes. Young people should never be held too strictly to such rules, and a chaperon's duties, as we all know, are often most successfully performed by a wise and salutary neglect. Our General Manager and even the Queen Dowager were considerate.

We generally started about half-past nine in the morning, half an hour earlier or later as the day's journey was to be long or short; and here let me record, to the credit of all, that not in any instance had we ever to wait for any of the party beyond the five minutes allowed upon all well managed lines for "variation of watches." The horn sounded, and we were off through the crowds which were usually around the hotel door awaiting the start. Nor even at meals were we less punctual or less mindful of the comfort of others. I had indeed a model party in every way, and in none more praiseworthy than in this, that the Charioteers were always "on time." The Prima Donna's explanation may have reason in it: "Who wouldn't be ready and waiting to mount the coach! I'd as soon be late, and a good deal sooner, maybe, for my wedding: and as for meals, there was even a better reason why we were always ready then: we couldn't wait." We did indeed eat like hawks, especially at luncheon—a real boy's hunger—the ravenous gnawing after a day at the sea gathering whilks. I thought this had left me, but that with many another characteristic of glorious youth came once more to make daft callants of us. O those days! those happy, happy days! Can they be brought back once more? Will a second coaching trip do it? I would be off next summer. But one hesitates to put his luck to the test a second time, lest the perfect image of the first be marred. We shall see.

During the evening we had learned the next day's stage—where we were to stay over night, and, what is almost as important, in what pretty nook we were to rest at midday; on the banks of what classic stream or wimpling burn, or in what shady, moss-covered dell. Several people of note in the neighborhood dropped into the inn, as a rule, to see the American coaching party, whose arrival in the village had made as great a stir as if it were the advance show-wagon of Barnum's menagerie. From these the best route and objects of interest to be seen could readily be obtained. The ordnance maps which we carried kept us from trouble about the right roads; not only this, they gave us the name of every estate we passed, and of its owner.

Aristocratic Gypsies.

The horses have to be considered in selecting a luncheon-place, which should be near an inn, where they can be baited. This was rarely inconvenient; but upon a few occasions, when the choice spot was in some glen or secluded place, we took oats along, and our horses were none the worse off for nibbling the road-side grass and drinking from the brook. Nor did the party look less like the aristocratic Gypsies they felt themselves to be from having their coach standing on the moor or in the glen, and the horses picketed near by, as if we were just the true-born Gypsies. And was there ever a band of Gypsies happier than we, or freer from care? Didn't we often dash off in a roar:

> "See! the smoking bowl before us,
> Mark our jovial ragged ring!
> Round and round take up the chorus,
> And in raptures let us sing.
> A fig for those by law protected!
> Liberty's a glorious feast!
> Courts for cowards were erected,
> Churches built to please the priest."

Halt! Ho for luncheon! Steps, Joe. Yes, sir! The committee of two dismount and select the choicest little bit of sward for the table. It is not too warm, still we will not refuse the shade of a noble chestnut or fragrant birk, or the side of a tall hedge, on which lie, in one magnificent bed, masses of honeysuckle, over which nod, upon graceful sprays, hundreds of the prettiest wild roses, and at whose foot grow the foxglove and wandering willie.

It is no easy matter to decide which piece of the velvety lawn is finest; but here come Joe and Perry with armfuls of rugs to the chosen spot. The rugs are spread two lengthwise a few feet apart, and one across at the top and bottom, leaving for the table in the centre the fine clovered turf with buttercups and daisies pied. The ladies have gathered such handfuls of wild flowers! How fresh, how unaffected, and how far beyond the more pretentious bouquets which grace our city dinners! These are Nature's own dear children, fresh from her lap, besprinkled with the dews of heaven, unconscious of their charms. How touchingly beautiful are the wild flowers! real friends are they, close to our hearts, while those of the conservatory stand outside, fashionable acquaintances only.

Wild Flowers.

Give us the wild flowers, and take your prize varieties; for does not even Tennyson (a good deal of a cultivated flower himself) sing thus of the harshest of them all, though to a Scotsman sacred beyond all other vegetation:

> . . . "the stubborn thistle bursting

> Into glossy purples, which outredden
> All voluptuous garden roses."

And in that wonder of our generation, the "Light of Asia," it is no garden beauties who are addressed:

> "Oh, flowers of the field! Siddârtha said,
> Who turn your tender faces to the sun—
> Glad of the light, and grateful with sweet breath
> Of fragrance and these robes of reverence donned,
> Silver and gold and purple—none of ye
> Miss perfect living, none of ye despoil
> Your happy beauty. . . .
> What secret know ye that ye grow content,
> From time of tender shoot to time of fruit,
> Murmuring such sun-songs from your feathered crowns?"

You may be sure that while in Scotland old Scotia's dear emblem, and that most graceful of all flowers, the Scottish bluebell, towered over our bouquets, and that round them clustered the others less known to fame.

It was an easy matter to tie the flowers round sticks and press these into the soft lawn, and then there was a table for you—equal it who can! Round this the travellers range themselves upon the rugs, sometimes finding in back to back an excellent support, for they sat long at table; and see at the head—for it's the head wherever she sits—the Queen Dowager is comfortably seated upon the smaller of the two hampers. The larger placed on end before her gives her a private table: she has an excellent seat, befitting her dignity. Joe and Perry have put the horses up at the inn, and are back with mugs of foaming ale, bottles of Devonshire cider, lemonade, and pitchers of fresh creamy milk, that all tastes may be suited. The stewardess and her assistants have set table, and now luncheon is ready. No formal grace is necessary, for our hearts have been overflowing with gratitude all the day long for the blessed happiness showered upon us. We owe no man a grudge, harbor no evil, have forgiven all our enemies, if we have any—for we doubt the existence of enemies, being ourselves the enemy of none. Our hearts open to embrace all things, both great and small; we are only sorry that so much is given to us, so little to many of our more deserving fellow-creatures. Truly, the best grace this, before meat or after!

> "He prayeth best who loveth best
> All things both great and small;
> For the dear God who loveth us,
> He made and loveth all."

In these days we feel for the Deevil himself, and wish with Burns that he would take a thought and mend; and, as Howells says, "if we had the naming of creation we wouldn't call snakes snakes" if the christening took place while we were coaching.

Good Appetites.

No one would believe what fearful appetites driving in this climate gives one. Shall we ever feel such tigerish hunger again! but, what is just as important, shall we ever again have such luncheons! "Give me a sixpence," said the beggar to the duke, "for I have nothing." "You lie, you beggar; I'd give a thousand pounds for such an appetite as you've got." Well, ours would have been cheap to you, my lord duke, at double the money. What a roar it caused one day when one of the young ladies was discovered quietly taking the third slice of cold ham. "Well, girls, you must remember I was on the front seat, and had to stand the *brunt* of the weather this morning." Capital! I had been there at her side, and got my extra allowance on the same ground; and those who bore the *brunt* of the weather claimed a great many second and even third allowances during the journey.

Aleck (*Aa*leck, not El-eck, remember), set the table in a roar so often with his funny sayings and doings that it would fill the record were I to recount them, but one comes to mind as I write which was a great hit.

A temperance—no, a total abstinence lady rebuked him once for taking a second or third glass of something, telling him that he should try to conquer his liking for it, and assuring him that if he would only resist the Devil he would flee from him. "I know," said the wag (and with such a comical, good-natured expression), "that is what the good book says, Mrs. — —, but I have generally found that I was the fellow who had *to get*." You couldn't corner Aaleck.

Although we were coaching, it must not be thought that we neglected the pleasures of walking. No, indeed, we had our daily strolls. Sometimes the pedestrians started in advance of the coach from the inn or the luncheon ground, and walked until overtaken, and at other times we would dismount some miles before we reached the end of the day's journey, and walk into the village. This was a favorite plan, as we found by arriving later than the main body our rooms were ready and all the friends in our general sitting-room standing to welcome us.

Hills upon the route were always hailed as giving us an opportunity for a walk or a stroll, and all the sport derivable from a happy party in country lanes. It was early June, quite near enough to

> "The flowery May who from her green lap throws
> The yellow cowslip and the pale primrose,"

and the hundreds of England's wild beauties with

> "quaint enamell'd eyes,
> That on the green turf suck the honeyed showers,
> And purple all the ground with vernal flowers."

Pleasures of Walking.

Many a time was Perry instructed to wait for us at the foot of the hill, or a mile or two in advance, while we spent the happy intervals in examining still closer than it was possible to do while driving the beauties which captivated us at every turn. The pleasures of walking set against those of coaching might well furnish matter for an evening's debate. Combined, as they were with us, the result was perfection, for they are indeed upon such a tour the complement of each other. If ever weary of the coach—which we never were—nothing like a walk along the hedge-rows as a substitute, with many a run into out-of-the-way paths, which tempted us by their loveliness, and many a minute stolen to explore the windings of the brooks we passed. I often felt that one of the prettiest pictures I had ever seen was that of our own party scattered about some bosky dell in the way I have described, while the towering coach-and-four stood out clear against the sky upon the hilltop, waiting for us to tear ourselves away from scenes among which we would linger till the daylight had passed. Let no one fail while coaching to work this mine of pure happiness to the full.

We carried perpetual flowering summer with us as we travelled from south to north, plucking the wild roses and the honeysuckles from the hedges near Brighton, never missing their sweet influences, and finding them ready to welcome us at Inverness, seven weeks later, as if they had waited till our approach to burst forth in their beauty in kindly greeting of their kinsmen from over the sea. A dancing, laughing welcome did the wild flowers of my native land give to us, God bless them!

On our arrival at the inn for the night, the General Manager examined the rooms and assigned them; Joe and Perry handed over the bags to the servants; the party went direct to their general sitting-room, and in a few minutes were taken to their rooms, where all was ready for them. The two American flags were placed upon the mantel of the sitting-room, in which there was always a piano, and we sat down to dinner a happy band.

The long twilight and the gloaming in Scotland gave us two hours after dinner to see the place; and after our return an hour of musical entertainment was generally enjoyed, and we were off to bed to sleep the sound, refreshing sleep of childhood's innocent days. The duties of the General Manager, however, required his attendance down stairs; he had to-morrow's route to learn and the landlord or landlady, as the case might be, to see. Some of the male members of the party were not loath to assist in this business, and I have heard many a story of the pranks played by them—for several of my friends are not unlike the piper, "Rory Murphy,"

> "Who had of good auld sangs the wale
> To please the wives that brewed good ale;
> He charmed the swats frae cog and pail
> As he cam through Dumbarton."

Coaching Weather.

No doubt the landlord's laugh was ready chorus, and the Gay Charioteers of this department, I make bold to say, tasted most of the "far ben" barrels of every landlord or landlady in their way northward. The question of the weather occurs to every one. "If you have a dry season, it may be done; if a wet one, I doubt it," was the opinion of one of my wisest friends in Britain. We were surprisingly fortunate in this respect. Only one day did we suffer seriously from rain. A gentle shower fell now and then to cool the air and lay the dust, or rather to prevent the dust, and seemingly to recreate vegetation. Who wouldn't bear a shower, if properly supplied with waterproofs and umbrellas, for the fresh glory revealed thereafter. Only a continual downpour for days could have dampened the ardor of the Gay Charioteers. Good coaching weather may be expected in June and July, if one may indulge any weather anticipations in England. After we left the deluge came; nothing but rain during August and September, at least such was the report—but the conveniences of living are so great and the discomforts so few in England that I incline to the opinion, especially when I take into consideration the well-known tendency of the islanders to grumble, that far too much is made out of the so-called bad weather. We had a curious illustration of this. One day we heard some rumbling sounds which would scarcely pass with us for thunder, and we were amused next morning to read in the newspapers of the terrific thunder-storm which had passed over the district. All things are gentle and well behaved in this sober, steady-going, conservative land. Even Jove himself "roars you as mildly as a sucking dove." Pluvius, too, is less terrible than he is painted, though the green, green grass, the smiling hedgerows, the luxuriant vegetation everywhere tells of a moist nature and a disposition to weep at short intervals; but the rain comes gently down as if all the while begging your pardon and explaining that it couldn't possibly help it, the sky being unable to keep it any longer in its overburdened bosom. Strong, thick shoes, one pair in reserve, and overshoes for the ladies, heavy woollen clothing—under and over—a waterproof, an umbrella, and a felt hat that won't spoil—these rendered us almost independent of the weather and prepared us to encounter the worst ever predicted of the British climate; and this is saying a great deal, for the natives do grumble inordinately about it. As I have said, however, our travelling was never put to a severe test. England and Scotland smiled upon the coaching party, and compelled us all to fall deeply in love with their unrivalled charms. We thought that even in tears this blessed isle must still be enchanting.

The same horses (with one exception) took us through from Brighton to Inverness. This has surprised some horsemen here, but little do they know of the roads and climate, or of Perry's care. Our average distance, omitting days when we rested, was thirty-two miles, and horses will actually improve on such a journey, as ours did, if not pushed too fast and not forced to pull beyond their strength up steep hills. The continual desire of most of our party to dismount and enjoy a walk gave our horses a light coach where the road was such as to bring them to a walk, and they were actually in better condition after the journey than when we started.

Wayside Inns.

For luncheon, "good my liege, all place a temple and all seasons summer," but for lodgings and entertainment for man and beast, how did we manage these? Shall we not take our ease in our inn? and shall not mine host of The Garter, ay and mine hostess too, prove the most obliging of people? I do not suppose that it would be possible to find in any other country such delightful inns at every stage of such a journey. Among many pretty objects upon which memory lovingly rests, these little wayside inns stand prominently forward. The very names carry one back to quaint days of old: "The Lamb and Lark," "The Wheat Sheaf," "The Barley Mow." Oh, you fat wight! your inn was in Eastcheap, but in your march through Coventry, when you wouldn't go with your scarecrows, it was to some wayside inn you went, you rogue, with its trailing vines, thatched roof, and pretty garden flower-pots in the windows; and upon such excursions it was, too, that you acquired that love of nature which enabled the master with six words to cover most that was un-unsavory in your character, and hand you down to generations unborn, shrived and absolved. Dear old boy—whom one would like to have known—for after all you were right, Jack: "If Adam fell in an age of innocency, what was poor Jack Falstaff to do in an age of villainy!" There was something pure and good at bottom of one who left us after life's vanities were o'er playing with flowers and "babbling o' green fields." These country hostelries are redolent of the green fields. It is in such we would take our ease in our inn. The host, hostess, and servants assembled at the door upon our arrival, and welcomed us to their home, as they also do when we leave to bid us God-speed. We mount and drive off with smiles, bows, and wavings of the hands from them; and surely the smiles and good wishes of those who have done so much to promote our comfort over night are no bad salute for us as we blow our horn and start on the fresh dewy mornings upon our day's journey.

British Honesty.

The scrupulous care bestowed upon us and our belongings by the innkeepers excited remark. Not one article was lost of the fifty packages, great and small, required by fifteen persons. It was not even practicable to get rid of any trifling article which had served its purpose; old gloves, or discarded brushes quietly stowed away in some drawer or other would be handed to us at the next stage, having been sent by express by these careful, honest people. It was a great and interesting occasion, as the reporters say, when the stowed-away pair of old slippers which she had purposely left, were delivered to one of our ladies with a set speech after dinner one evening. Little did she suspect what was contained in the nice package which had been forwarded. Our cast-off things were veritable devil's ducats which would return to plague us. To the grandest feature of the Briton's character, the love of truth, let one more cardinal virtue be added—his downright honesty. More Englishmen of all ranks, high and low, in proportion to population, will escape conviction upon two counts of the general indictment, "Thou shalt not bear false witness," and "Thou shalt not steal," than those of any other nationality; but upon a collateral count a larger proportion of Englishmen of position will have difficulty in clearing themselves than of any other race of which I have knowledge; for while the true Briton will tell the truth, if he has to speak at all, he will conceal his honest convictions upon social and political subjects to such an extent in public as to seem to you almost hypocritical when compared with what he will say freely in private. The M.P. of the smoking room of the House of Commons and the same man on the floor of the House, for instance, are two distinct personages, for it is understood that whatever is said below is to be above as if unsaid. I have often wondered how they merge the one character into the other when the day's words and acts come under review ere the eyes close in sleep—there is such a miserable fear in the breast of the free-born Briton that he will in an unguarded moment say something which he feels to be true, but which society will not think "good form." The great difference between a Radical and a Liberal in England is, it seems to me, that the one holds the same opinions in public and in private, while the other has two sets of opinions, the one for public, the other for private use. The maintenance of old forms, from which the life has passed out, is no doubt the real cause of this phase of English political life, apparently so inconsistent with the Saxon love of truth; one sham requires many shams for its support.

We all have our special weaknesses as to the articles we leave behind at hotels. Mine is well known; but I smile as I write at the cleverness shown in preventing my lapses during the excursion from coming before the congregation. It was a wary eye which was kept upon forwarded parcels, mark you, and not once was I presented with a left article. The eleventh commandment is, not to be found out.

Wild Flowers.

With these general observations we shall not "leave the subject with you," but, retracing our steps to the hills overlooking Brighton, we shall mount the coach waiting there for us at the King's Cross Inn; for you remember we dismounted there while the horses were watered for the first time. Ten miles of bewildering pleasure had brought us here; some of us pushed forward and had our first stroll, but we scattered in a minute, for who could resist the flowers which tempted us at every step! The roses were just in season; the honeysuckle, ragged robin, meadow sweet, wandering willie, and who can tell how many others whose familiar names are household words. What bouquets we gathered, what exclamations of delight were heard as one mass of beauty after another burst upon our sight! We began to realize that Paradise lay before us, began to know that we had discovered the rarest plan upon earth for pleasure; as for duty that was not within our horizon. We scarcely knew there was work to do. An echo of a moan from the weary world we had cast behind was not heard. Divinest melancholy was out of favor; Il Penseroso was discarded for the time, and L'Allegro, the happier goddess, crowned, bringing in her train—

> "Sport, that wrinkled Care derides,
> And Laughter, holding both his sides;
> Come and trip it as you go,
> On the light, fantastic toe."

That does not quite express it, for there was time for momentary pauses now and then, when the heart swelled with gratitude. We were so grateful for being so blessed. It was during this stroll that Emma came quietly to my side, slipped her arm in mine, and said in that rich, velvety English voice which we all envy her: "Oh, Andrew, when I am to go home you will have to tell me plainly, for indeed I shall never be able to leave this of my own accord. I haven't been as happy since I was a young girl." "Do you really think you could go all the way to Inverness?" "Oh, I could go on this way forever." "All right, my lady, 'check your baggage through,' as we say in Yankeedom;" and never did that woman lose sight of the coach till it was torn away from her at Inverness.

Some of us dismounted before reaching Horsham, and went in pursuit of adventure. In an old tan-yard by the wayside, where men were making leather in the crude, old-fashioned way, with horses instead of a steam engine for the motive power, we had our first conversation with the British rural workman, whose weekly earnings do not exceed $3.50. Now, this was not more than thirty miles from London, and only twenty-one from the sea at Brighton, and yet the oldest man of the party, who was the most talkative, had never seen the sea. He had been in London once, during the great Exhibition in 1851, having been treated to the journey by his employer; but his brother, who lived only a few miles beyond, had never been in a railway carriage. Their old master had died recently and had left a pound ($5) to every workman who had been with him for a certain number of years—I think ten. Good old master! The owners had new-fangled notions, he said, and were spending "heaps o' money" in building a steam engine which was not yet ready, but which he invited us to go and see. This was to do the work much faster; but (with a shake of the head) "I've 'earn tell by some as knows it's na sae gid for the leather."

Rip Van Winkles.

Could we really be within an hour's ride of the capital of the world, and yet in the midst of a Sleepy Hollow like this, peopled by Rip van Winkles! This incident gives a just idea of the tenacity with which the English hold to what their fathers did before them. This man's father could not have seen the sea at Brighton, nor have visited London short of spending a week's earnings. His successor goes along as his father did—what was good enough for his father is good enough for him,

> "Chained to one spot,
> They draw nutrition, propagate and rot."

But the next generation is to see all this changed, for even southern England is under the compulsory education act, and the rural population is to have the political franchise and a voice in the election of county boards.

At Horsham we lunched at the King's Arms, walked about its principal square, and were off again for Guildford. As we leave the sea the soil becomes richer, and ere we reach Horsham we say, yes, this is England indeed; but I forgot we passed through the Weald of Sussex before reaching Horsham. The cloudy sky cast deep shadows with the sunbeams over the rich, wooded landscape, as no clear blue sky has power to do, and brought to my mind Mrs. Browning's lines:

> . . . "my woods in Sussex have some purple shades at gloaming,
> Which are worthy of a king in state, or poet in his youth.

* * * * * * * * * *

> Oh, the blessed woods of Sussex, I can hear them still around me,
> With their leafy tide of greenery still rippling up the wind!"

And many a stately home did we see, fit for her "who spake such good thoughts natural."

Mrs. Browning is said to have written Lady Geraldine in a few hours, lying upon a sofa. This is one of the proofs cited that genius does its work as if by inspiration, without great effort. What nonsense! The Agave Americana bursts into flower in a day; but, look you, a hundred years of quiet, unceasing growth, which stopped not night nor day, was the period of labor preceding the miracle—a hundred years, during all of which it drank of the sunshine and the dews. Scott wrote some of his best works in a few weeks, but for a lifetime he never flagged in his work of gathering the fruits of song and story. Burns dashed off "A man's a man for a' that" in a jiffy. Yes, but for how many years were his very heartstrings tingling and his blood boiling at the injustice of hereditary rank! His life is in that song, not a few hours of it.

* * * * *

GUILDFORD, June 17.

A Generous Squire.

The approach to Guildford gives us our first real perfect English lane—so narrow and so bound in by towering hedgerows worthy the name. Had we met a vehicle at some of the prettiest turns there would have been trouble, for, although the lane is not quite as narrow as the pathway of the auld brig, where two wheelbarrows trembled as they met, yet a four-in-hand upon an English lane requires a clear track. Vegetation near Guildford is luxuriant enough to meet our expectations of England. It was at the White Lion we halted, and here came our first experience of quarters for the night. The first dinner en route was a decided success in our fine sitting-room, the American flags, brought into requisition for the first time to decorate the mantel, bringing to all sweet memories of home. During our stroll to-day we stopped at a small village inn before which pretty roses grew, hanging in clusters upon its sides. It was a very small and humble inn indeed, the tile floors sanded, and the furniture of the tap-room only plain wood—there were no chairs, only benches around the table where the hinds sit at night, drinking home-brewed beer, smoking their clay pipes, and discussing not the political affairs of the nation, but the affairs of their little world, bounded by the hall at one end of the estate, and the parsonage at the other. The merits of the gray mare, or the qualities of the last breed of sheep at the home farm, or the new-fangled plough which the squire has been rash enough to order. The landlady told us that she had recently moved from one of the midland towns to this village to secure purer air for the children, who had not been thriving well. Her husband was a gardener and worked for the squire. Two pretty little girls were brought in for us to see, true Saxons, with blue eyes and light colored hair, but with less color in their sweet innocent faces than usual—the result of dirty, crowded Leeds, no doubt—but soon to be changed by the country air. The eldest girl could not have been more than six or seven years old, but when she was given a few pence she went to the next room and brought a sheet of paper upon which were pasted some penny postage stamps. She was going at once to the post office to buy more stamps with her pennies. On inquiring we learned that the Post Office Department receives deposits of a shilling in stamps and allows two and a half per cent. interest I think, upon them, and "the squire" God bless him! had promised all the children upon his estates, which I trust vast, that whenever they saved eleven stamps he would give the last one to complete the shilling. In this way he hopes to instil into the young the importance of beginning early to save something for a rainy day. The still younger girl had also her stamp paper. The English are an improvident race, not given to denying themselves to-day that they may feast later on. "Do not put off till to-morrow what can be done to-day" is generally construed to mean, that the cake may as well be eaten at once, so that upon the whole we were not displeased to see these children trained to accumulate; but nevertheless it did seem pitiful that the dear little lambs, instead of sporting without a care, should have so early to learn that life is to the mass mainly a struggle for subsistence. Civilization is a failure till all this be changed. What a pity the name and address of that squire are mislaid. He evidently feels that property has its duties as well as its rights. The village and the inn and all the surroundings showed that the Hall was, in this instance, as it is in so many others, the centre and source of good influences. "He has a good wife and earnest thinking and working daughters," said one of the party. Surely he has and they do their part or he could not succeed. It was quite safe to infer this, was the verdict. Man is a poor agency for such work, left to himself. It needs woman's patience and glowing sympathy to work improvement in the manners and customs of the rural population. Man may supply the money, which corresponds only to barren faith among the virtues; it is to woman we must look for the harvest—good works.

When we remounted the coach, one regret found loud expression, and as the Scribe writes to-day, he wishes the omission could be remedied. Why did not we give these children a shilling each, with strict injunctions to gorge themselves with taffy and gingerbread, not a penny of it to be saved. A regular spree regardless of consequences! "Oh! it would have made them ill," said one. Well, suppose it did, just think of the legacy left them, a dream for years that they had been brought to death's door by too much taffy! Why, the sweet taste would have lingered in the pretty little mouths till womanhood, and they would have thought about their illness as Conn in the Shaughraun did about his month in jail for taking the squire's horse for a run with the hounds: "Begorra! it was worth it!"

Franklin's Proverb.

It might have given them a taste for dissipation, and they would have ceased to gather stamps, and turned out badly, was the next suggestion. This was seemingly agreed to by the majority, but there was one who wished he had secretly conveyed to the cherubs, at least a six-pence each to be entirely devoted to gormandizing. "Take care of your pence and the pounds will take care of themselves," the Queen Dowager remarked, is one of Ben Franklin's wisest proverbs. There was one at least of her children who had good reason to remember that favorite axiom. During his temporary absence from school, good Mr. Martin had instituted a rule that each one in the class should repeat a proverb before the lessons began. Her offspring was at the foot of the class, from absence it is to be hoped, and as each boy and girl spoke his proverb (they were taught together in those days, much to the advantage of both sexes, for who wanted to be a dunce before pretty and clever A. R.) they had an unfamiliar sound, but when his turn came he innocently gave them his mother's favorite from Franklin. It was like introducing a strange dog into a crowded church. After the uproar had subsided, the teacher said that while it was no doubt a very good proverb, it was not just in place among the sacred proverbs of Solomon. Another story was related of one of the Charioteers who, when told that he ought to sing when the others did in church, struck up, at the top of his shrill piping voice, "Come under my plaidie, the night's going to fa';" when the congregation began the Psalm. His uncle was so convulsed that, notwithstanding the angry glances of many near him, he could not stop the performance in time to prevent an unseemly interruption.

We had done our first day's coaching, and a long day at that, and looking back it is amusing to remember how anxiously we awaited the reports of the ladies of our party; for it was not without grave apprehension that some must fall by the wayside, as it were, as we journeyed on. One who had tried coaching upon this side had informed us that few ladies could stand it; but it was very evident that the spirits and appetites of ours were entirely satisfactory, and they all laughed at the idea that they could not go on forever. The Queen Dowager was quite as fresh as any. It was a shame that general orders consigned to bed at an early hour two of the ladies thought least robust, while the others walked about the suburbs of Guildford until late. We stood in the thickening twilight in front of an ivy-clad residence for some time, and asked each other if anything so exquisite had ever been seen, so full of rest, of home. The next morning all were fresh and happy, without a trace of fatigue—full of yesterday, and quite sure that no other day could equal it. But this was often said: many and many a day was voted the finest yet, only to be eclipsed in its turn by a later, till at last an effort to name our best day led to twenty selections, and ended in the general conclusion that it was impossible to say which had crowded within its hours the rarest treat, for none had all the finest, neither did any lack something of the best. But there is one point upon which a unanimous verdict can always be had from the Gay Charioteers, that to such days in the mass none but themselves can be their parallel.

We ran into a book-shop in the morning and obtained a local guide-book, that we might cull for you the proper quotations therefrom. It consists of 148 pages, mostly given up to notices of the titled people who visited the old town long ago; but who cares about them? Here, however, is something of more interest than all those nobodies. Cobbett says of Guildford, in his "Rural Rides:"

Cobbett's Opinion.

"I, who have seen so many towns, think this the prettiest and most happy looking I ever saw in my life." There's praise for you! But, then, he had never seen Dunfermline. Here is a characteristic touch of that rare, horse-sense kind of a man. He is enraptured over the vale of Chilworth.

"Here, in this tranquil spot, where the nightingales are to be heard earlier and later in the year than in any other part of England, where the first budding of the trees is seen in the spring, where no rigor of seasons can ever be felt, where everything seems framed for precluding the very thought of wickedness—this has the devil fixed on as one of his seats of his grand manufactory, and perverse and even ungrateful man not only lends his aid, but lends it cheerfully."

Since those days, friend Cobbett, the devil has much enlarged his business in gunpowder and bank notes, of which you complain. He was only making a start when you wrote. The development of manufactures in America (under a judicious tariff, be it reverently spoken), amazing as it has been, and carried on as a rule by the saints, is slow work compared with what his satanic majesty has been doing in these two departments. We must bestir ourselves betimes.

You remember Artemus Ward's encounter with the colporteur. After a long, dusty day's journey, arriving at the hotel, he applied to the barkeeper for a mint-julep, and just as Artemus was raising the tempting draught to his lips, a hand was laid upon his arm and the operation arrested. The missionary in embryo said in a kind of sepulchral tone, for he was only a beginner and had not yet reached that true professional voice which comes only after years of exhortation: "My friend, look not upon the wine when it is red. It stingeth like a serpent and it biteth as an adder." "Guess not, stranger," replied Artemus, "not if you put sugar in it."

It is just so with bank-notes, friend Cobbett. They don't bite worth a cent, neither do they sting, if you have government bonds behind them. But this was not understood in your day. The Republic had not then shown to the world the model system of banking. The objection made to it by others, viz., that founded as it is upon the obligations of the nation, its discredit involves the fall of private credit, counts for little to a republican. We would not give much for the man who is not willing to stake "his life, his fortune, and his sacred honor" upon the solvency of the Republic. Pitiable is the man who could think of his petty private means when his country was in peril. When the Republic falls, let us also fall.

There is a funny thing in this guide-book. "There also resides Mr. Martin Farquhar Tupper, the author of 'Proverbial Philosophy,' etc. He has eulogized the scene around as follows." Then come two pages of Tupper. I naturally looked to see the name of the author of the book, but none was given. Such modesty! But the case is a clear one, for who but Tupper would quote Tupper! "Sir," said Johnson to Bossy, "Sir, I never did the man an injury in my life, and yet he would persist in reading his tragedy to me." Here's the concluding quotation from the guide-book of Guildford, and the Scribe promises not to quote much more from any similar source. Cobbett says that in Albury Park he saw some plants of the "American cranberry, which not only grow here, but bear fruit, and therefore it is clear that they may be cultivated with great ease in this country."

American Blessings.

Potatoes, tomatoes, and cranberries—look at the great blessings America has bestowed upon the "author of her being;" and what won't grow in the rain and fog of the old home, doesn't she grow for her and send over by every steamer, from canvas-back ducks to Newtown pippins! Thackeray was right in saying one night, when some friends were disposed to criticise America, "Ah! well, gentlemen, much can be pardoned to a country which produces the canvas-back duck." At dinner-tables in England, nowadays, to the usual grace, "O Lord! for what we are about to receive make us truly thankful," should be added, "and render us truly grateful to our big son Jonathan, God bless him!"

One could settle down at the White Lion in Guildford, and spend a month, at least, visiting every day fresh objects of interest, and I have no doubt becoming day by day more charmed with the life he was leading. In every direction historical scenes, crowded full of instructive stories of the past, invite us: and yet to-morrow morning the horn will sound, and we shall be off, reluctantly saying to ourselves, we must return some day when we have leisure, and wander in and around, absorb and moralize. This rapid survey is only to show us what we can do hereafter. A summer to each county would not be too much, and here are eight hundred miles from sea to firth to be rushed over in seven weeks. Guildford, farewell!—on "to fresh woods and pastures new."

* * * * *

SATURDAY, June 18.

After a delightful breakfast we mount the coach and are off through the crowd of lookers-on for our second day's journey. During this stage we learned the valuable lesson that we should not attempt to coach through England without having the ordnance survey maps, and paying close attention to them. In this part of the country, so near to monster London, the roads and lanes are innumerable, and run here, there, and everywhere. You can reach any point by many different roads. Guide-posts have a dozen names upon them. We did some sailing out of our course to-day, and found many charming spots not down in the chart, which the straight line would have caused us to miss; it was late ere Windsor's towers made their appearance. The day was not long enough for us, long as it was, but the fifty miles we are said to have traversed were quite enough for the horses. But next day would be Sunday, we said, and they had a long rest to look forward to at Windsor.

* * * * *

WINDSOR, June 18-20.

The Scribe as a Whip.

Upon reaching the forest, the General Manager insisted that the Scribe should take the reins and drive his party through the royal domain. This was his first trial as the whip of a four-in-hand, and not a very successful one either. It's easy enough to handle the ribbons, but how to do this and spare a hand for the whip troubles one. As Josh Billings remarks in the case of religion, "It's easy enough to get religion, but to hold on to it is what bothers a fellow. A good grip is here worth more than rubies." The Scribe had not the grip for the whip, but it did give him a rare pleasure when he got a moment or two now and then (when Perry held the whip), to think that he was privileged to drive his friends in style up to Her

Majesty's very door at Windsor. Only to the door, for that good woman was not at home, but in bonnie Scotland, sensible lady! As we were en route ourselves, we were quite in the fashion; some of her republican subjects, however, were quite disappointed at not getting a glimpse of her during the tour.

The drive through the grounds gave to some of our party the first sight of an English park, and it is certain that the impression it made upon them will never be effaced.

Windsor at last, a late dinner and a stroll through the quaint town, the castle towering over all in the cloudy night, and we were off to bed, but not before we had enjoyed an hour of the wildest frolic, though tired and sleepy after the long drive. We laughed until our sides ached, but how vain to attempt to describe the fun! To detail the trifles light as air which kept us in a roar during our excursion is like offering you stale champagne. No, no, gone forever are those rare nothings which were so delicious when fresh; but, for the benefit of the members of the Circle, I'll just say "Poole." It was a happy thought to put the General Manager's suit of new clothes in Davie's package and await results. We had ordered travelling suits in London, and when they arrived we all began to try them on at once. Davie's disappointment at getting an odd-looking suit fancied by the General Manager was so genuine! But such a perfect fit, though a mistake, maybe, as to material; and then, when he tried his own suit, what a misfit it was! The climax: "David, if you are going to"—but this is too much! The tears are rolling down my cheeks once more as I picture that wild scene.

Gladstone.

We heard the chimes at midnight, and then to bed. Windsor is nothing unless royal. It is all over royal, although Her Majesty was absent. But the Prince of Wales was there, and a greater than he—Mr. Gladstone—had run down from muggy London to refresh his faded energies by communing with nature. It is said that his friends are alarmed at his haggard appearance toward the close of each week; but he spends Saturday and Sunday in the country, and returns on Monday to surprise them at the change. Ah! he has found the kindest, truest nurse, for he knows—

> . . . "that Nature never did betray
> The heart that loved her; 'tis her privilege,
> Through all the years of this our life, to lead
> From joy to joy; for she can so inform
> The mind that is within us, so impress
> With quietness and beauty, and so feed
> With lofty thoughts, that neither evil tongues,
> Rash judgments, nor the sneers of selfish men,
> Nor greetings where no kindness is, nor all
> The dreary intercourse of daily life,
> Shall e'er prevail against us, or disturb
> Our cheerful faith, that all which we behold
> Is full of blessings."

Mr. Gladstone's fresh appearance Monday mornings gratifies his friends, and pleases even his opponents, for such a man can have no ill-wishers, surely. When Confucius had determined to behead the emperor's corrupt brother, his counsellors endeavored to dissuade him, from a just fear that the criminal's friends would rise and avenge his death. "Friends!" said the sage, "such a character may have adherents, but friends never." The result proved his wisdom. No revolt came, though Confucius stood by to see justice done, refusing to listen to the petition of the emperor for his own brother's life. In like manner, Mr. Gladstone may have opponents—enemies never. All Englishmen must in their hearts honor the man who is a credit to the race. By the way, he's Scotch, let me note, and never fails to bear in mind and to mention this special cause for thankfulness. I suspect that this fact has not a little to do with the intense enthusiasm of Scotland for him. We are a queer lot, up in the North Countrie, and he is our ain bairn. Blood is thicker than water everywhere, but in no part of this world is it so *very much thicker* as beyond the Tweed.

We attended church at Windsor and saw the great man and the Prince come to the door together. There the former stopped and the other walked up the aisle, causing a flutter in the congregation. Mr. Gladstone followed at a respectful distance, and took his seat several pews behind. How absurd you are, my young lady republican! Can you not understand? One is only the leading man in the empire—a man who, in a fifty years' tussle with the foremost statesmen of the age, has won the crown both for attainments and character; but the other, bless your ignorant little head!—he is a prince.

Kings and Princes.

Well, if he is, he has never done anything, you say. True, but what are kings and princes for? The people of England, my dear, not so very long ago, used to have it beaten into them that "the king can do no wrong." As this is historically the true doctrine and has antiquity on its side, it would have been very un-English to reject it; so they quietly accepted the dogma and made it true by arranging that the king should never be allowed to do anything—it's a way these islanders have—the form may be what it likes, the substance must be as they wish. They never revolutionize in England—they transform. What you complain of then, my red republican miss, is really the best proof that the prince will make that modern article called a Constitutional Monarch, and spend his days as the English man-milliner Worth—setting the fashions, laying foundation stones, and opening fancy bazars. Oh! you would not be such a prince or such a king. The Bruce at Bannockburn, at the head of his countrymen striking for the independence of Scotland, and King Edward leading his hosts, these were *real* kings, you say? The kings of to-day are shadows. I am not going to dispute that with you, Miss; times have changed and kings with them; but were I Prince of Wales, I would be in Ireland to-day investigating the causes of discontent and devising a remedy; and above all showing my deep and abiding sympathy with that portion of my people. This would be better than leading men to murder their fellows—as your heroes did. Oh yes, indeed, says my young lady politician, I should like to be the Prince of Wales just to do that. What a hero it would make him! Why, he would rank with Alfred the Good, or George Washington. Why doesn't Mr. Gladstone suggest this to him? I believe the Prince would just jump at the chance. Well, my dear girl, drop a postal card to the grand old man, and you will get his views upon the subject by return mail. The conversation ended by a toss of the head, and "Well, I would if I were a man. I should like a chance 'to talk it up' to the Prince." As the Prince is an admirer of pretty American young ladies, our friend might get a hearing and astonish him.

In the afternoon we attended St. George's Chapel. In one of the stalls we saw again that sadly noble lion-face—no one ever mistakes Gladstone. He sat wrapped in the deepest meditation. He is very pale, haggard, and careworn—the weight of empire upon him!

> "I tell thee, scorner of these whitening hairs,
> When this snow melteth there shall come a flood."

I could not help applying to him Milton's lines:

> . . . "with grave
> Aspect he rose, and in his rising seem'd
> A pillar of state: deep on his front engraven
> Deliberation sat and public care;
> And princely counsel in his face yet shone,
> Majestic though in ruin."

He has work to do yet. If he were only fifty instead of seventy odd! Well, God bless him for what he has done; may he rule England long!

The Queen Dowager.

A memorable event occurred at Windsor, Sunday, June 19th—the Queen Dowager reached her seventy-first year. At breakfast Mr. B. rose, and addressing himself to her, made one of the sweetest, prettiest speeches ever heard. He presented to her an exquisite silver cup, ornamented with birds and flowers, and inscribed: "Presented to Mrs. M. C. at Windsor, by the members of the coaching-party, upon her seventy-first birthday." Mr. B.'s reference to her intense love of nature in all its glorious forms, from the tiny gowan to the extended landscape, was most appropriate.

We were completely surprised; and when the speaker concluded, the Scribe was about to rise and respond, but a slight motion from Her Majesty apprized him that she preferred to reply in person. She acquitted herself grandly. Her speech was a gem (Mem.—it was so short). After thanking her dear friends, she said:

"I can only wish that you may all have as good health, as complete command of all your faculties, and enjoy flowers and birds and all things of nature as much as I do at seventy-one." Here the voice trembled. There were not many dry eyes. The quiver ran through the party, and without another word the Queen sat slowly down. I was very, very proud of that seventy-year old (I am often that), and deeply moved, as she was, by this touching evidence of the regard of the coaching-party for her.

This incident led to some funny stories about presentation speeches. Upon a recent occasion, not far from Paisley, Aggie told us, a worthy deacon had been selected to present a robe to the minister. The church was crowded, and the recipient stood expectantly at the foot of the pulpit, surrounded by the members of his family. Amid breathless silence the committee entered and marched up the aisle, headed by the deacon bearing the gift in his extended arms. On reaching the pulpit a stand was made, but never a word came from the deacon, down whose brow the perspiration rolled in great drops. He was in a daze, but a touch from one of the committee brought him back to something like a realizing sense of his position, and he stammered out, as he handed the robe to the minister:

> "Mr. Broon,
> Here's the goon."

You need not laugh. It is not likely that you could make as good a speech, which, I'll wager, is far better than the one over which he had spent sleepless nights, but which providentially left him at the critical moment.

Windsor, seen from any direction at a distance, is *par excellence* the castle—a truly royal residence; but, seen closely, it loses the grand and sinks into something of prettiness. It is no longer commanding, and is insignificant in comparison with the true castles of the North, the surroundings of which are in keeping with the idea of a stronghold, and take you at once to the times of the chieftain and his armed men. There is nothing of this at Windsor, and the glamour disappears when you begin to analyze. Royalty's famous abode should be looked at, as royalty itself should be—at a safe distance.

St. George's Chapel.

Service at St. George's Chapel will not soon be forgotten by our party. The stalls of the Knights of the Garter, over the canopies of which hang their swords and mantles surmounted by their crests and armorial bearings, carry one far back into the days of chivalry. One stall arrested and held my attention—that of the Earl of Beaconsfield. When I was not gazing at Gladstone's face, I was moralizing upon the last Knight of the Garter, whose flag still floats above the stall. Disraeli won the blue ribbon about as worthily as most men, and by much the same means—he flattered the monarch. But there is this to be said of him: he had brains and made himself.

What a commentary upon pride of birth, the flag of the poor literary adventurer floating beside that of my lord duke's! It pleased me much to see it. How that man must have chuckled as he bowed his way among his dupes, from Her Majesty to Salisbury, and passed the radical extension of the suffrage that doomed hereditary privilege to speedy extinction. But where will imperialism get such another leader, after all? It has not found him yet.

"What is that up there?" asked one of our party. "The royal box, miss." Were we really at the opera, then? A royal box in a church for the worship of God! Did you ever hear anything like that! There is a royal staircase, too. Why not? You would not have royalty on an equality with us, would you, even if we are all alike miserable sinners and engaged in the worship of that God who is no respecter of persons.

"Well, I think this is awful," said one of the party. "I don't believe the good Queen would go to church in this way, if she only thought of it. Our President and family have their pew just like the rest of us." Our English members were equally surprised that the American should see anything shocking in the practice, and the ladies fought out the matter between themselves; the Americans insisting that the Queen should attend worship as other poor sinners do, since all are equal in God's eyes; and the English saying little, but evidently harboring the idea that even in heaven special accommodations would probably be found reserved for royalty, with maybe a special staircase to ascend by. Early education and inherited tendencies account for much.

Royal Etiquette.

The staircase question led to the story that the Marquis of Lorne was not allowed to enter some performance by the same stair with his wife. The American was up at this. "If I had a husband, and he couldn't come with me, I wouldn't go." This made an end of the discussion, for the English young lady's eyes told plainly of her secret vow that wherever she went — — must go too. All were agreed on this point; but on the general question it was a drawn battle, the one side declaring that if they were men they would not have a princess for a wife under any circumstances, and the other insisting that, if they were princesses, they would not have anybody but a prince for a husband.

We were honored while here by the presence of Mr. Sidney G. Thomas and his sister, who came down from London and spent the day with us. Mr. Thomas is the young chemist, who, in conjunction with his cousin Mr. Gilchrist, would not accept the dictum of the authorities that phosphorus, that fiend of steel manufacturers, cannot be expelled from iron ores at a high temperature. They set to work over a small toy pot, which deserves to rank with Watt's tea-kettle, to see whether the scientific world had not blundered. Let me premise that the presence of phosphorus in pig iron to the extent of more than about one tenth of one per cent. is fatal to the production of good steel by the Bessemer or open hearth processes. Do what you will, this troublesome substance persists in remaining with the iron. If there be phosphorus in the iron-stone you smelt, every atom of it will be found in the resulting iron; and if there be any in the limestone, or the coke or coal used, every atom of it also will find its way into the iron.

It is essential, therefore, that iron-stone should be found practically free from phosphorus; but unfortunately such ore is scarce, and therefore expensive. The great iron-stone deposits of England are full of the enemy; so are those of America; hence, both countries depend largely upon ores which have to be transported from Spain and other countries. One authority estimates that if all the high phosphorus ores in Britain could be made as valuable as those free from the objectionable ingredient, the saving per annum would go far to pay the interest upon the national debt. Many have been the attempts to devise some tempting bait to coax this fiend to forego his strange affinity for iron, and unite with some other element;

but no, his satanic majesty would cling to the metal.

Messrs. Thomas and Gilchrist, in studying some highly creditable experiments made by my friend Lothian Bell, Esq. (for he was upon the right track), discovered an oversight which seemed to qualify the results which he reached, and to render his experiments inconclusive. It was possible, they thought, that his failure might have resulted from the fiend not being *kept* out when he *was* out. So they went quietly to work with their toy pot, and Eureka! Their charm had not only exorcised the fiend, but they had discovered how to lead him away from the molten metal into the refuse and shut the door on him there. Here was a triumph indeed! I fancy they neither ate nor slept till repeated experiments proved that the true charm had been found at last.

Iron and Phosphorus.

Mr. E. Windsor Richards, the broad manager of the largest manufactory of iron and steel in the world, was soon acquainted by them with the discovery. He tried it upon a large scale, and announced the end of the reign of King Phosphorus; but he dies hard. This was some years ago, for I read the good news a few minutes after I had landed at Naples from the East, on my way round the world in the year 1879. Many obstacles had yet to be surmounted, but now every ton of steel manufactured at Mr. Richards's great works is made from iron stone which a few years ago was counted worthless for steel. Enough iron stone can be had for three dollars to make a ton of pig iron suitable for steel rails. The same amount of low phosphorus stone at Pittsburgh cost last year sixteen dollars, and yet there are intelligent people who do not understand why we cannot make rails as cheap as the English.

I wonder if I could explain to the general reader how Messrs. Thomas and Gilchrist succeeded. It always seems to me like a fairy tale—I will try. In making steel, ten tons of molten pig iron is run into a big pot called a converter, and hundreds of jets of air are blown up through the mass to burn out the silica and carbon, and finally to make it steel. Now, phosphorus has a greater affinity for lime than for iron when it reaches a certain temperature, and when the air blast brings the mass to the required heat, the million particles of phosphorus, like so many tiny ants disturbed, run hither and thither, quite ready to leave the iron for the lime. These clever young men first put a lot of lime in the bottom of the pot as a bait, and into this fly the ants, perfectly delighted with their new home. The lime and slag float to the top and are drawn off—but mark you, let the temperature fall and the new home gets too cold to suit these salamanders, although the temperature may be over 2,000 degrees, hot enough to melt a bar of steel in a moment if thrown into the pot. No, they must have 2,500 degrees in the lime or they will rush back to the metal.

But here lay a difficulty: 2,500 degrees is so very hot that no ordinary pot lining will stand it, and of course the iron pot itself will not last a moment. If ganister or fire brick is used it just crumbles away, and besides this, the plaguey particles of phosphorus will rush into it and tear it all to pieces. The great point is to get a basic lining, that is, one free from silica. This has at last been accomplished, and now the basic process is destined to revolutionize the manufacture of steel, for out of the poorest ores, and even out of puddle cinder, steel or iron much purer than any now made for rails or bridges can be obtained, and the two young chemists, patentees of the Thomas-Gilchrist process, take their rank in the domain of metallurgy with Cort, Nelson, Bessemer and Siemens. These young men have done more for England's greatness than all her kings and queens and aristocracy put together.

A Modern Moses.

It was this pale Gladstonian-looking youth we had with us for the day and for our Sunday evening dinner at Windsor. He wears no title—he is too sound a Radical, and too sensible a man to change the name his honored father gave him—but nevertheless we felt we had one of the great men of our generation as our guest. If it be true, as it is, that he who causes two blades of grass to grow where but one grew before is a benefactor to the race, what is the magician who takes from the bowels of the earth a ton of dross, and transforms it into steel before our eyes— strikes with his enchanted wand a hundred mines of worthless stone and turns it into gold, as the prophet struck the dry rock and called water forth? The age of real miracles is not over, you see, it has only begun, and Thomas is our modern Moses; his miracle seems as much greater than that of his prototype as the nineteenth century is advanced beyond that of the Jewish dispensation.

Monday was another thoroughly English day. The silver Thames, that glistened in the sun, was enlivened by many stately swans. The castle towered in all its majesty, vivified by the meteor flag which fluttered in the breeze. The grounds of Eton were crowded with nice-looking English boys as we passed. Many of us walked down the steep hill and far into the country in advance of the coach, and felt once more that a fine day in the south of England was perfection indeed. The sun here reminds one of the cup that cheers, but does not inebriate: its rays cheer, but never scorch. You could not tell whether, if there were to be any change, you would prefer it to be a shade cooler or a shade warmer.

The swans of Windsor are an institution almost as old as the castle itself, for they are mentioned in records more than five hundred years ago. The swan is indeed a royal bird, and it is said that no subject can own them when at large in a public river except by special grant from the crown. Such a grant is accompanied by a swan-mark for each *game* of swans—the proper term, mark you, for a collection of the noble birds. You may say a flock of geese but not of swans; a game of swans, please, if you would "speak by the card." The corporation of Windsor has possessed the right of keeping swans in the Thames almost from time immemorial. Formerly the king's swanherd made an annual expedition up the river to mark them. He and his assistants chased the poor frightened birds in boats, caught them roughly with long hooks, with little deference to their beautiful plumage, and marked them by cutting one or more nicks in the upper mandible of their beaks. This expedition, called swan-upping (corrupted into swan-hopping), is still made by the deputies of the Dyers' and Vintners' companies, now the principal swan owners on the Thames, the mark of the former being one nick and of the latter two nicks on the bill.

Villiers, but as he was poor his suit had been rejected. A turn came in the tide. Coke, shorn of most of his honors, was in disgrace, and the Duke of Buckingham, Sir John's brother, was King James's favorite and the dispenser of immense patronage. Coke, with the object of winning back the royal favor and of humbling Bacon, his great enemy, now determined to ally himself with the rising house, and offered his daughter to Villiers. Lady Hatton, who had not been consulted in the matter, refused her consent, ran away with her daughter, and concealed her in the house of a kinsman. But Coke found out her hiding place, and with a dozen stout fellows broke into the house and seized his daughter. Lady Hatton, aided by Bacon, carried her case to the privy council and Coke was proceeded against in the Star Chamber. But with Buckingham behind him the old lawyer proved too strong for Bacon this time, and succeeded in throwing his wife into prison and in forcing her to consent to the match.

The marriage took place at Hampton Court in the presence of the king, the queen, and the most distinguished of the nobility, and Frances became Lady Villiers. Stoke Pogis was settled on the bridegroom, who was shortly raised to the peerage as Viscount Purbeck and Baron Villiers, of Stoke Pogis, and Coke flattered himself that his troubles had at last ended. But the marriage resulted like many another ill-assorted union. Lady Villiers, after driving her husband nearly to the verge of distraction, eloped with Sir Robert Howard, and lived for many years an eventful and scandalous life, which finally brought its reward in her degradation, imprisonment, and death.

If the course of true love never runs smooth, it may be taken for granted that the stream is even more tempestuous when marriage is made a matter of family alliance with no love at all in the matter. Our young ladies were unanimous upon this point, and one and all declared their firm resolve and readiness to trust to "true love" with all its risks. The Queen Dowager, being appealed to by them for support, settled the matter by reciting the lines of an old Scotch song:

> "Lassie tak the man ye loe
> Whate'er ye're minnie say,
> Though ye sud mak ye're bridal bed
> Amang pea strae."

So ta-ta all worldly considerations and family alliances, and the rest of it, say the wild romps of the Gay Charioteers.

Royal Visits.

Several years after the death of Coke, Stoke Pogis was for a short time the place of confinement of Charles I., who could see from its windows the towers of Windsor Castle, which he was never again to enter except as a headless corpse. On the death of Viscount Purbeck, who resided in the manor house after Coke's decease, Stoke Pogis passed by purchase into the hands of the Gayer family. When Charles II. came to his own again the then possessor of the mansion was knighted, and became so devoted in his affection for the Stuarts that when in after time King William desired to visit Stoke Pogis to see a place so rich in historical associations, the old knight would not listen to it. In vain did his wife intercede: he declared that the usurper should not cross his threshold, and he kept his word. So it came to be said that Stoke Pogis had sumptuously entertained one sovereign, been the prison of another, and refused admission to a third.

We were told that quite recently Queen Victoria had visited it in person, with a view to its purchase for her daughter, and while walking through its magnificent suite of rooms she expressed the wish that her own Windsor had their equal. She finally decided to purchase Claremont, the price demanded for Stoke, it is said, having been too great to square with her majesty's estimate of value. It is in the market to-day. If any of our bonanza kings want one of the stately homes of England, rich in historical associations and "looking antiquity," here is his chance.

In still later times the old place came into possession of the Penn family, the heirs of our William Penn of Pennsylvania, and it was by one of them, John Penn, that the cenotaph to Gray was erected—for the poet, it will be remembered, was laid in his mother's tomb. This same Penn pulled down much of the old house and rebuilt is as it is to-day.

Our luncheon was to be upon the banks of the Thames to-day, the Old Swan Inn, where the stone bridge crosses the stream, being our base of supplies; but ere this was reached what a lovely picture was ours between Stoke Pogis and the Swan! All that has been sung or written about the valley of the Thames is found to be more than deserved. The silver stream flows gently through the valley, the fertile land rises gradually on both sides, enabling us to get extensive views from the top of the coach. Our road lies over tolerably high ground some distance from the river. Such perfect, quiet, homelike, luxuriant beauty is to be seen nowhere but in England. It is not possible for the elements to be combined to produce a more pleasing picture; and now, after seeing all else between Brighton and Inverness that lay upon our line, we return to the region of Streatley and Maple Durham, and award them the palm as the finest thoroughly English landscape.

We say to the valley of the Thames what the Eastern poet said to the Vale of Cashmere, which is not half so pretty:

"If there be a paradise upon earth,
It is here, it is here."

The Old Swan proved to be, both in structure and location, a fit component part of the sylvan scene around. There ran the Thames in limpid purity, a picturesque stone bridge overhanging it, and the road-side inn within a few yards of the grassy bank.

Skylarks.

The rugs were laid under a chestnut tree, and our first picnic luncheon spread on the buttercups and daisies. Swallows skimmed the water, bees hummed above us—but stop! what's that, and where? Our first skylark singing at heaven's gate! All who heard this never-to-be-forgotten song for the first time were up and on their feet in an instant; but the tiny songster which was then filling the azure vault with music was nowhere to be seen. It's worth an Atlantic voyage to hear a skylark for the first time. Even luncheon was neglected a while, hungry as we were, that we might if possible catch a glimpse of the warbler. The flood of song poured forth as we stood wrapt awaiting the descent of the messenger from heaven. At last a small black speck came into sight. He is so little to see—so great to hear!

I know several fine things about the famous songster:

> "In the golden lightning
> Of the sunken sun,
> O'er which clouds are bright'ning,
> Thou dost float and run,
> Like an unbodied joy whose race is just begun."

An "unbodied joy!" That's a hit, surely!

Here is Browning on the thrush, which I think should be to the lark:

> "He sings each song twice over,
> Lest you should think he never could recapture
> The first fine careless rapture."

The third is just thrown in by the prodigal hand of genius in a poem not to a lark but to a daisy:

> "Alas! it's no thy neebor sweet,
> The bonnie lark, companion meet,
> Bending thee 'mang the dewy weet,
> Wi' speckl'd breast,
> When upward springing, blithe, to greet
> The purpling east."

How fine is Wordsworth's well known tribute:

> "Type of the wise, who soar but never roam,
> True to the kindred points of Heaven and Home!"

And now I remember Shakespeare has his say too about the lark—what is it in England he has not his say about? or in all the world for that matter; and how much and how many things has he rendered it the highest wisdom for men to keep silent about after he has said his say, holding their peace forever.

Reading Abbey.

A row upon the silver Thames after luncheon, and we are off again for Reading, where we are to rest over night at the Queen's. Reading has a pretty, new park and interesting ruins within its boundaries which we visited before dinner. There are but few traces left of the once famous Abbey, founded early in the twelfth century by Henry I. In the height of its prosperity more than two hundred monks fattened at its hospitable board, and its mitred abbot sat as a peer in Parliament. It was noted, too, as a centre of learning, but the jolly brethren must have sadly degenerated in this respect, if we can believe the report of the royal commissioners in temp. Henry VIII., for Hugh Cook, the last abbot, who was hanged and quartered near his own door in 1539, is described as a "stubborn monk, absolutely without learning." But, of course, all who believe that the much-married Henry was a monster of iniquity will put no faith in the reports of his minions, and will continue to believe that Abbot Hugh was a holy man of God, whose shortcomings in the small matters of orthography and syntax were more than made up by his proficiency in vigils, fastings, and prayers. That he was the "right man in the right place" is proven by the inventory of the relics found in his keeping by the aforesaid minions at the time of the suppression of the monastery. Among these sacred objects were "twoo peces of the holye crosse," "Saynt James hande," "a bone of Marye Magdelene," "a pece of Saynt Pancrat' arme," and "a bone of Saynt Edwarde the martyr is arme." Can it be possible that this saintly man, who so zealously guarded such treasures to the last moment of his life, should still be allowed to suffer under the imputation of stubbornness and ignorance! He mightn't just have been "one of those literary fellers," but it is very clear he had a firm grasp of the "fundamentals" of the faith. What is learning compared to a "bone of Saynt Edwarde" as a means of keeping the sheep in the true fold! The old abbot knew his business better than Henry's commissioners. The tooth of Buddha, which I went to see when in Ceylon, draws crowds from all parts of the island, and excites more piety than the tomtom, or the incantations of the most learned priest. Truly there's nothing like a relic as a means of grace.

A pretty lawn in the rear of our hotel gave us an opportunity for a game of lawn tennis in the twilight after dinner, and in the morning we were off for Oxford. The editorial in the Reading paper that morning upon emigration struck me as going to the root of the matter. Here is the concluding paragraph:

"Already the expanding and prospering industries of the New World are throwing an ominous shadow across the Old World and are affecting some of its habits and practices. But over and above and beyond all these, the free thought, the liberty of action, the calm independence and the sense of the dignity of man as man, and the perfect equality of all before the law and in the eye of the constitution now existing in America, are developing a race of men who, through correspondence with home relations, the intercourse of free travel, the transaction of business, and the free, outspoken language of the press, are gradually disintegrating the yet strong conservative forces of European society, and thus preparing the downfall of the monarchical, aristocratic, military, and ecclesiastic systems which shackle and strangle the people of the Old World. These thoughts seem to me to convey the meaning of the great exodus now going on, and he is a wise statesman who reads the lesson aright."

There's a man after my own heart. He grasps the subject.

Causes of Emigration.

The editor tells one of the several causes of the exodus which is embracing many of the most valuable citizens of the old lands where class distinctions still linger. Man longs not only to be free but to be equal, if he has much manhood in him; and that America is the home for such men, numbers of the best are fast finding out. But England will soon march forward; she is not going to rest behind very long. There will soon be no superior political advantages here for the masses, nor educational ones either. England is at work in earnest, and what she does, she does well. I prophecy that young England will give young America a hard race for supremacy.

Some of us walked ahead of the coach for several miles, and I had a chat with a man whom we met. He was a rough carpenter and his wages were sixteen shillings per week ($4). A laborer gets eleven shillings (not $2.75), but some "good masters" pay thirteen to fourteen shillings ($3.25 to $3.50), and give their men four or five pounds of beef at Christmas. Food is bacon and tea, which are cheap, but no beef. Men's wages have not advanced much for many years (I should think not!), but women's have. An ordinary woman for field work can get one shilling per day (24 cents); a short time ago ninepence (18 cents) was the highest amount paid. Is it not cheering to find poor women getting an advance? But think what their condition still is, when one shilling per day is considered good pay! I asked whether employers did not board the workers in addition to paying these wages, but he assured me they did not. This is southern England and these are agricultural laborers, but the wages seem distressingly low even as compared with British wages in general. The new system of education and the coming extension of the suffrage to the counties will soon work a change among these poor people. They will not rest content crowding each other down thus to a pittance when they can read and write and vote. Thank fortune for this.

Our ladies were unusually gay in their decorations to-day, with bunches of wild flowers on their breasts and hats crowned with poppies and roses. They decked the Queen Dowager out until she looked as if ready to play Ophelia. Their smiles too were as pretty as their flowers. What an embodied joy bright, happy ladies are under all conditions, and how absolutely essential for a coaching party! Was it not Johnson's idea of happiness to drive in a gig with a pretty woman? He wasn't much of a muff! If anything could have kept him in good humor, this would have done it. If he could have been on top of a coach with a bevy of them, not even he could have said a rude thing.

Oxford.

Oxford was reached before the sun went down. Its towers were seen for miles—Magdalen, Baliol, Christ Church, and other familiar names. We crossed the pretty little Isis, marvelling at every step, and drove up the High Street to the Clarendon.

The next day was to be Commencement, and only a few rooms were to be had in the hotel, but we were distributed very comfortably among houses in the neighborhood. Several hours before dinner were delightfully spent in a grand round of the colleges. We peeped into the great quads, walked the cloisters, and got into all kinds of queer old-fashioned places. But the stroll along the Isis, and past Magdalen Tower, and up the long walk—that was the grand finish! We pardon Wolsey his greed of getting, he was so princely in giving. To the man who did so much for Oxford much may be forgiven.

* * * * *

OXFORD, June 21.

This morning was devoted to visiting the principal colleges more in detail, and also to the ascent of the tower of the Sheldonian Theatre, which no one should ever miss doing. Below us lay the city of palaces, for such it seems, palaces of the right kind too—not for idle kings or princes to riot in, and corrupt society by their bad example, but for those who "scorn delights and live laborious days."

Our Cambridge member, Mr. B., tells us it does not cost more than £200 ($1,000) per annum for a student here. This seems very cheap. The tariff which we saw in one of the halls gave us a laugh:

"Commons.

Mutton,   long,   11*d*.

Mutton,   short,   9*d*.

Mutton,   half,   7*d*."

The long and the half we could understand, but how could they manage the short? This must be a kind of medium portion for fellows whose appetites are only so-so. You see how fine things are cut even in Oxford. Our party thought if the students were coaching there would be little occasion for them to know anything of either short or half. At least we were all in for long commons at eleven pence.

Martyrs.

We drove past the martyrs' memorial, Latimer and Ridley's. Cranmer does not deserve to be named with them. A visit to such a monument always does me good, for it enables me to say to those who doubt the real advancement of mankind: Now look at this, and think for what these grand men were burnt! Is it conceivable that good, sterling men shall ever again be called upon in England to die for opinion's sake! That Cranmer wrote and advocated the right and necessity of putting to death those who differed from him, and therefore that he met the fate he considered it right to mete to others, shows what all parties held in those dark days. I claim that the world has made a distinct and permanent advance in this department which in no revolving circle of human affairs is ever to be lost. The persecution of the Rev. Mr. Green, of Professor Robertson Smith, and of Bishop Colenso in the present day proves, no doubt, that there is much yet to be done ere we can be very proud of our progress; but these are the worst of to-day's persecutions, and could occur only in England and Scotland. There is a long gap between them and burning at the stake! Grand old Latimer was prophetic when he called out from amid the faggots to his colleague: "Be of good comfort and play the man; we shall this day light such a candle by God's grace as I trust shall never be put out!"

I think it certain that the candle will never again be put out. The bigots of to-day can annoy only in Britain. In other English-speaking communities even that power has passed away, and persecution for opinion's sake is unknown. "A man may say the thing he will"—there is a further and a higher stage yet to be reached when a man will consider it a man's part to have an opinion upon all matters and say what he thinks boldly, concealing nothing.

We left Oxford with just a sprinkle of rain falling, but we had scarcely got fairly out of the city when it ceased and left the charming landscape lovelier than ever. Banbury Cross was our destination, and on our route lay magnificent Blenheim, the estate given by the nation to the Duke of Marlborough. See what the nations do for the most successful murderers of their fellows! and how insignificant have ever been the rewards of those who preserve, improve, or discover—for a Marlborough or a Wellington a fortune, for a Howard or a Wilberforce a pittance. It is only in heathen China that the statesman, the man of letters, heads the list. No military officer, however successful as a destroyer, can ever reach the highest rank there, for with them the victories of peace are more renowned than those of war; that is reserved for the men who know—the Gladstones and the Disraelis, the Darwins and the Spencers, the Arnolds and the Ruskins. It is only in civilized countries that the first honors are given to butchers.

Blenheim.

Blenheim is superb, grand, and broad enough to satisfy princely tastes. And that noble library! As we walked through it we felt subdued, as if in the presence of the gods of ages past, for a worthy collection of great books ever breathes forth the influence of kings dead yet present, of

> "Those dead but sceptred sovereigns
> Whose spirits still rule us from their urns."

And to think that this library, in whose treasures we revelled, reverently taking one old tome after another in our hands, has since then been sold by auction! Degenerate wretch! but one descended from Marlborough can scarcely be called degenerate. You may not even be responsible for what seems like family dishonor; some previous heir may have rendered the sale necessary; but the dispersion of such treasures as these must surely open the eyes of good men in England to the folly of maintaining hereditary rank and privilege. Perhaps, however, the noble owner had no more use for his books than the lord whose library Burns was privileged to see, which showed no evidences of usage. The bard wrote in a volume of Shakespeare he took up:

> "Through and through the inspired leaves,
> Ye maggots, make your windings;
> But oh! respect his lordship's taste
> And spare his golden bindings."

With many notable exceptions, the aristocracy of Britain took its rise from bad men who did the dirty work of miserable kings, and from women who were even worse than their lords. It seems hastening to an end in a manner strictly in accordance with its birth. Even Englishmen will soon become satisfied that no man should be born to honors, but that these should be reserved for those who merit them. But what kind of fruit could be expected from the tree of privilege? Its roots lie in injustice, and not the least of its evils are those inflicted upon such as are born under its shadow. The young peer who succeeds in making somebody of himself does so in spite of a vicious system, and is entitled to infinite praise; but though our race is slow to learn, the people hear a wee bird singing these stirring days, and they begin to like the song. The days of rank are numbered.

* * * * *

BANBURY, June 22.

Banbury Cross.

Banbury Cross was reached about five o'clock, and few of us were so far away in years or feeling from the days of childhood as not to remember the nursery rhyme which was repeated as we came in sight of the famous Cross. We expected to see a time-worn relic of days long past, and I verily believe that some of us hoped for a glimpse of the old lady on the white horse, with "rings on her fingers, and bells on her toes." Imagine our disappointment, then, when we saw an elaborate Gothic structure, looking as new and modern as if it had received its finishing touches but yesterday. And so indeed it had, for it was recently erected by public subscription. The charm was gone.

I like new political institutions for my native land, but prefer the old historical structures; and as we drove past this spick-and-span imitation of antiquity I felt like criticising the good people of Banbury for the sacrilege I supposed they had committed in thus supplanting the ancient landmark which had made their town known the wide world over. I could not help entertaining a hope, too, that the original "goodly Crosse with many degrees about it," had been put away in some museum or other safe place where it could receive the homage of all devoted lovers of Mother Goose. Alas! inquiry developed the fact that the Puritanic besom of destruction, which demolished so many images and other ornaments in the churches in good Queen Bess's time, swept away Banbury Cross as early as 1602, and that not a piece of it remains to tell of its ancient glory.

Banbury was early noted as a stronghold of Puritanism, and was famous, as Fuller says, for "zeale, cheese and cakes." The zeal and the cheese are not now as strong as they were, but Banbury cakes are still in as high repute as ever, and are largely made and exported. They are probably the same now as in the days of Ben Jonson, who tells of them in "Bartholomew Fair," — a kind of miniature mince pie, generally lozenge-shaped, consisting of a rich paste with a filling of Zante currants and other fruits.

Banbury has the celebrated works of my friend, Mr. Samuelson, M.P.; and before dinner I walked out to see them, and if possible to learn something of Mr. Samuelson's whereabouts. Upon returning to the hotel I found that he was at that moment occupying the sitting-room adjoining ours. We had an evening's talk and compared notes as brother manufacturers. If England and America are drawing more closely together politically, it is also true that the manufacturers of the two countries have nearly the same problems to settle. Mr. Samuelson was deep in railway discriminations and laboring with a parliamentary commission to effect changes, or rather, as he would put it, to obtain justice.

I gave an account of our plans, our failures, and our successes, of which he took note. This much I am bound to say for my former colleagues upon this side (for before I reformed I was a railway manager), that the manufacturers of Britain have wrongs of which we know nothing here, though ours are bad enough. I add the last sentence lest Messrs. Vanderbilt, Roberts, Cassatt, and the Garretts (father and son), might receive a wrong impression from the previous admission; for these are the gentlemen upon whom our fortunes hang.

Political Economy Club.

The evidence given before the Parliament Commission in Britain, proves that the people there are subjected to far worse treatment at the hands of railway companies than we are here. American grain is transported from Liverpool to London, for one-half the rate charged upon English grain from points near Liverpool—I give this as one instance out of hundreds. The defence of the railway company is that unless they carry the foreign article at half rates the ships will carry it to London direct, or that it will go by sea from Liverpool. I attended a meeting of the Political Economy Club, in London, where the question of legislative interference with railway charges was ably discussed. The prevalent opinion seemed to be that it was doubtful whether the evils could be cured by legislation. Being called upon to state our experience here, I gave them an account of the unwise policy pursued by the Pennsylvania Railroad Company (now happily reversed) at Pittsburgh and its consequences; for the great riot in Pittsburgh had for its real source the practice of the Railway Company of carrying the manufactures of the East, from New York and Philadelphia, through the city of Pittsburgh to the West for less than it would carry the same articles for from Pittsburgh, although the distance was twice as great. Many such anomalies as this still exist in England.

The members seemed interested in hearing that the result was that the railway company finally agreed that in no case should the rates to and from the shorter exceed those charged for the greater distance, and Pittsburgh manufactures are now taken East and West at ten per cent. less than the through rates between Chicago and the seaboard, no matter how these may be forced by competition. While this rule does not ensure exact justice nor cover all cases, it is nevertheless a great step in advance and removes most of the more serious causes for just complaint.

The club spoken of is a notable one. It consists of twenty-five members, only vacancies caused by death being filled by election. Admission is considered a great honor. It is said that every question within the range of practical politics upon which the club has declared its opinion, has been legislated upon within a short time in accordance with its decision. Every member is well known and must have a national reputation. Among those present were Sir John Lubbock, who learnt early in youth a rare secret, the way to learn—*"consider the ways of the ant, and be wise"*—and Mr. Fawcett, the blind Postmaster-General, a man whose career proves, as clearly perhaps as ever was proved, the truth that there is no difficulty to him who wills.

Mr. Leonard Courtney, one of the coming men, took a leading part in the discussion on railways; Mr. Giffen, however, read the paper of the evening, which of course was able, although on the wrong side, as I think. He is the noted man of figures, whose recent article, read before the Statistical Society, showing the hundreds of millions America is soon to contain, produced so startling an effect here, as well as in Europe. Mr. Shaw Le Fevre, Lord Sherbrooke (Robert Lowe), and the father of the Corn Law Repeal movement, Mr. Villiers, and several others of note were present.

Satires and Epigrams.

I was indebted to one of the members, my friend Prof. Thorold E. Rogers, M.P., for the coveted opportunity to visit this club. By the way, I wonder the Professor's book of Satires and Epigrams has not been republished in America. It is wonderfully clever, and the Charioteers have had many a laugh and many a pleasant half hour enjoying it.

Here is a specimen, which I may be pardoned quoting, as I found upon inquiry that the hero Brown was no less than one of my own friends, a Dunfermline man too, at that, Mr. Reid, M.P.:

> "Sent to a distant land in early youth,
> Brown made his way by honor, thrift, and truth;
> Ten years he worked and saved, then, satisfied,
> Back to his native land our merchant hied.
> A man of worth as well as wealth, he sought
> How he might wisely use the cash he'd brought:
> He clearly saw his fortune could be graced
> Only by prudence, candor, judgment, taste;
> Assumed no airs, indulged in no pretence,
> Guided his words, his acts, by common sense;
> Maintained his self-respect, though glad to please,
> Seemed not to aim, but won his aims with ease,
> And proved that he had learnt the highest tact,
> When no one feared and no one dared detract.
> (I don't say hate, for some men are so nice
> They cannot bear a man without a vice);
> Well, such a hater, with a well-bred sneer,
> (He took good care that all the room could hear):
> Said, 'Dawdle asked me, Brown, if I could tell
> What are your shield, your arms, your motto?' Well,
> Brown winced, grew red, looked puzzled for a while,
> Then answered gayly with a pleasant smile,
> 'My shield is *or*, sir, and the arms I bear,
> Three mushrooms rampant.'—Motto, '*Here we are.*'"

There are many similar good things in the book, so I venture to point it out to the enterprising publishers of America as something worthy of—"conveying."

There is much discussion this morning as to the best route to take, there is so much to tempt us on either of several ways. Shall we go by Compton Verney (there is a pretty English name for you), Wellesbourn, and Hastings? or shall we take our way through Broughton Castle, Tadmarton, Scoalcliffe, Compton Wynyate, and Oxhill? In one way Wroxton Abbey, one of the real genuine baronial abbeys, if one may say so, and Edgehill. Surely no good Republican would miss that! But on the other route we shall see the stronghold of Lord Saye and Sele, older yet than Wroxton, and Compton Wynyate, older and finer than all—"a noble wreck in ruinous perfection," and a third route still finer than either as far as scenery is concerned. Such is this treasure house, this crowded grand old England, whose every mile boasts such attractions to win our love.

> "Look where we may, we cannot err
> in this delicious region—change of place
> Producing change of beauty—ever new."

Every day's journey only proves to us how little of all there is to see we can see; how much we miss on the right and on the left. One might coach upon this Island every summer during his whole life and yet die leaving more of beauty and of interest to visit than all that he had been able to see. When one does not know how to spend a summer's holiday let him try this coaching life and thank heaven for a new world opened to him.

Wroxton Abbey.

We chose the first route, and whatever the others might have proved we are satisfied, for it is unanimously decided that in Wroxton Abbey we have seen our most interesting structure. Though it dates only from the beginning of the seventeenth century, it is a grand building and a fine example of the domestic architecture of the period. Its west front is a hundred and eighteen feet long, and its porch is an elegant specimen of the Italian decorated entrances of the time. Blenheim and Windsor are larger, but had we our choice we would take Wroxton in preference to either. With what interest did we wander through its quaint irregular chambers and inspect its treasures! James I. slept in this bed, Charles I. in that, and George IV. in another; this quilt is the work of Mary Queen of Scots—there is her name; Queen Elizabeth occupied this chamber during a visit, and King William this. Then the genuine old pictures, although in this department Blenheim stands unrivalled. Marlborough knew the adage that "to the victor belongs the spoils," and acted upon it too, for he had rare opportunities abroad to gather treasures. But for a realization of your most picturesque ideal of a great old English house, betake yourselves to Wroxton Abbey. Its little chapel, rich in very old oak carving, is in itself worth a journey to see.

A pretty story is told of the visit of James I. to the Abbey. The wife of Sir William Pope, the owner, had lately presented him with a daughter, and on the King's arrival the babe was brought to him bearing in her little hand a scroll containing the following verses:

> "See this little mistres here,
> Did never sit in Peter's chaire,
> Or a triple crowne did weare;
> And yet she is a Pope.

"No benefice she ever sold,
Nor did dispence with sins for gold;
She hardly is a sev'nnight old,
And yet she is a Pope.

"No King her feet did ever kisse,
Or had from her worse look than this:
Nor did she ever hope
To saint one with a rope;
And yet she is a Pope.
A female Pope, you'll say, a second Joan;
No sure—she is Pope Innocent or none."

Edgehill.

We lunched off deal tables and drank home-brewed ale in the tap-room of the Holcroft Inn, a queer old place, but we had a jolly time amid every kind of thing that carried us back to the England of past centuries. Beyond Holcroft we came suddenly upon the grandest and most extensive view by far that had yet rejoiced us. We were rolling along absorbed in deep admiration of the fertile land that spread out before us on both sides of the road, and extolling the never-ceasing peacefulness and quiet charm of England, when, on passing through a cut, a wide and varied panorama lay stretched at our feet. A dozen picturesque villages and hamlets were in sight, and by the aid of our field-glass a dozen more were brought within range. The spires of the churches, the poplars, the hedgerows, the woods, the gently undulating land apparently giving forth its luxuriant harvest with such ease and pleasure, all these made up such a picture as we could not leave. We ordered the coach to go on and wait at the foot of the hill until we had feasted ourselves with the view. We lay upon the face of the hill and gazed on Arcadia smiling below. Very soon some of the neighboring residents came, for one is never long without human company in crowded England; and we found that we were indeed upon sacred ground. This was Edgehill! As sturdy republicans we lingered long upon the spot, gazing on the scene of that bloody fight between king and people which, however, was almost without immediate result—for it was a drawn battle—but which eventually led to so much. Charles's army lay at Banbury, whence we had just come, that of the Parliament at Kineton yonder, and spread out before us was the plain where they met. The ground is now occupied by two farms called the Battle Farms, distinguished as Battleton and Thistleton. Between the farm-houses, on the latter place, are the places where the slain were buried, appropriately called the Grave Fields. A copse of fir trees in one place is said to mark the site of a pit into which five hundred were thrown.

Some of the royalist writers have tried to prove that Cromwell was not present at Edgehill, and one has even countenanced an idle tale that he witnessed the battle from a steeple on one of the neighboring hills, and that he incontinently took to his heels, or rather to his horses' legs, when he thought the meeting had resulted disastrously to the forces of the Parliament. But Carlyle characterizes this story as it deserves, for Lord Nugent expressly mentions Cromwell's troop of dragoons as among those that charged at the close of the battle. No, no, stern old Oliver was not the man to stand aloof when he once had scent of a battle; and we may be sure, although he was then but a captain of horse, that he did good service at Edgehill.

There were good men on both sides that day, and not the least among them was brave Sir Jacob Astley, who commanded Charles's foot. He was withal a man of piety, for the Parliamentarians did not have a monopoly in that line, however much their chroniclers may claim it; and I have always regarded his prayer on that momentous Sunday morning as a model which many clergymen might study with profit to themselves and to their congregations. "O Lord!" said he, as he settled himself firmly in the saddle, "Thou knowest how busy I must be this day. If I forget Thee, do not Thou forget me. March on, boys!" Is not that to the purpose?

Let such as are at their appointed work have no fear that they will ever be forgotten—the performance of a duty ranks before the offering of a prayer, any day—nay, is of itself the best prayer. There's plenty of time for lip service when we have served the Lord by hard work in a good cause. When people have nothing better to do let them pray, but don't let them be too greedy and ask much for themselves.

Warwick Castle.

Our route lay through Warwick and Leamington. The view of the castle from the bridge is, I believe, the best of its kind in England. "From turret to foundation stone" it is all perfect. The very entrance tells of the good old days. As we pass beneath the archway, over the drawbridge, and under the portcullis, it all comes back to us.

> "Up drawbridge, grooms. What, Warder, ho!
> Let the portcullis fall!
> To pass there was such scanty room
> The bars descending razed his plume."

Warwick, the king-maker! This was his castle. His quarrel with the king was one of our most taking recitations. The Scribe was considered heavy in this:

> "Know this, the man who injured Warwick
> Never passed uninjured yet."

He found that out, did he not, my lord of the ragged staff!

The view from the great hall looking on the river below is fixed in my mind. Don't miss it; and surely he who will climb to the top of Guy's Tower will have cause for thankfulness for many a year thereafter. You get a look at more of England there than is generally possible. I sympathize with Ruskin in his rage at the attempt to raise funds by subscription to mend the ravages of a recent fire in the castle. A Warwick in the rôle of a Belisarius begging for an obolus! If the king-maker could look upon this! But historical names are now often trailed in the dust in England; and it must be some consolation to him, wherever he may be, to know that the bearer of the title, if responsible for this, is no scion of the old stock.

Guy of Warwick.

The legend of Guy of Warwick, accepted as an historical fact by the early writers, has been relegated to the garret of monkish superstition, with the ribs of the dun cow and other once undoubted relics; but its romance will always lend an interest to the old castle and attract the traveller to the site of the hermitage on Guy's Cliff where the fabled hero died and was buried. You must not suppose that Guy's Tower had any connection with the original Guy, for the building dates only from the close of the fourteenth century, while the latter boasts an antiquity of nearly a thousand years. Indeed, we can place him to a dot, for the antiquary Rous is very precise in his statement. He says: "On the twelfth of June, 926, being the third year of the reign of Athelstan, a most terrible single combat took place between the champions of the kings of England and Denmark—Guy, Earl of Warwick, and Colebrand the Pagan, an African giant; through the mercy of God the Christian undertook the combat, being advised thereto by an angel; and the faithful servant of God and the Church fortunately vanquished the enemy of the whole realm of England."

Is it not dreadful to contemplate what might have been the consequences if Colebrand the African had got the upper hand of that faithful servant of God and the Church! But it was not to be. The Pagan had a lost fight from the start, for, though the chronicle does not expressly say so, it is very evident to the reflecting mind that Guy was backed throughout by the angel—a mean advantage which, but for the immensity of the stake, would have led any ordinary lover of fair play to side with the weaker party. But not so with the wily monks of those days. In their easy consciences the end justified the means, and so they glorified Guy as the champion of all that was good, and so sedulously trumpeted his fame that the Norman barons who succeeded to the ownership of the old Saxon stronghold saw their interest in adopting the victor as an ancestor. In time these Normans came to believe implicitly in the family tree with Guy at the root, just as some silly people pin their faith to the parchment evidences of the professional genealogists proving their descent from some fabulous hero who followed William and his crew from Normandy. They named their sons after Guy, called the tower his tower, and hung up his arms and armor in the great hall, while their wives and daughters worked his exploits in tapestry.

These proud descendants of a fabulous ancestor remind one of the general in the "Pirates of Penzance" who is found weeping at the tomb in the abbey belonging to the property he has purchased. When it is suggested to him that his tears are misplaced, he replies: "Sir, when I bought this property I bought this abbey and this tomb with its *contents*. I do not know whose ancestors these *were*, but I do know whose ancestors they *are*." And he falls to sobbing again, bound to have an ancestry of some kind, the more important the more to belittle himself by comparison. But the general is very English for all that. Tennyson's lines,

> "Trust me, Clara Vere de Vere,
> From yon blue heavens above us bent
> The grand old gardener and his wife
> Smile at the claims of long descent,"

are well known and repeated by the school children all over the land, but the grown men and women, entirely free from the weakness of trying to figure out a family tree of respectable antiquity, will be found unexpectedly small in this old land. Josh Billings settled the matter as far as Americans are concerned, for the malady is even more ridiculous in the New World. "We can't boast old family here," says he, "the country ain't *long* enough, unless a feller has Injun in him." That is what the lawyers call an estoppel, I take it.

Kenilworth Castle.

Driving through Leamington we reached Kenilworth Castle for luncheon, to which we had looked forward for several days. Alas! the keeper informed us that no picnic parties are admitted since the grounds have been put into such excellent order by the kind Earl Clarendon (for which thanks, good earl). But he was a man of some discrimination, this custodian of the ruins, and when he saw our four-in-hand and learned who we were—Americans! Brighton to Inverness!—he made us an exception to the rule, of which I trust his lordship will approve, if he ever hears. We had one of our happiest luncheons beneath the walls under a large hawthorn tree, which we decided was the very place where the enraged Queen Bess discovered dear Amy Robsart on that memorable night.

A thousand memories cluster round this ruin; but what should we have known of it had not the great magician touched with his wand this dead mass of stone and lime and conferred immortality upon the actors and their revels? In his pages we live over again the days of old, and take part with the Virgin Queen and her train of lords and ladies in the grand reception so lavishly prepared for her amusement by the then reigning favorite; ruined walls and towers and courts assume their ancient proportions and resound with music and revelry, and the noble park, now so quiet, is alive once more with huntsmen and gayly clad courtiers. But vivid as is Scott's picture, it is exceeded in quaint interest by the original account of the festivities from which the great romancer drew his facts, but which is as little known to the ordinary reader of "Kenilworth" as is the prototype of Hamlet to the common play-goer. Master Robert Laneham, the writer, was a sort of hanger-on of the court, and appears to have accompanied Leicester to Kenilworth. His account is in the form of a letter addressed to "my good friend, Master Humfrey Martin, Mercer," in London, and is written, says Scott, "in a style of the most intolerable affectation, both in point of composition and orthography."

After a brief account of the preliminary journey of the queen, this veracious chronicler informs us that she was "met in the Park, about a flight shoot from the Brayz and first gate of the castl" by a person representing "one of the ten Sibills, comely clad in a Pall of white Sylk, who pronounced a proper Poezi in English Rime and meeter."... "This her majestie benignly accepting, passed foorth untoo the next gate of the Brayz, which, for the length, largenes, and use they call now the Tylt-yard; whear a Porter, tall of Person, big of lim and stearn of countinance, wrapt also all in Sylke, with a club and keiz of quantitee according, had a rough speech full of Passions, in meeter aptly made to the purpose."

A Giant's Portrait.

Be it here recorded that the Charioteers had the pleasure while in London of looking upon the portrait of this giant porter, which hangs in the King's Guard Chamber at Hampton Court Palace. It is supposed to have been painted by the Italian artist Ferdinando Zucchero, who, it will be remembered, visited England. The fellow is truly called "big of lim," for the canvas is more than nine feet high and the figure, which is said to be of life size, measures eight and a half feet. His hand is seventeen inches long. He stands with his left hand on his hip and his right on a long rapier; is dressed in large balloon breeches, with black stockings, and a white quilted vest with a black waistcoat over it; and wears a cap with a feather in it and a small ruff. The picture was painted after the queen's visit to Kenilworth, for the date 1580 is plainly to be seen in one of the upper corners.

When the great porter had concluded, "six Trumpetoours, every one an eight foot hye in due proportion of Parson beside, all in long garments of Sylk suitabl," who stood upon the wall over the gate, sounded a "tune of welcum." These "armonious blasterz mainteined their music very delectably," while the queen rode into the inner gate, "where the Ladye of the Lake (famous in King Arthurz Book) with two Nymphes waiting uppon her, arrayed all in Sylks, attended her highness' coming. From the midst of the Pool, whear uppon a moovable Iland bright blazing with Torches, she floating to land, met her majestie with a well-penned meeter," expressive of the "Anncientie of the castl" and the hereditary dignity of its owners.

"This Pageant was cloz'd up with a delectabl harmony of Hautboiz, Shalmz, Cornets, and such oother loord Muzik," that held on while her majesty crossed a bridge over a dry valley in front of the castle gate, the different posts of which were decorated with fruits, flowers, birds, and other decorations emblematic of the gifts of Sylvanus, Pomona, Ceres, Neptune, and other divinities. Having passed this, the main gate of the castle was reached. Over it, on a "Tabl beautifully garnisht aboove with her Highness' Arms" was inscribed a Latin poem descriptive of the various tributes paid to her arrival by the gods and goddesses. The verses were read to her by a poet "in a long ceruleoous garment, with a side and wide sleevz Venecian wize drawn up to his elboz, his dooblet sleevz under that Crimson, nothing but Sylk: a Bay garland on his head, and a skro in his hand."... "So passing into the inner Coourt, her majesty (that never rides but alone), thear sat down from her palfrey, was conveied up to Chamber: When after did follo so great peal of gunz, and such lightning by fyrwork a long space toagither, as Jupiter woold sheaw himself too be no furthur behind with his welcoom than the rest of his gods."

The chronicler then gives an account of the festivities, which lasted seventeen days and comprised nearly every amusement known to the period. On Sunday, after "divine servis and preaching," the afternoon was spent in "excellent muzik of sundry swet Instruments and in dauncing of Lordes and Ladiez, and other woorshipfull degreez, uttered with such lively agilitee and commendable grace az whither it moought be more straunge too the eye, or pleazunt too the minde, for my part indeed I coold not discern."

Bearbaiting.

One morning was devoted to a bearbaiting, in which thirteen bears and bandogs took part, "with such fending and prooving, with plucking and tugging, skratting and byting, by plain tooth and nayll a to side and toother, such expens of blood and leather waz thear between them, as a moonths licking I ween will not recoover."

Refined amusement, you say, for the Queen of England and her court only three hundred years ago. But not so fast, my dear lady; think what three hundred years hence will say of you and your amusements. Did you not give us a lively description the other evening of your riding after the hounds? Lady Gay Spanker herself, I thought, could not have done it better, and I am sure she was not more fascinating than you. But long before one hundred years shall pass, my friend, ladies in your station will be equally amazed that you could so torture a poor hare or fox and feel it to be not only not *unworthy of a lady* but a source of enjoyment to you. I say your grandchild will blush for her grandma as she shows to her children the picture of your lovely face. What Queen Elizabeth is now in your eyes, what Roman emperors in the bloody Coliseum were in hers, you will be in the eyes of the third generation after you. Think of this. Remember what Cowper says:

> "I would not rank among my list of friends,
> Though graced with polished manners and fine sense,
> That man who needlessly sets foot upon a worm."

Men will give up such sports after a time; but surely we may expect women to find even in this day not only no pleasure but even positive pain in such sports and leave them to coarser natures.

Sunday Amusements.

Another day was marked by the exhibition of an Italian tumbler, who displayed "such feats of agilitee, in goinges, turninges, tumblinges, castings, hops, jumps, leaps, skips, springs, gambaud, soomersauts, caprettiez, and flights; forward, backward, sydewize, a doownward, upward, and with sundry windings, gyrings and circumflexions; allso lightly and with such eaziness, as by me in feaw words it is not expressibl by pen or speech I tell yoo plain." On the second Sunday, after a "frutefull Sermon," a "solemn Brydeale of a proper Coopl was appointed in the tylt-yard," attended by all the country folk in holiday costume. This was followed by Morris dances, a Coventry play, and other games. "By my troth, Master Martyn, 'twaz a lively pastime; I beleeve it woold have mooved sum man to a right meerry mood, though had it be toold him hiz wife lay a dying." And all this on the Holy Sawbath—for shame, Queen Bess!

Nearly every hour had its appointed sport, one amusement following another in endless variety, and the park was peopled with mimic gods and goddesses who surprised the queen with complimentary dialogues and addresses at every turn. Dancing and feasting were kept up all day long and far into the night, for no note was taken of time. "The clok bell sang not a note all the while her highness waz thear; the clok also stood still withall; the handz of both the tablz stood firm and fast, allwayz poynting at two a clok," the hour of banquet.

The day of our visit to Kenilworth was very warm, even for Americans, and after luncheon we became a lazy, sleepy party. I have a distinct recollection of an upward and then a downward movement which awoke me suddenly. One after another of the party, caught asleep on a rug, was treated to a tossing amid screams of laughter. We were all very drowsy, but a fresh breeze arose as the sun declined, and remounting the coach late in the afternoon we had a charming drive to Stratford-on-Avon.

* * * * *

STRATFORD-ON-AVON, June 23.

Our resting-place was the Red Horse Inn, of which Washington Irving has written so delightfully. One can hardly say that he comes into Shakespeare's country, for one is always there, so deeply and widely has his influence reached. We live in his land always; but, as we approached the quiet little village where he appeared on earth, we could not help speculating upon the causes which produced the prodigy. One almost expects nature herself to present a different aspect to enable us to account in some measure for the apparition of a being so far beyond all others; but it is not so—we see only the quiet beauty which characterizes almost every part of England. His sweet sonnets seem the natural outbirth of the land. Where met he the genius of tragedy, think you? Surely not on the cultivated banks of the gentle Avon, where all is so tame.

Shakespeare's Tomb.

But as Shakespeare resembled other burghers of Stratford so much, not showing upon the surface that he was that

> "largest son of time
> Who wandering sang to a listening world,"

our search for external conditions as to his environment need not be continued. Ordinary laws are inapplicable—he was a law unto himself. How or why Shakespeare was Shakespeare will be settled when there shall be few problems of the race left to settle. It is well that he lies on the banks of the Avon, for that requires us to make a special visit to his shrine to worship him. His mighty shade alone fills the mind. True monotheists are we all who make the pilgrimage to Stratford. I have been there often, but I am always awed into silence as I approach the church; and when I stand beside the ashes of Shakespeare I cannot repress stern, gloomy thoughts, and ask why so potent a force is now but a little dust. The inexplicable waste of nature, a million born that one may live, seems nothing compared to this—the brain of a god doing its work one day and food for worms the next! No wonder, George Eliot, that this was ever the weight that lay upon your heart and troubled you so!

A cheery voice behind me. "What is the matter? Are you ill? You look as if you hadn't a friend in the world!" Thanks, gentle remembrancer. This is no time for the Scribe to forget himself. We are not out for lessons or for moralizing. Things are and shall be "altogether lovely." One must often laugh if one would not cry.

Here is a funny conceit. A worthy draper in the town has recently put an upright stone at the head of his wife's grave, with an inscription setting forth the dates of her birth and death, and beneath it the following verse:

"For the Lord has done great things for us, whereof we are exceeding glad."

The wretch! One of the wives of our party declared that she could not like a man who could think at such a crisis of such a verse, no matter how he meant it. She was confident that he was one of those terribly resigned kind of men who will find that the Lord has done great things for him in the shape of a second helpmeet within two years.

This led to a search for other inscriptions. Here is one which struck our fancy:

> "Under these ashes lies one close confined,
> Who was to all both affable and kind;
> A neighbor good, extensive to ye poor,
> Her soul we hope's at rest forevermore."

This was discussed and considered to go rather too far. Good Swedenborgians still dispute about the body's rising again, and make a great point of that, as showing their superior wisdom, as if it mattered whether we rise with this body or another, any more than whether we wear one suit of clothes or another; the great matter being that we rise at all. But this good friend seems to bespeak rest forever for the soul. One of us spoke of having lately seen a very remarkable collection of passages from Scripture which seemed to permit the hope that all for whom a kind father has nothing better in store than perpetual torture will kindly be permitted to rest. One of the passages in question was: "For the wicked shall *perish* everlastingly." The question was remitted to the theologians of our party, with instructions to give it prayerful consideration and report.

Everlasting Punishment.

If there be Scriptural warrant for the belief, I wish to embrace it at once. Meanwhile I am not going to be sure that any poor miserable sinner is to be disturbed when after "life's fitful fever he sleeps well" on the tender, forgiving bosom of mother earth, unless he can be *finally* fitted for as good or a better life than this. Therefore, good Emma and Ella and the rest who are staunch dogmatists, be very careful how you report, for it is a fearful thing to charge our Creator unjustly with decreeing everlasting torture even to the worst offender into whom He has breathed the breath of life. Refrain, if possible,

> "Under this conjuration speak;
> For we will hear, note, and believe in heart
> That what you speak is in your conscience washed
> As pure as sin with baptism."

I have not yet been favored with the report asked for, and therefore the question rests.

The Charioteers got upon delicate ground occasionally, as was to be expected, and although in all well regulated families two subjects—politics and religion—

are proscribed, we came near running foul of the latter to-day. There were wide differences of opinion among us, of course, from the true blue Presbyterian, strong for all the tenets of Calvin, down to the milder Episcopalian who took more hopeful views and asked:

> "Shall there not be as good a 'Then' as 'Now'?
> Haply much better! since one grain of rice
> Shoots a green feather gemmed with fifty pearls,
> And all the starry champak's white and gold
> Lurks in those little, naked, gray spring-buds."

I related an incident which happened in Rome. As I entered the general drawing room one evening, an exciting discussion was going forward on the very subject which we were then considering. A lady of rank was giving expression to very advanced ideas which others were combatting. An old gentleman at last said: "Ladies and gentlemen, all this reminds me of a discussion we young men were having once in my good old father's hall, when my father happened to enter. After listening to us a few minutes he said: 'Young men, you may as well cease your arguing. I'll tell you all about it. In this life

> "Our ingress is naked and bare,
> Our progress is trouble and care,
> Our egress is—no one knows where.
> If you do well here, you'll do well there,—
> I could tell you no more if I preached for a year.'"

The effect was instantaneous. Unanimous adhesion was given to the old gentleman's conclusion, and the party bid each other a cordial good night and went reconciled to bed. I am happy to record that such was also the effect upon the Charioteers.

Shakespeare Stories.

It will be taken for granted that while the Charioteers were in this hallowed region many stories were told about Shakespeare. Two of the gentlemen of our party, at least, dated our love of letters to the circumstance that we were messenger boys in the Pittsburgh telegraph office; and when we carried telegrams to the managers of the theatre, good kind Mr. Porter (followed by one equally kind to us, Mr. Foster) permitted us after delivering them to pass up to the gallery among the gods, where we heard now and then one of the immortal plays. Having heard the melodious flow of words, which of themselves seem to have some spiritual meaning apart from the letter—differing in this from all other combinations of words—how could we rest till we got the plays and learnt most of the notable passages by heart, crooning over them till they became parts of our intellectual being? One story, I remember, shows how completely the master pervades literature. It is authentic, too, for the teller was one of the actors in it.

Visiting friends in a country town, he went with the family to church Sunday morning. The clergyman called in the evening and seeing upon the parlor table an open copy of Shakespeare, perhaps suspecting (which was true) that our friend had been entertaining the ladies with selections from it, Sunday evening as it was, he felt moved to say that it was the worldling's bible, which for himself he thought but little of and never recommended for general reading. It was the mainstay of the theatre. That is very strange, said our friend, for we have all been saying that the finest part of your sermon was a short quotation from Shakespeare, and I have been reading the whole passage to the ladies. Here it is:

> "The quality of mercy is not strained;
> It droppeth, as the gentle rain from heaven,
> Upon the place beneath: it is twice blessed;
> It blesses him that gives, and him that takes."

Imagine the feelings of the narrow, ignorant man, who really thought he had a call from God to teach mankind. But he could not help it. A man can no more escape the influence of Shakespeare than he can that of surroundings. Shakespeare is the environment of all English-speaking men.

Davie's Shakespearean story was of a fellow in Venango County who, having just "struck ile," bought from a pedler a copy of "As You Like It." He was so pleased with Touchstone that he wrote to the pedler: "If that fellow Shakespeare ever writes anything more, be sure to get me one of the first copies—and d— the expense!"

We had one of the loveliest mornings imaginable for leaving Stratford. Many had assembled to see the start, and our horn sounded several parting blasts as we crossed the bridge and rode out of the town. Our destination was Coventry, twenty-two miles away, and the route lay through Charlecote Park and Hampton Lucy. This was one of the most perfect of all our days. The deer in hundreds gazed on us as we passed. There were some noble stags in the herd, the finest we had seen in England, and Charlecote House was the best specimen of an Elizabethan mansion.

Sir Thomas Lucy.

It was built about 1558 by the very Sir Thomas Lucy whom Shakespeare satirized as Justice Shallow. The original family name was Charlecote or Cherlcote, but about the end of the twelfth century William, son of Walter de Cherlcote, assumed the name of Lucy and took for his arms three luces (pike fish); so Justice Shallow was warranted in affirming that his was an "old coat." The poet's verses will stick to him as long as the world lasts; but judging from other circumstances, Sir Thomas was a very good sort of a man and no doubt a fair specimen of the English Squire of the time. His effigy may still be seen on his tomb in Charlecote Church, beside that of his wife—a not unintelligent face, with moustache and peaked beard cut square at the end, surrounded by the ruff then in fashion. There is no epitaph of himself, but the marble bears a warm memorial of his wife, who died five years before him, concluding thus:

> "Set down by him that best did know
> What hath been written to be true."

Thomas Lucy.

It is commonly said that Shakespeare was arrested for poaching in this very park, but the antiquaries have decided that it was the old park of Fulbrook on the Warwick road, where Fulbrook Castle once stood. But it makes little difference where the precise place was. That is of interest only to the Dryasdusts. All we care to know is that Shakespeare wanted a taste of venison which was denied him, and took it without leave or license. The descendant of that squire, my gentle Shakespeare, would give you the entire herd for another speech to "the poor sequestered stag," which you could dash off—no, you never dashed off anything; create? no; evolved? that's nearer it; *distilled*—there we have it—distilled as the pearls of dew are distilled by nature's sweet influences unknown to man. He would exchange Charlecote estate, man, for another Hamlet or Macbeth, or Lear or Othello, and the world would buy it from him for double the cost of all his broad acres, and esteem itself indebted to him forever. The really precious things of this world are its books.

To *do* things is not one-half the battle. Carlyle is all wrong about this. To be able to tell the world what you have done, that is the greater accomplishment! Cæsar is the greatest man of the sword because he was in his day the greatest man of the pen. Had he known how to fight only, tradition would have handed down his name for a few generations with a tolerably correct account of his achievements; but now every school-boy fights over again his battles and surmounts the difficulties he surmounted, and so his fame goes on increasing forever.

What a man says too often outlives what he does, even when he does great things. General Grant's fame is not to rest upon the fact that he was successful in killing his fellow-citizens in a civil war, all traces of which America wishes to obliterate, but upon the words he said now and then. His "Push things!" will influence Americans when Vicksburg shall be forgotten. "I propose to fight it out on this line" will be part of the language when few will remember when it was spoken; and "Let us have peace" is Grant's most lasting monument. Truly, both the pen and the tongue are mightier than the sword!

Beautiful Trees.

The drive from Warwick to Leamington is famous, but not comparable to that between Leamington and Coventry. Nowhere else can be found such an avenue of stately trees; for many miles a strip about two hundred feet wide on both sides of the road is wooded. In passing through this plantation many a time did we bless the good, kind, thoughtful soul who generations ago laid posterity under so great an obligation. Dead and gone, his name known to the local antiquary and appreciated by a few of the district, but never heard of beyond it. "So shines a good deed in a naughty world." Receive the warm thanks and God bless you of pilgrims from a land now containing the majority of the English-speaking races, which was not even born when you planted these stately trees. Americans come to bless your memory; for what says Sujata:

> "For holy books teach when a man shall plant
> Trees for the travellers' shade, and dig a well
> For the folks' comfort, and beget a son,

It shall be good for such after their death."

Who shall doubt that it is well with the dear, kind soul who planted the thousand trees which delighted us this day, nodding their graceful boughs in genial welcome to the strangers and forming a triumphal arch in their honor.

* * * * *

COVENTRY, June 24.

George Eliot.

Coventry in these days has a greater than Godiva. George Eliot stands alone among women; no second near that throne. We visited the little school-room where she learnt her first lessons; but more than that, the Mayor, who kindly conducted us through the city, introduced us to a man who had been her teacher. "I knew the strange little thing well," he said. A proud privilege indeed! I would have given much to know George Eliot, for many reasons. I heard with something akin to fellowship that she longed to be at every symphony, oratorio, or concert of classical music, and rarely was that strong, brooding face missed at such feasts. Indeed, it was through attending one of these that she caught the cold which terminated fatally. Music was a passion with her, as she found in it calm and peace for the troubled soul tossed and tried by the sad, sad things of life. I understand this. A friend told me that a lady friend of hers, who was staying at the hotel in Florence where George Eliot was, made her acquaintance casually without knowing her name. Something, she knew not what, attracted her to her, and after a few days she began sending flowers to the strange woman. Completely fascinated, she went almost daily for hours to sit with her. This continued for many days, the lady using the utmost freedom, and not without feeling that the attention was pleasing to the queer, plain, and unpretending Englishwoman. One day she discovered by chance who her companion really was. Never before, as she said, had she felt such mortification. She went timidly to George Eliot's room and took her hand in hers, but shrank back unable to speak, while the tears rolled down her cheeks. "What is wrong?" was asked, and then the explanation came. "I didn't know who you were. I never suspected it was *you!*" Then came George Eliot's turn to be embarrassed. "You did not know I was George Eliot, but you were drawn to plain me all for my own self, a woman? I am so happy!" She kissed the American lady tenderly, and the true friendship thus formed knew no end, but ripened to the close.

The finest thing not in her works that I know this genius to have said is this: Standing one day leaning upon the mantel she remarked: "I can imagine the coming of a day when the effort to relieve human beings in distress will be as involuntary upon the part of the beholder as to clasp this mantel would be this moment on my part were I about to fall." There's an ideal for you! Christ might have said that.

The state here imagined is akin to her friend Herbert Spencer's grand paragraph.

"Conscientiousness has in many outgrown that stage in which the sense of a compelling power is joined with rectitude of action. The truly honest man, here and there to be found, is not only without thought of legal, religious, or social compulsion, when he discharges an equitable claim on him; but he is without thought of self-compulsion. He does the right thing with a simple feeling of satisfaction in doing it, and is indeed impatient if anything prevents him from having the satisfaction of doing it." Who is going to cloud the horizon of the future of our race with traitor-doubts when already, in our own day, amid much which saddens us, the beams of a brighter sun, herald of a better day, already touch the mountain tops, for such are this woman and this man towering above their fellows. By and by these beams will reach the lesser heights—and anon, the very plains will be transformed by them, and

> "Man to man the world o'er shall brothers be,
> And a' that."

I think that because we are so happy in this glorious life we are now leading, we are disposed to be so very kind to each other. The Charioteers, one and all, seem to me to have reached Mr. Spencer's ideal. If there's a thing that can be done to promote the happiness of others, they are only impatient till they have the satisfaction of doing it. Happiness is known to be a great beautifier—but is it not also a great doer of good to others? It was resolved to debate the question whether the happy person is not also the one who really thinks most and does most for others—not for hope of reward or fear of punishment, but simply because he has reached the stage where he has a simple satisfaction in doing it.

George Eliot's Poetry.

Here is George Eliot's greatest thing in poetry, for her poems are much less known than they should be.

> "O may I join the choir invisible
> Of those immortal dead who live again
> In minds made better by their presence: live
> In pulses stirred to generosity,
> In deeds of daring rectitude, in scorn
> For miserable aims that end with self,
> In thoughts sublime that pierce the night like stars,
> And with their mild persistence urge men's search
> To vaster issues.
> *
>
> "May I reach
> That purest heaven, be to other souls
> The cup of strength in some great agony,
> Enkindle generous ardor, feed pure love,
> Beget the smiles that have no cruelty—
> Be the sweet presence of a good diffused,
> And in diffusion ever more intense.
> So shall I join the choir invisible
> Whose music is the gladness of the world."

One thing more about our heroine, and a grand thing, said by Colonel Ingersoll. "In the court of her own conscience she sat pure as light, stainless as a star." I believe that, my dear Colonel. Why can you not give the world such gems as you are capable of, and let us alone about future things, concerning which you know no more than a new-born babe or a D.D.?

There is a good guide-book for Coventry, and there's much to tell about that city. It was once the ecclesiastical centre of England. Parliaments have sat there and great things have been done in Coventry. Many curious and valuable papers are seen in the hall. There is the order of Queen Elizabeth to her truly and well-beloved Mayor of Coventry, directing him to assist Earls Huntingdon and Shrewsbury in good charge of Mary Queen of Scots. There is a mace given by Cromwell to the corporation. You see that ruler of men could bestow maces as well as order his troopers to "take away that bauble" when the commonwealth required nursing. These and many more rare treasures are kept in an old building which is not fire-proof—a clear tempting of Providence. If I ever become so great a man as a councillor of Coventry, my maiden speech shall be upon the enormity of this offence. A councillor who carried a vote for a fire-proof building should some day reach the mayorship. This is a hint to our friends there.

The land question still troubles England, but even in Elizabeth's time it was thought not unconstitutional to fix rents arbitrarily. Here lies an edict of Her Majesty good Queen Bess, fixing the rates for pasturage on the commons near Coventry: "For one cow per week, one penny; for one horse, two-pence." Our agriculturists should take this for a basis, a Queen Elizabeth valuation! I suppose some expert or other could figure the "fair rent" for anything, if given this basis to start upon.

Coventry Cathedral.

The churches are very fine, the stained-glass windows excelling in some respects any we have seen, the amount of glass is so much greater. The entire end of one of the cathedral churches is filled by three immense windows reaching from floor to roof, the effect of which is very grand. The choir of this church is not in line with the other portion of the building. In reply to my inquiry why this was so, the guide boldly assured us, with a look of surprise at our ignorance, that all cathedrals are so constructed, and that the crooked choir symbolizes the head of Christ, which is always represented leaning to one side of the cross. This idea made me shiver; I felt as if I should never be able to walk up the aisle of a cathedral again without an unpleasant sensation. Thanks to a clear-headed, thorough-going young lady, who, "just didn't believe it," we soon got at the truth about cathedrals, for she proved that they are everywhere built on straight lines. This guide fitly illustrates the danger of good men staying at home in their little island. His cathedral is crooked, and therefore all others are or should be so. Very English this. Very. There are many things still crooked in the dear old tight little isle which other lands have straightened out long ago, or rather never built crooked. Hurry up, you leader of nations in generations past! It's not your rôle in the world to lag behind; at least it has not been till lately, when others have "bettered your instruction." Come along, England, you are not done for; only stir yourself, and the lead is still yours. The guide was a theological student, and therefore could not be expected to have much general knowledge, but he surely should have known something about cathedrals.

It rained at Coventry during breakfast, and friend G. ventured to suggest that perhaps some of the ladies might prefer going by rail to Birmingham and join the coach there, at luncheon; but

> "He did not know the stuff
> Of our gallant crew, so tough,
> On board the Charioteer O."

He was "morally sat upon," as Lucy says. Not a lady but indignantly repelled the suggestion. Even Mrs. G., a bride, and naturally somewhat in awe of her husband yet, went so far as to say "Tom is a little queer this morning."

Waterproofs and umbrellas to the front, we sallied forth from the courtyard of the Queen's in a drenching down-pour.

> "But what care we how wet we be,
> By the coach we'll live or die."

That was the sentiment which animated our breasts. For my part I was very favorably situated, and I held my umbrella very low to shield my fair charge the better. Of course I greatly enjoyed the first few miles under such conditions. My young lady broke into song, and I thought I caught the sense of the words, which I fondly imagined was something like this:

> "For if you are under an umbrella
> With a very handsome fellow,
> It cannot matter much what the weather may be."

I asked if I had caught the words correctly, but she archly insinuated there was something in the second line that wasn't quite correct. I think, though, she was only in fun; the words were quite right, only her eyes seemed to wander in the direction of young B.

The Oxford Don.

None of the ladies would go inside, so Joe had the compartment all to himself, and no doubt smiled at the good joke as we bowled along. Joe was dry inside, and Perry, though outside, was just the same ere we found an inn. This recalled the story of the coachman and the Oxford Don, when the latter expressed his sympathy at the condition of the former; so sorry he was so wet. "Wouldn't mind being so wet, your honor, if I weren't so *dry*." But I think R. P.'s story almost as good as that. A Don tried to explain to the coachman the operation of the telegraph as they drove along. "They take a glass about the size of an ordinary tumbler, and this they fill with a liquid resembling—ah—like—ah—" "Anything like beer, your honor, for instance?" If Jehu didn't get his complimentary glass at the next halt, that Don was a muff.

The rain ceased, as usual, before we had gone far, and we had a clear dry run until luncheon. We see the Black Country now, rows of little dingy houses beyond, with tall smoky chimneys vomiting smoke, mills and factories at every turn, coal pits and rolling mills and blast furnaces, the very bottomless pit itself; and such dirty, careworn children, hard-driven men, and squalid women. To think of the green lanes, the larks, the Arcadia we have just left. How can people be got to live such terrible lives as they seem condemned to here? Why do they not all run away to the green fields just beyond? Pretty rural Coventry suburbs in the morning and Birmingham at noon; the lights and shadows of human existence can rarely be brought into sharper contrast. If

> "Better fifty years of Europe than a cycle of Cathay"

surely better a year in Leamington than life's span in the Black Country! But do not let us forget that it is just Pittsburgh over again; nay, not even quite so bad, for that city bears the palm for dirt against the world. The fact is, however, that life in such places seems attractive to those born to rural life, and large smoky cities drain the country; but surely this may be safely attributed to necessity. With freedom to choose, one would think the rush would be the other way. The working classes in England do not work so hard or so unceasingly as do their fellows in America. They have ten holidays to the American's one. Neither does their climate entail such a strain upon men as ours does.

Overworked Americans.

I remember after Vandy and I had gone round the world and were walking Pittsburgh streets, we decided that the Americans were the saddest-looking race we had seen. Life is so terribly earnest here. Ambition spurs us all on, from him who handles the spade to him who employs thousands. We know no rest. It is different in the older lands—men rest oftener and enjoy more of what life has to give. The young Republic has some things to teach the parent land, but the elder has an important lesson to teach the younger in this respect. In this world we must learn not to lay up our treasures, but to enjoy them day by day as we travel the path we never return to. If we fail in this we shall find when we do come to the days of leisure that we have lost the taste for and the capacity to enjoy them. There are so many unfortunates cursed with plenty to retire upon, but with nothing to retire to! Sound wisdom that school-boy displayed who did not "believe in putting away for to-morrow the cake he could eat to-day." It might not be fresh on the morrow, or the cat might steal it. The cat steals many a choice bit from Americans intended for the morrow. Among the saddest of all spectacles to me is that of an elderly man occupying his last years grasping for more dollars. "The richest man in America sailing suddenly for Europe to escape business cares," said a wise Scotch gentleman to me, one morning, as he glanced over the *Times* at breakfast. Make a note of that, my enterprising friends, and let it be recorded here that this was written before my friend Herbert Spencer preached to us the gospel of relaxation.

It has always been assumed that dirt and smoke are necessary evils in manufacturing towns, but the next generation will probably wonder how men could be induced to live under such disagreeable conditions. Many of us will live to see all the fuel which is now used in so thriftless a way converted into clean gas before it is fed to the furnaces, and thus consumed without poisoning the atmosphere with smoke, which involves at the same time so great a loss of carbon. Birmingham and Pittsburgh will some day rejoice in unsullied skies, and even London will be a clean city.

We spent the afternoon in Birmingham, and enjoyed a great treat in the Public Hall, in which there is one of the best organs of the world. It is played every Saturday by an eminent musician, admission free. This is one of the little—no, one of the great—things done for the masses in many cities in England, the afternoon of Saturday being kept as a holiday everywhere.

Here is the programme for Saturday, June 25:

TOWN HALL ORGAN RECITAL.

BY MR. STIMPSON

From 3 till 4 o'clock.
Programme for June 25, 1881:

1. Overture to A Midsummer Night's Dream,　　　　*Mendelssohn.*

(It will only be necessary to state this descriptive Overture was written in Berlin, August 6, 1826. Shakespeare and Mendelssohn must have been kindred spirits, for surely no more poetic inspiration ever came from the pen of any musical composer than the Overture of the great German master.)

2. Romanza,　　　　　　　　　　　　　　　*Haydn.*

(This charming Movement is taken from the Symphony which Haydn wrote in 1786, for Paris, entitled "La Reine de France," and has been arranged for the organ by Mr. Best, of Liverpool.)

3. Offertoire, in F major,　　　　　　　　　　*Batiste.*

(All the works of the French masters, Wely, Batiste, Guilmant, and Saint-Saens, if not severely classical, have a certain grace and charm which make them acceptable to even the most prejudiced admirers of the ancient masters; and this Offertoire of Batiste is one of the most popular of his compositions.)

4. Fugue in G minor, J. S.　　　　　　　　　*Bach.*

(It may interest connoisseurs to know this grand Fugue was selected by the Umpires for the trial of skill when the present Organist of the Town Hall was elected.)

5. Jaglied (Hunting Song),　　　　　　　　*Schumann.*

6. Selection from the Opera "Martha"　　　　*Flotow.*

(The Opera from which this selection is taken was written in Vienna, in 1847, and, in conjunction with "Stradella," at once stamped the name of the author as one of the most popular of the dramatic composers of the present day.)

7. Dead March in Saul,　　　　　　　　　　*Handel.*

IN MEMORIAM, SIR JOSIAH MASON.

Price One Halfpenny.

The next Free Organ Recital will be given on July 2d,

AT THREE O'CLOCK.

A HISTORY of the TOWN HALL ORGAN (a New Edition,
Revised and Enlarged,) by Mr. STIMPSON,

Is now ready, and may be had in the Town Hall, and the Midland Educational Co.'s Warehouse, New Street.

**NOTICE.— A box will be placed at each door to receive contri-
butions, to defray the expenses of these recitals.**

The Prima Donna said she had never before heard an organ so grandly played, and she knows. The management of the left hand in the fugue she declared wonderful. It is best to give the best for the masses, even in music, the highest of our gifts. John Bright has made most of his speeches in this hall, but it is no longer large enough for the Liberal demonstrations, and a much larger structure has been erected.

We are behind in providing music for the people, but it says much for the progress of the Republic in these higher domains, from whence come sweetness and light, that the greatest tragic singer, Frau Materna, said to a friend that she would tell Herr Wagner upon her return that if he wished to hear his greatest music performed better than ever it had been before he must come to New York. Alas! even as I re-write these pages comes the sad news that we can reap no more from that genius. He has made his contribution to the world, and a noble one it is, rejoicing many hearts and lifting many above their surroundings to exquisite enjoyments beyond; and now he closes his eyes and vanishes; the long day's task is ended and he must sleep.

To-night the Symphony Society substitutes for another number of their programme his Funeral March. It will seem like a voice from the grave; not a dry eye, nor a cold heart will be in the house. A soul has taken flight to whom we are under obligation, which must increase and increase the longer we live, for it has given expression to much that is of our highest and best, and suggested a thousandfold more than ever could be expressed. Our benefactor is indeed gone, in a sense material, but his soul lives with us and his voice will still be heard calling us up higher. The man who reveals new beauties in music enriches human life in one of its highest phases, and is to be ranked with the true poet. He who composes great music is the equal of him who writes great words; Beethoven, Handel, and Wagner are worthy compeers of Shakespeare, Milton, and Burns.

Furnaces and Coalpits.

The eleven miles between Birmingham and Wolverhampton are nothing but one vast iron-working, coal-mining establishment. There is scarcely a blade of grass of any kind to be seen, and not one real clean pure blade did we observe during the journey. It was Saturday afternoon and the mills were all idle, and the operatives thronged the villages through which we drove. O mills and furnaces and coal-pits and all the rest of you, you may be necessary, but you are no bonnie! Pittsburghers though many of us were, inured to smoke and dirt, we felt the change very deeply from the hedgerows, the green pastures, the wild flowers and pretty clean cottages, and voted the district "horrid." Wolverhampton's steeples soon came into sight, and we who had been there and could conjure up dear, honest, kindly faces waiting to welcome us with warm hearts, were quite restored to our usual spirits, notwithstanding dirt and squalor. The sun of a warm welcome from friends gives many clouds a silver lining, and it did make the black country brighter. The coach and horses, and Joe and Perry, not to mention our generalissimo, belong to Wolverhampton, as you know, and our arrival had been looked for by many. The crowd was quite dense in the principal street as we drove through. One delegation after another was left at friends' houses, the Charioteers having been billeted upon the connection; and here for the first time we were to enjoy a respite.

* * * * *

WOLVERHAMPTON, June 25-30.

We were honored by an entertainment at his Honor the Mayor's. As usual on fine days in England, the attractions of the mansion (and they are not small in this case) gave place to open-air enjoyments on the lawn—the game, the race, the stroll, and all the rest of the sports which charm one in this climate. The race across the lawn was far better fun than the Derby, but our gentlemen must go into strict training before they challenge those English girls again. It is some consolation that Iroquois has since vindicated the glory of the Republic.

We coached one day about fourteen miles to Apley House, and had a joyous picnic day with our friends Mr. and Mrs. S——, of Newton. The party numbered seventy odd, great and small. That day the Charioteers agreed should be marked as a red-letter day in their annals, for surely never was a day's excursion productive of more enjoyment to all of us. There are few, if any, prettier views in England than that from the terrace at Apley House. The Vale of Severn deserves its reputation. We had a trip on the river for several miles from Bridgenorth to the grounds as part of the day's pleasure.

Small Rivers.

How very small England's great rivers are! I remember how deeply hurt Mr. F—— was when his Yankee nephew (H. P. Jr., Our Pard) visited him for the first time, and was shown the river by his uncle, who loved it. "Call this a river?" exclaimed he, "why, it's only a creek! I could almost jump across it there." But H. P. was young then, and would not have hesitated to "speak disrespectfully of the equator" upon occasion. I won the good man's heart at once by saying that small though it was in size (and what has either he or I to boast of in that line, I wonder?) little Severn filled a larger space in the world's destiny and the world's thoughts than twenty mighty streams. Listen:

"Three times they breathed and three times did they drink
Upon agreement of swift Severn's flood,
Who then, affrighted with their bloody looks,
Ran fearfully among the trembling reeds
And hid his crisp head in the hollow bank,
Blood-stained with these violent combatants."

Why, you have not a river like that in all America. H. P. was judiciously silent. But I do not think he was ever quite forgiven. These Americans have always such big ideas.

The free library at Wolverhampton interested me. I do not know where better proof of the advantages of such an institution is to be found. It was started upon a small scale, about fifteen thousand dollars being expended; now some forty thousand dollars have been spent upon the building. Last year eighty-six thousand books were issued. I counted at noon, June 30th, sixty-three persons in the reading-room, and at another time nearly two hundred readers. On Saturdays, between two and ten P.M., the number averages fully a thousand. In addition to the circulating library, there are a reference library, a museum, and large reading-rooms. Several courses of lectures are connected with the institution, with teachers for the various branches. One teacher, a Mr. Williams, has "passed" scholars in the science and art department every year, and one year every one of his scholars passed the Kensington examination. A working plumber who attended these classes gained prizes for chemistry and electricity, and is now secretary of the water-works at Chepstow. We may hear more of that climber yet. Plenty of room at the top! No sectarian papers are subscribed for, but all reputable publications are received if sent. In this way all sects are represented by their best, if the members see fit to contribute them. This is the true plan. "Error may be tolerated if truth be free to combat it. Let truth and error grapple." This city levies one penny per pound upon the rates, as authorized by the Libraries act. This nets about four thousand dollars per annum. Just see what powerful agencies for the improvement of the people can be set on foot for a trifling sum.

A People's Library.

And do not fail to note that this library, like all others in Britain organized under the Libraries act, does not pauperize a people. It is no man's library, but the library of the people—their own, maintained and paid for by public taxation to which all contribute. An endowed library is just like an endowed church, at best half and generally wholly asleep. It is a great mistake to withdraw from such an institution the healthy breeze of public criticism; besides this, people never appreciate what is wholly given to them so highly as that to which they themselves contribute.

Wolverhampton is a go-ahead city (I note a strong Scotch element there). A fine park, recently acquired and laid out with taste, shows that the physical well-being of the people is not lost sight of. The administration of our friend ex-Mayor D. is to be credited with this invaluable acquisition. Mr. D. took the most prominent part in the matter, and having succeeded he can consider the park his own estate.

It is not in any sense taken away from him, nor one of its charms lessened, because his fellow-citizens share its blessings. Indeed as I strolled through it with him I thought the real sense of ownership must be sweeter from the thousands of his fellows whom we saw rejoicing within it than if he were indeed the lordly owner in fee and rented it for revenue. This whole subject of meum and tuum needs reconsideration. If Burns, when he held his plough in joy upon the mountain-side and saw what he saw, felt what he felt, was not more truly the real possessor of the land than the reputed nominal landlord, then I do not grasp the subject. There are woeful blunders made as to the ownership of things. Who owns the treasures of the Sunderland or Hamilton libraries? and who will shed the tears over their dispersion, think you, chief mourner by virtue of deepest loss, the titled dis-graces, in whose names they stand, or the learned librarian whose days have been spent in holy companionship with them? It is he who has made them his own, drawn them from their miserable owners into his heart. I tell you a man cannot be the real owner of a library or a picture gallery without a title from a much higher tribunal than the law. Nor a horse either, for that matter. Who owns your favorite horse? Test it! I say the groom does. Call Habeeb or Roderick. So slow their response! I won't admit they don't know and like me too. John knows my weakness and stands out of sight and lets me succeed slowly with them; but after that, see at one word from him how they prick up their ears and neigh, dance in their boxes, push their grand heads under his arm, and say as plainly as can be, "This is our man." I'm only a sleeping partner with John in them after all. It's the same all through; go to your dogs, or out to your flocks, and see every sheep, and even the little lambs, the cows with their kind, glowering eyes, the chickens, and every living thing run from you to throng round the hand that feeds them. There is no real purchase in money, you must win friendship and ownership in the lower range of life with kindness, companionship, love; the coin of the realm is not legal tender with Trust, or Habeeb, or Brownie, nor with any of the tribe.

Sister Dora.

Let us not forget to chronicle a visit paid to Walsall, the scene of Sister Dora's labors. It is only seven miles from Wolverhampton in the very heart of the black country. Dr. T. drove us out to the crowded smoky town, and we followed him through the hospital and heard from the officials many interesting stories of that wonderful woman. Our friend the Doctor also knew her well. She has been known to rush through a crowd and separate brutal men who were fighting. The most debased of that ignorant mining and iron manufacturing population seemed under her influence to an incredible degree; but then her sympathy and her tender devotion to every human being in distress were no doubt the secret of her power. A desperate case was brought into the hospital late one night. The physicians pronounced his recovery hopeless, but Sister Dora was not satisfied; indeed, she seemed to feel instinctively that the man had still a chance. She told the physicians to leave him, as she felt that they could do little good after they had given up hope, and took charge of the case herself. She told the poor wretch that she was going to stand by him all night and bring him through; and having faith herself she inspired it in the patient, and the result was that she actually saved the man's life.

Here is the very material for a saint. Had this occurred a few generations ago, or were it to occur in some parts of Italy to-day, Saint Dora would surely be added to the calendar, and why not! Let us dispute over the miraculous and supernatural as we may, who will deny that the faith of this noble woman and the faith transmitted from her sympathetic heart to the poor sufferer were the foundation upon which his recovery was built up?

This incident gave rise to a discussion upon the coach one day as to the influence of faith in one's ability to do certain things affecting the result. The man who goes in to win may win: the one who goes in to lose can't win. So far all were agreed. Some of our party were disposed to lament the lack of faith which characterizes this age. "There are no Abrahams now-a-days," said one. "What would you do, Tom, if you should receive a message commanding you to offer up your son upon the altar?" "Well," said Tom, who was a telegraph operator in his early days, "I think I should first ask to have that message repeated." All right. So would we all of us. Still there is a wide province for faith. If it does not exactly remove mountains now a days, it at least enables us to tunnel them, which is much the same thing as far as practical results are concerned.

English Hospitality.

We can tell you nothing of the hotels of Wolverhampton, but the fourteen of us can highly recommend certain quarters where it was our rare privilege to be honored guests. Whether the English eat and drink more than the Americans may be a debatable question, but they certainly do so oftener. The young ladies quartered at Newbridge reported this the only bar to perfect happiness; they never wanted to leave the garden for meals nor to remain so long at table. As the Prima Donna reported, they "just sound a gong and *spring* luncheons and teas and suppers on you." The supper is an English institution, even more sacred than the throne, and destined to outlive it. You cannot escape it, and to tell the truth, after a little you have no wish to do so. There is much enjoyment at supper, and in Scotland this is the toddy-time, and who would miss that hour of social glee!

Mention must be made of the private theatricals at Merridale and of the amateur concert at Clifton House, both highly creditable to the talented performers and productive of great pleasure to the guests. I find a programme of the latter and incorporate it as part of the record:

Clifton House, Wolverhampton,

June 29th, 1881.

Programme of Music

Pianoforte Duet	"Oberon"	*René Favayer*
	Misses A. J. B. and A. C. B.	
Song	"Twenty-one"	*Molloy*
	Miss S. D.	
Song	"The Raft"	*Pinsuti*

	Mr. B. P.	
LADIES' TRIO	"O Skylark, for thy wing"	*Smart*
	The Misses B. and Miss D.	
SONG	"A Summer Shower"	*Marziales*
	Miss D.	
SONG	"The Better Land"	*Cowen*
	Miss M. B.	
SONG	"The Lost Chord"	*Sullivan*
	Miss P.	
PIANOFORTE SOLO	"La Cascade"	*Pauer*
	Miss A. D.	
SONG	"Let me dream again"	*Sullivan*
	Miss R.	
SONG	"The Diver"	*Loder*
	Mr. A. B.	
SONG	"My Nannie's awa'"	– –
	Miss J. J.	
DUET	"When the Wind blows in from the Sea"	*Smart*
	Miss M. B. and Mr. B. P.	
SONG	"For ever and for ever"	*Paolo Tosti*
	Miss A. J. B.	
SONG	"The Boatswain's Story"	*Molloy*
	Mr. B. P.	
	GOD SAVE THE QUEEN.	

Private Theatricals.

A great many fine compliments have been paid to performers in this world, but do you remember one much better than this? Our Prima Donna sang "My Nannie's awa'," my favorite among twenty favorites; and she did sing it that night to perfection. We were all proud of her. When she returned to her seat next to M., there was whispered in her ear: "Oh, Jeannie, the lump's in my throat yet!" All the hundred warm expressions bestowed upon her did not weigh as much as that little gem of a tribute. When you raise the lump in the throat by a song you are upon the right key and have the proper style, even if your teacher has been no other than your own heart, the most important teacher of all.

After the theatricals at Merridale came the feast. The supper-table comes before me, and the speeches. The orator of the Wolverhampton connection is ex-Mayor B. He speaks well, and never did he appear to greater advantage than on that evening. It's a sight "gude for sair een" to see a good-natured, kindly English gentleman presiding at the festive board, surrounded by his children and his children's children, and the family connections to the number of seventy odd. They are indeed a kindly people, but oh dear! those who have never been out of their little island, even the most liberal of them, have such queer, restricted notions about the rest of mankind! This, however, is only natural; travel is in one sense the only possible educator. England has been so far ahead of the world until the present generation, that it is difficult for her sons to believe she is sleeping too long. The best speech of the evening upon our side was made by Our Pard, who said he felt that after he had forgotten all else about this visit, the smiling faces of the pretty, rosy-cheeked English young ladies he had been admiring ever since he came to Wolverhampton, and never more ardently than this evening, would still haunt his thoughts; and then, with more emphasis, he closed with these memorable words: "And I tell you, if ever young men ask me where they can find the nicest, sweetest, prettiest, and best young ladies for wives, they won't have to ask twice." (Correct! shake, Pard!)

We were fortunate in seeing the statue of Mr. Villiers unveiled. Earl Granville spoke with rare grace and ease, his style being so far beyond that of the other speakers that they suffered by comparison. The sledge-hammer style of oratory is done. Let ambitious youngsters make a note of that, and no longer strut and bellow, and tear a passion all to tatters, to very rags. Shakespeare understood it:

> "In the very tempest and I may say whirlwind of your passion,
> You must beget a temperance to give it utterance."

Coffee Houses.

The effort now making throughout Great Britain to provide coffee-houses as substitutes for the numerous gin palaces has not been neglected in Wolverhampton. The Coffee House Company which operates in the city and neighborhood has now fourteen houses in successful operation, and, much to my astonishment and gratification, I learned that seven and a half per cent. dividends were declared and about an equal amount of profit reserved for contingencies. In Birmingham there are twenty houses, and cash dividends of ten per cent. per annum have been made. If they can be generally made to pay even half as well, a grand advance has been made in the war against intemperance. I visited one of the houses with ex-Mayor D., who, I rejoice to say, is Chairman of the Company, and in this great office does more for the cause than a thousand loud-mouthed orators who only denounce the evil about which we are all agreed, but have no plan to suggest for overcoming it. It is so easy to denounce and tear down; but try to build up once and see what slow, discouraging labor is involved.

The prices in these coffee-houses are very low: one large cup of good tea, coffee, or cocoa, at the counter, 1*d.* (2 cents); one sandwich, 1*d.* (2 cents). If taken upstairs in a room at a table, one-half more.

There is a reading-room with newspapers free, bagatelle-table, and comfortable sitting-rooms; also a ladies' room and a lavatory, and cigars, tobacco, and all non-alcoholic drinks are provided. Men go there at night to read and to play games. The company has been operating for three years, and the business increases steadily. We saw similar houses in most of the towns we passed, and wished them God-speed.

A chairman of a company like this has it in his power to do more good for the masses, who are the people of England, than if he occupied his time as member of Parliament; but the English exalt politics unduly and waste the lives of their best men disputing over problems which the more advanced Republicans have settled long ago and cleared out of their way. They will learn better by and by. We must not be impatient. They are a slow race and prone to makeshifts politically.

Lincoln and the Deserter.

A delegation of the Charioteers passed a happy day visiting one of the celebrated homes of England, Bilton Grange, near Rugby, the residence of Mr. John Lancaster, whom Americans will remember as the owner of the yacht "Deerhound," who rescued Commander Semmes, when the "Kearsarge" swept the infamous "Alabama" from the seas. Mr. Lancaster showed us the pistols presented to him by the Confederate Officer as token of gratitude. This seems like ancient history already, so rapidly has the Rebellion and all thoughts thereof faded away. Jefferson Davis goes to and fro exciting no remark, arousing some pity. Had he been invested with the crown of martyrdom, how different would be the feeling of his people to-day! It is with Davis as with the deserter of whom Hon. Daniel J. Morrell tells: He took the mother of the runaway to see President Lincoln, in Washington, to plead for the life of her darling boy, who had been court-martialed and was to be shot in a few days. Lincoln first upbraided my friend for subjecting him to such an ordeal, but the poor woman was already in the room, sobbing as if her heart would break, and there was no help for it. Lincoln conducted her to a seat, asked a great many questions, learned that the boy had returned to work at Johnstown, and provided for his mother and sister from his earnings, giving as an excuse for leaving the army, that it was lying idle on the banks of the Potomac and he knew it could not move until spring.

The President mused a few moments, apparently undecided what action to take. Even the woman held her breath for the time and awaited in silence the word which was to rejoice her or doom her to misery forever.

"Well, I don't believe it would do him any good to shoot him, do you, madam?" asked Father Abraham of the mother, in a tone of inquiry so natural that one would have thought he was actually in doubt upon the subject himself and wanted the opinion of the person who knew the boy best.

The mother was speechless. During the inquiry the President had been rolling a small strip of paper into a ball. He handed this to Mr. Morrell, saying: "Read that when you get out, Daniel, but mind you don't tell Stanton."

Mr. Morrell beckoned the woman to the door, placed her in the carriage, read the slip, and ordered the coachman to drive at once to the office of the Provost Marshal. Here is what he found in that tiny strip: "P.M. Washington—Send Private Johnston, Company B, 9th Penn. Infantry, to his regiment. A. L."

That is the kind of thing that took our trusting hearts and gave this wood-chopper of Illinois such power as all the hereditary monarchs of the world can never hope to acquire. Just so with Jefferson Davis:—it wouldn't do anybody any good to shoot him. Happy America! strong enough to laugh at all powers which talk of assailing you.

Moral for Englishmen.

In driving to and from Bilton Grange, we passed famous Rugby and talked of our favorite Tom Brown. What a sad pity that Mr. Hughes was carried away by the fascinations of a scheme for transplanting gentle manly Englishmen to the Rugby colony in Tennessee! It was foredoomed to failure, and to much heart-burning and recrimination. Of all men in the world, your well-educated young Englishman is least adapted for such a life as Tennessee has to offer. Had the West or North-west been selected, the result should have been different so far as pecuniary consider-ations are concerned, for even poor management there could not have kept the land from rising in value. The stream of emigration from the older States to the new might have told these men where to go; but it seems that whenever foreigners attempt to do anything in America through an organization, their first thought is how to do it in a manner as far as possible from that of the Americans. The consequence is, they generally lose their money. Moral for our English cousins: "When in America do as the Americans do." If they settle in Iowa do you go and sit down beside them there. And to my iron and steel friends in this little island, just one word: If Americans are not overpoweringly anxious to develop the wonderful resources, say of Alabama, for instance, just you take Rip Van Winkle's plan "go home and t'ink about it jest a leetle" before you undertake the task. These Americans do not know everything, of course, but it is just possible they may know something about their own country.

> "Nae man can tether time nor tide,
> The hour approaches, Tam maun ride."

Our six days at Wolverhampton had passed rapidly away in one continual round of social pleasures, and now we were off again to fresh woods and pastures new. The horn sounds. We call the roll once more. Mr. B., Senior, had left us at Windsor, but the Junior B. he sent us fitly represented the family. If he couldn't tell as many funny stories nor quote as much poetry as his sire, the young Cambridge wrangler could sing college songs and give our young ladies many glimpses of young England. He was a great favorite was Theodore (young Obadiah).

Miss B. and he left us at Banbury, much to our regret, but London engage-ments were imperative. Mr. and Mrs. K. arrived. If ever a couple received a warm-er welcome I never saw nor heard of it. It seemed as if we had been separated for years, and how often during our journey had one or another of the party regretted that Aggie and Aaleck were missing all this.

It was upon the ocean that Ben and Davie conceived the idea that a run to Paris would be advisable. Leave of absence for two week was accordingly granted to four—Mr. and Mrs. McC., Miss J. and Mr. V.

We bade them good-bye at Wolverhampton, Thursday, June 30th, and saw them fairly off, not without tears upon both sides from the weaker sex. These partings are miserable things always. Their places were taken by Miss J. R. (a Dunfermline bairn), Miss A. B., and Mr. D. Next morning we gathered the clans at Mr. G.'s, calling at the houses of several other friends for the contingent they had so kindly entertained; thence to Merridale for the remainder and the final start.

It was a sight to see the party on the lawn there as we drove off, giving three hearty cheers for Wolverhampton. In special honor of the head of the clan there, the master of Merridale, we had just sung "For he is an Englishman." Yes, he is the Englishman all over. Our route for many miles was still in the black country, but near Lichfield we reached again the rural beauties of England. How thankful to get away once more from the dirt and smoke and bustle of manufactories!

The new members had not gone far before they exhibited in an aggravated form all the usual signs of the mania which had so seriously affected all who have ever mounted our coach. The older members derived great pleasure from seeing how completely the recent acquisitions were carried away. Their enthusiasm knew no bounds, and we drove in to the Swan at Lichfield brimful of happiness. We had left Wolverhampton about noon, the stage for the day being a short one, only twenty miles.

* * * * *

LICHFIELD, July 1.

Lichfield Cathedral.

The cathedral deserves a visit, out of the way of travel as it is. Its three spires and its chapter house are the finest we have yet seen; and then Chantrey's sleeping children is worth travelling hundreds of miles to see. Never before has marble been made to express the childish sleep of innocence as this does.

It was strange that I should stumble upon a monument in the cathedral to Major Hodson, whose grave I had seen in India. He lies with Havelock and Lawrence in the pretty little English cemetery at Lucknow, poor fellow, and here his friends and neighbors away in quiet Lichfield have commemorated his valor.

How well do I remember my visit to that historic burial place in far off India and the impression made upon me as I stood beside the tombs of the heroes who fell in the days of the great mutiny! The inscription on Lawrence's is: "Here lies Henry Lawrence, who tried to do his duty." What could you add that would not weaken that?

We talked, standing by Hodson's monument, of the long struggle and the relief at Lucknow, and of what I had written of it in my "Notes of a Trip round the World." As it pleased the Charioteers, perhaps I may be pardoned for quoting a part of it.

"Our first visit was to the ruins of the Residency, where for six long months

Sir Henry Lawrence and his devoted band were shut up and surrounded by fifty thousand armed rebels. The grounds, which I should say are about thirty acres in extent, were fortunately encompassed by an earthern rampart six feet in height. You need not be told of the heroic resistance of the two regiments of British soldiers and one of natives, nor of the famous rescue. Hour after hour, day after day, week after week, and month after month, the three hundred women and children, shut in a cellar under ground, watched and prayed for the sound of Havelock's bugles, but it came not. Hope, wearied out at last, had almost given place to despair. Through the day the attacks of the infuriated mob could be seen and repelled, but who was to answer that as darkness fell the wall was not to be pierced at some weak point of the extended line? One officer in command of a critical point failing—not to do his duty, there was never a fear of that—but failing to judge correctly of what the occasion demanded, and the struggle was over. Death was the last of the fears of those poor women night after night as the days rolled slowly away. One night there was graver silence than usual in the room; all were despondent and lay resigned to their seemingly impending fate. No rescue came, nor any tidings of relief. In the darkness one piercing scream was heard from the narrow window. A Highland nurse had clambered up to gaze through the bars and strain her ears once more. The cooling breeze of night blew in her face and wafted such music as she could not stay to hear. One spring to the ground, a clapping of hands above her head, and such a shriek as appalled her sisters who clustered around; but all she could say between the sobs—'The slogan! the slogan!' Few knew what the slogan was. 'Didna ye hear? Didna ye hear?' cried the almost demented girl, and then listening one moment that she might not be deceived, she muttered, 'It's the Macgregors Gathering, the grandest o' them a',' and fell senseless to the ground.

Jessie of Lucknow.

"Truly, my lassie, the 'grandest o' them a',' for never came such strains before to mortal ears. And so Jessie of Lucknow takes her place in history as one of the finest themes for painter, dramatist, poet, or historian, henceforth and forever. I have some hesitation whether the next paragraph in my note-book should go down here or be omitted. Probably it would be in better taste if quietly ignored, but then it would be so finely natural if put in. Well, I shall be natural or nothing, and recount that I could not help rejoicing that Jessie was Scotch, and that Scotchmen first broke the rebel lines and reached the fort, and that the bagpipes led the way. That's all. I feel better now that this also is set down."

In Lichfield cathedral are seven very fine stained-glass windows which were found stowed away in a farm-house in Belgium, and purchased by an English gentleman for £200, and now they rank among the most valuable windows in the world. What a pity that the treasures wantonly destroyed during the Reformation had not found similar shelter, to be brought from their hiding-places once more to delight us!

Church Music.

We heard service Saturday morning, and mourned over the waste of exquisite music—twenty-six singers in the choir and only ten persons to listen in the vast cathedral, besides our party. It is much the same throughout England. In no case during week days did we ever see as many persons in the congregation as in the choir. Surely the impressive cathedrals of England are capable of being put to better uses than this. It seems a sin to have such choirs and not conduct them in some way to reach and elevate greater numbers. In no building would an oratorio sound so well. Why should not these choirs be made the nucleus for a chorus in every district, and let us have music which would draw the masses within the sacred walls? But maybe this would be sacrilegious. Theological minds may see in the music suggested an unworthy intruder in domains sacred to dogma; but they should remember that the Bible tells us that in heaven music is the principal source of happiness—the sermon seems nowhere—and it may go hard with such as fail to give it the first place on earth. In this view of the case it was decided to-day upon the coach that what some had hitherto thought a scandal, viz., that the choirs of most of our fashionable churches cost more than all the other expenses of the church, and that organists and sopranos receive a much larger salary considering the time given than the ministers; or, as one of the young ladies put it, "More is paid for music than for religion"—all this, instead of being reprehensible, as some have unthinkingly believed, may really be, and probably is, quite in accordance with the proper order of worship. Well, I am not going to grudge Miss B. her three thousand dollars a year any longer, said a vestryman; so he was converted to the theory that music stands upon strong ground. Some day, however, my lord bishop and lazy crew, the cathedrals of England will not be yours alone to drone in, but become mighty centres of grand music, from which shall radiate elevating influences over entire districts; and the best minds of the nation, remembering how narrow and bigoted the church was when these structures were built, will change the poet's line and say:

"To what great uses have they come at last!"

The world moves and the church establishment must move with it, or—this is a splendid place to stop—there is as great virtue in your "or" as in your "if," sometimes. Here is the best description of service in an English cathedral:

"And love the high embower'd roof,
With antique pillars massy proof,
And storied windows richly dight,
Casting a dim religious light:
There let the pealing organ blow,
To the full voic'd choir below,
In service high and anthems clear,
As may with sweetness, through my ear,
Dissolve me into ecstasies,
And bring all heaven before mine eyes."

The music at Lichfield does indeed draw you into regions beyond and intimates immortality, and we exclaim with friend Izaak Walton, "Lord, what music hast thou provided for the saints in heaven, when thou affordest bad men such music on earth!"

I remember that when in China I read that Confucius was noted for his intense passion for music. He said one day to his disciples that music not only elevates man while he is listening, but that to those who love it music is able to create distinct images which remain after the strains cease and keep the mind from base thoughts. Think of the sage knowing this when he had probably only the sing-song Chinese fiddle to console him! I forget, he had the gongs, and a set of fine gongs of different tones make most suggestive music, as I have discovered.

The position of Lichfield Cathedral is peculiarly fine. Three sides of the square surrounding it are occupied by splendid ecclesiastical buildings connected with the diocese, including the bishop's palace. A beautiful sheet of water lies upon the lower side, so that nothing incongruous meets the eye.

We obtained there a better idea of the magnitude of the church establishment and its to us seemingly criminal waste of riches than ever before. To think of all this power for good wasting itself upon a beggarly account of empty benches, the choir outnumbering the congregation!

The Coach.

We had ordered the coach to come and await us at the cathedral, but had not expected Perry to drive up to the very door. There the glittering equipage was, however, surrounded by groups of pretty, rosy children and many older people gazing respectfully. There is something about a well-appointed coach and four which is calculated to puff a man up with vanity. I remember I had been absorbed in the service, and afterward in wandering about the cathedral had had my thoughts carried back to India. I was again in the crowded streets of Benares mounted upon the richly caparisoned elephants of the Rajah, and anon strolling upon the Apollo Bunder in Bombay, one of a crowd the gorgeous coloring of which equals any scene ever given in grand opera. I reached the cathedral door in a kind of trance; the gay coach, the horses and their sparkling harness, and Joe and Perry in their livery burst upon me, and looking up and around I did feel that we were a "swell" party, and had ever so much to be thankful for. It is a source of never failing pleasure to stand and see the Charioteers mount the coach—they are all so happy, and I am "so glad they are glad." And so we mounted and drove off, taking a last fond look of grand old Lichfield.

* * * * *

DOVEDALE, July 2-3.

Our objective point was Dovedale, thirty miles distant. When three miles out we stopped at Elmhurst Hall for Miss F., who had preceded us to pay a visit to Mr. and Mrs. F—x, who very kindly invited the party to dismount and lunch with them; but the thirty miles to be done would not permit us the pleasure. The next time we pass, however, good master and mistress of Elmhurst Hall, you shall certainly have the Charioteers within your hospitable walls, if you desire it, for such an inviting place we have rarely seen.

Sudbury Park.

We were to lunch in Sudbury Park, the residence of Lord Vernon. This was the first grassy luncheon of the five new-comers, and we were all delighted to see their enjoyment of this most Arcadian feature of our coaching life. It proved to be one of our pleasantest luncheons, for there is no finer spot in England than Sudbury Park. Of course it is not the glen nor the wimpling burn of the Highlands, but for quiet England it is superb.

The site chosen was near a pretty brook. Before us was the old-fashioned brick Queen Anne mansion, and behind us in the park was a cricket ground, where a match between two neighboring clubs was being worthily contested. The scene was indeed idyllic. There was never more fun and laughter at any of our luncheons. Aaleck had to be repressed at last, for several of the members united in a complaint against him. Their sides ached, but that they did not mind so much; their anxiety was about their cheeks, which were seriously threatened with an explosion if they attempted to eat. To avoid such results it was voted that no one should make a joke nor even a remark. Silence was enjoined; but what did that amount to! The signs and grimaces were worse than speech. Force was no remedy. It took time to get the party toned down, but eventually the lunch was finished.

We strolled over and watched the cricketers. It all depends upon how you look at a thing. So many able-bodied perspiring men knocking about a little ball on a warm summer's day, that is one way; so many men relieved from anxious care and laying the foundation for long years of robust health by invigorating exercise in the open air, that is the other view of the question. The ancients did not count against our little span of life the days spent in the chase; neither need we charge those spent in cricket; and as for our sport, coaching, for every day so spent we decided that it and another might safely be credited. He was a very wise prime minister who said he had often found important duties for which he had not time; one duty, however, he had always *made* time for, his daily afternoon ride on horseback. Your always busy man accomplishes little; the great doer is he who has plenty of leisure. The man at the helm turns the wheel now and then, and so easily too, touching an electric bell; it's the stoker down below who is pitching into it with his coat off. And look at Captain McMicken promenading the deck in his uniform and a face like a full moon; quite at his ease and ready for a story. And there is Johnnie Watson, chief engineer, who rules over the throbbing heart of the ship; he is standing there prepared for a crack. Moral: Don't worry yourself over work, hold yourself in reserve, and sure as fate, "it will all come right in the wash."

Leaving the contestants, we walked down to the lake in front of the mansion, and with our usual good fortune we were just in time to see the twenty acres of ornamental water dragged for pike, which play such havoc with other fish. The water had been drained into a small pond, which seemed alive with bewildered fish. We sat and watched with quiet interest the men drawing the net. Hundreds were caught at every haul, from which the pike were taken. A tremendous eel gave the men a lively chase; three or four times it escaped, wriggled through their legs and hands one after the other, and made for the water. Had the gamekeeper not succeeded in pinning it to the ground with a pitchfork, the eel would have beaten the whole party.

Adam and Eve.

Lord Vernon's park is rich in attractions. An old narrow picturesque arched bridge, which spans the pretty lake, has a statue of Adam at one end and Eve at the other. Over the former the ivy clusters so thickly as to make our great prototype a mass of living green; poor Eve has been less favored, for she is in a pitiable plight for a woman, with "nothing to wear."

But Eve was not used to kind treatment. Adam was by no means a modern model husband, and never gave Eve anything in excess except blame. Here she is still, the Flora McFlimsy of my friend William Allen Butler (minus the flora as I have said); but let her be patient, her dress is sure to come, for kind nature in England abhors nakedness. She is ever at work clothing everything with her mantle of green.

> "Ever and ever bringing secrets forth,
> It sitteth in the green of forest glades
> Nursing strange seedlings at the cedar's root,
> Devising leaves, blooms, blades.
> This is its touch upon the blossomed rose,
> The fashion of its hand-shaped lotus leaves;
> In dark soil and the silence of the seeds
> The robe of Spring it weaves."

We had rare enjoyment at the lake, and envied Lord Vernon his princely heritage. The old forester who once showed me over a noble estate in Scotland was quite right. I was enchanted with one of the views, and repeated.

> "Where is the coward who would not dare
> To fight for such a land!"

"Aye," said the old man, "aye, it's a grand country, *for the lairds.*" It will be a grander country some day when it is less "for the lairds" and more for the toiling masses; but may the destroying angel of progress look kindly upon such scenes of beauty as Sudbury Park. The extensive estate may be disentailed and cultivated by a thousand small owners in smiling homes, with educated children within them, and the land bring forth greater harvests touched by the magic wand of the sense of ownership—for it makes an infinite difference to call a thing your own—and yet the mansion and park remain intact and give to its possessor rarer pleasures than at present. I think one of the greatest drawbacks to life in Britain in grand style must be the contrast existing between the squire and the people about him. It is bad enough even in Chester Valley, where the average condition and the education of the inhabitants are probably equal to any locality in the world, but in England it is far too marked for comfort, I should think.

While we were still lingering on the banks of the lake Perry's horn sounded from the main road to call us from the enchanting scene, and we were off for Dovedale through pretty Ashbourne.

Horseback Riding.

As we bowled along the conversation turned upon horseback riding, and some one quoted the famous maxim, "the outside of a horse for the inside of a man." "But what about a woman?" asked F. "Oh," answered Puss, "the outside of a horse for the inside of a woman and the outside as well, for in no other position can a woman ever possibly look so captivating as on a horse. Girls who ride in the park have double chances." A voice from the front—"You are right." Our Pard there admits that he had no idea of falling in love with Annie until he saw her on horseback; and when he had ridden with her a few times he was conquered. A woman looks her loveliest on horseback.

"That is not Mrs. Parr's opinion," rejoined a young lady on the front seat. "I think it is in her splendid 'Dorothy Fox' she says that a woman never shows so clearly the angel of beauty which dwells in a good woman's heart as when she murmurs her yes to her lover."

"Oh, that's not fair," came from the back row. "That's too short, only a moment; and besides only one man sees it. That doesn't count. We mean that a woman shows off better on horseback than anywhere else."

"Oh!" said the cynic, "is that it, Miss? Nothing counts without the showing off, *eh!*" And so we rattled on interrupted at intervals by exclamations called forth by England's unique beauty.

Can any one picture a resting-place so full of peace and beauty as the old Izaak Walton Inn? We arrived there in the twilight, and some of us walked down the long hill and got our first sight of the Dove from the bridge at the foot across the stream.

I got the memorable verses near enough from memory to repeat them on the bridge. Let me put them down here, for in truth, simple as they are, who is going to predict the coming of the day when they will cease to be prized as one of the gems of literature?

> "She dwelt among the untrodden ways,
> Beside the springs of Dove,
> A maid whom there were none to praise,
> And very few to love.
>
> "A violet by a mossy stone,
> Half hidden from the eye;
> Fair as a star when only one
> Is shining in the sky.
>
> "She lived unknown, and few could know
> When Lucy ceased to be;
> But she is in her grave, and oh,
> The difference to me!"

But think of dear old Izaak and of his fishing excursions to this very spot. He actually stayed at our inn! He too is secure of his position as the author of a classic for as long a time as we care to look forward to. Is it not strange that no one has ever imitated this man's unique style? "God leads us not to heaven by many nor by hard questions," says the fisherman, and he knew a thing or two. There is a flavor about him peculiarly his own, but especially rich when read in this old inn, sacred to his memory. I enjoyed him with a fresh relish during the few hours of Sunday which I could devote to him, for there is a good sermon in many a sentence of the "Complete Angler." Dear old boy, your place in my library and in my heart too is secure.

Ilam Hall.

Ilam Hall, near the inn, is the great place, and there is a pretty little church within a stone's throw of it. We walked over on Sunday morning and saw the squire come into church with his family and take his seat among his people, for I take it most of the congregation were connected with the hall. The parson, no doubt, was the appointee of the squire, and we tried to estimate the importance of these two men in the district, their duties and influence—both great—for to a large extent the moral as well as the material well-being of a community in rural England depends upon the character of the hall and parsonage. The squire was Mr. Hanbury, M.P., who courteously invited our party to visit the hall after service, and to stroll as we pleased through his grounds. He had been in America, and knew our erratic genius and brother iron-master Abram S. Hewitt. In the evening we received from him some fine photographs of the hall (a truly noble one), which we prize highly. The accompanying note was even more gratifying, for it said that he had been so warmly received in America that it was always a pleasure when opportunity offered to show Americans such attentions as might be in his power. It is ever thus, cold indifference between the two English-speaking branches is found only among the stay-at-homes. The man who knows from personal experience the leading characteristics of the people upon both sides of the ferry is invariably a warm and sincere friend. The two peoples have only to become acquainted to become enthusiastic over each other's rare qualities.

This is a sheep-grazing district, quite hilly, and the rainfall is much beyond the average; but the weather question troubles us little; the Charioteers carry sunshine within and without. Our afternoon walk was along the Dove, which we followed up the glen between the hills for several miles, finding new beauties at every turn. Mr. H. has the stream on his estate reserved for five miles for his own fishing, but our landlord said he was very generous and always gave a gentleman a day's sport when properly applied for. We were offered free range by Mr. H., a privilege which Davie and I hold in reserve for a future day, that we may most successfully conjure the shade of our congenial brother of the angle; "for you are to note," saith he, "that we anglers all love one another." We at least all love Izaak Walton, "an excellent angler and now with God." Reading the ingenious defence of fishing by our author, "an honest man and a most excellent fly-fisher," is not waste time in these days of violent anti-vivisectionists, who have seen poor hares chased down for sport all their lives, and their Prince shoot pigeons from a trap without a protest, but who affect to feel pity for a cat sacrificed upon the holy altar of science. Miserable hypocrites, who swallow so large a camel and strain at so very small a gnat! It shows what demoralization is brought about in good people by rank and fashion; one rule for the Prince who disgraces himself by cruel sports, another for the medical student who exalts himself working for the good of his race.

Izaak Walton.

But to quaint Izaak's defence; and first as to the fish themselves.

"Nay, the increase of these creatures that are bred and fed in water is not only more and more miraculous, but more advantageous to man, not only for the lengthening of his life, but for the preventing of sickness; for 'tis observed by the most learned physicians that the casting off of Lent and other fish days hath doubtless been the chief cause of those many putrid, shaking, intermitting agues into which this nation of ours is now more subject than those wiser countries which feed on herbs, salads, and plenty of fish. And it is fit to remember that Moses (Levit. 11: 9; Deut. 14: 9) appointed fish to be the chief diet for the best commonwealth that ever yet was; and it is observable not only that there are fish, as namely the whale, three times as big as the mighty elephant that is so fierce in battle, but that the mightiest feasts have been of fish."

Is not that capital? It calls to mind Josh Billings' answer to his correspondent who wrote saying that he had heard many times that a fish diet was most favorable for increase of brain power, but he had never been able to find out the best kind of fish for the purpose. Could he inform him? "In your case," replied Josh, "try a whale or two."

Fishing.

Here is Izaak's argument for the lawfulness of fishing:

"And for the lawfulness of fishing it may very well be maintained by our Saviour's bidding St. Peter cast his hook into the water and catch a fish for money to pay tribute to Cæsar. And it is observable that it was our Saviour's will that four fishermen should have a priority of nomination in the catalogue of his twelve disciples (Matt. 10: 2, 4, 13), as namely: St. Peter, St. Andrew, St. James, and St. John, and then the rest in their order. And it is yet more observable that when our blessed Saviour went up into the mount when he left the rest of his disciples and chose only three to bear him company at his transfiguration, that those three were all fishermen; and it is to be believed that all the other apostles after they betook themselves to follow Christ, betook themselves to be fishermen too: for it is certain that the greater number of them were found together fishing by Jesus after his resurrection, as it is recorded in the 21st chapter of St. John's Gospel, v. 3, 4. This was the employment of these happy fishermen, concerning which choice some have made these observations: first that he never reproved these for their employment or calling as he did the scribes and the money-changers; and secondly, he found that the hearts of such men were fitted for contemplation and quietness, men of mild, and sweet, and peaceable spirits, as indeed most anglers are; these men our blessed Saviour, who is observed to love to plant grace in good natures, though indeed nothing be too hard for him, yet these men he chose to call from their irreprovable employment of fishing and gave them grace to be his disciples and to follow him and do wonders. I say four of twelve."

There I think we may safely rest the defence of our favorite sport, especially upon secondly; for it is all very well to say animals must be slain that we may live, and yet it does not give one a high idea of the fineness of the man who chooses the occupation of a butcher, and is happiest when he is killing something. Blood! Iago, blood! For my part, while recognizing the necessity that the sheep should bleat for the lamb slain that I may feast, I don't profess to see that the arrangement is anything to rave over as an illustration of the wisdom or the goodness of God. Let us eat, asking no questions, but trusting that some day we shall see clearly that all is well. Meanwhile I give up coursing, fox hunting, and pigeon shooting as unworthy sports, and never again will I kill a deer in sport. I once saw the mild, reproachful eyes of one turned upon me as it lay, wounded, as much as to say: "I am so sorry it was *you* who did this." So was I, poor innocent thing. It is years since I saw that look, but it haunts me yet at intervals. It is one of the many things I have done for which I am ever sorry.

Too much fishing! It is no use to try to give you the good things of Izaak Walton, for it is with him as with Shakespeare. Two volumes of his "beauties" handed to gentle Elia. "This is all very well, my friend, but where are the other five volumes?" We must get out of Dovedale—that is clear. *Allons donc!*

Our stage to-day was to Chatsworth, twenty-four miles, where our Fourth of July dinner was to be celebrated. As we passed Ilam Hall we stopped, sounded our horn, and gave three cheers for the squire who had been so kind to his "American cousins."

Our luncheon was beside the pretty brook at Youlgreaves, on the estate of the Duke of Rutland, and a beautiful trout-stream it is. We could see the speckled beauties darting about, and were quite prepared to believe the wonderful stories told us of the basketfuls taken there sometimes. There is something infectious in a running stream. It is the prettiest thing in nature. Nothing adds so much to our midday enjoyment as one of these babbling brooks,

> "Making music o'er the enamelled stones,
> And giving a gentle kiss to every sedge
> It overtaketh in its pilgrimage."

If there be "sermons in stones," I think it must be when the pure water sings as it rushes over them.

The Burnie.

The Charioteers demanded that I should repeat "The Burnie," a gem by a true poet, Ballantyne. Would you, my gentle reader, like also to know it? I think you would, for such as have followed me so far must have something akin to me and surely will sometimes like what I like, and I like this much:

> "It drappit frae a gray rock upon a mossy stane,
> An doon amang the green grass it wandered lang alane.

It passed the broomie knowe beyond the hunter's hill;
It pleased the miller's bairns an it ca'd their faether's mill.

"But soon anither bed it had, where the rocks met aboon,
And for a time the burnie saw neither sun nor moon.
But the licht o' heaven cam' again, its banks grew green and fair,
And many a bonnie flower in its season blossomed there;

"And ither burnies joined till its rippling song was o'er,
For the burn became a river ere it reached the ocean's shore.
And the wild waves rose to greet it wi' their ain eerie croon.
Working their appointed wark and never, never done.

"Nae sad repinings at the hardness o' their lot,
Nae heart-burnings at what anither got;
The good or ill, the licht or shade, they took as it might be,
Sae onward ran the burnie frae the gray rock to the sea."

There's a moral for us! There is always peace at the end if we do our appointed work and leave the result with the Unknown. Let us, then, follow Mrs. Browning,

"And like a cheerful traveller, take the road,
Singing beside the hedge. What if the bread
Be bitter in thine inn, and thou unshod
To meet the flints?—At least it may be said,
'Because the way is short, I thank thee, God!'"

And so at the sea the burnie's race was run and it found peace. Immensity gives peace always. It is so vain to strive in the presence of the ocean, for it tells of forces irresistible. It obeys its own laws, caring for nought:

"Libel the ocean on its tawny sands, write verses
In its praise; the unmoved sea erases both alike.
Alas for man! unless his fellows can behold his deeds,
He cares not to be great."

Not so. O poet, when man stands on the shore and *thinks*, for then he feels his nothingness, and the applause of his fellows is valued as so much noise merely, except as it serves as proof that he has stirred them for the right. This state lasts unless he lifts his eyes to the skies above the waste, and renews his vows to the Goddess of Duty. He learns, not in the depths nor on the level of ocean's surface, but from higher and beyond—that life is worth living, then he takes up his task and goes on, saying

"And whether crowned or crownless when I fall
It matters not, so as God's work is done.
I've learned to prize the quiet lightning deed—
Not the applauding thunder at its heels
Which men call fame."

Daft Callants.

The Queen Dowager and Aggie were off to paidle in the burn after luncheon, and as a fitting close they kilted their petticoats and danced a highland reel on the greensward, in sight of the company, but at some distance from us. They were just wee lassies again, and to be a wee lassie at seventy-one is a triumph indeed; but, as the Queen Dowager says, that is nothing. She intends to be as daft for many years to come, for my grandfather was far older when he alarmed the auld wives of the village on Halloween night, sticking his false face through the windows. "Oh!" said one, recovering from her fright, "it is just that daft callant, Andrew Carnegie!" I remember one day, in Dunfermline, an old man in the nineties—a picture of withered eld, a few straight, glistening white hairs on each side of his head, and his nose and chin threatening each other—tottered across the room to where I was sitting, and laying his long, skinny hand upon my head, murmured:

"An' ye're a gran'son o' Andrew Carnegie's! Aye, maan, I've seen the day when your grandfaether an' me could have hallooed ony reasonable maan oot o' his judgment."

I hope to be a daft callant at seventy-one—as daft as we all were that day. Indeed, we were all daft enough while coaching, but the Queen Dowager really ought to have been restrained a little. She went beyond all bounds, but life is an undoubted success if you can laugh till the end of it.

Let me try to give an idea how this blessed England is crowded. Here is a sign-board we stopped at to-day, to make sure we were taking the right way; for, even with the Ordnance map upon one's knee, strict attention is required or you will be liable to take the wrong turn.

A voice from the General Manager: "Perry, stop at the post and let us be sure."

"Right, sir."

The post points four ways, east, west, north, and south.

First arm reads as follows: Tissington, 3; Matlock Bath, 10; Chesterfield, 21.

Second arm: Ashbourne, 3; Derby, 16; Kissington, 19.

Third arm: Dovedale, Okedon, Ilam.

Fourth arm: New Haven, 6; Buxton, 17; Bakewell, 13; Chatsworth, 16.

All this the guide-post said at one turn, and fortunate it was that Chatsworth, our destination, happened to be upon the fourth arm, for had the worthy road-surveyors not deemed it necessary to extend their information beyond Bakewell, you see we might as well have consulted the Book of Days.

Tissington Hall.

The entrance to Tissington estate was near the post, and we were very kindly permitted to drive through, which it was said would save several miles and give us a view of another English hall. We managed, however, to take a wrong turn somewhere, and added some eight miles to our journey; so much the better—the longer the route the happier we were.

Every English hall seems to have some special features in which it surpasses all others. This is as it should be, for it permits every fortunate owner to love his home for acknowledged merits of its own. If one has the nobler terrace, another boasts a finer lawn; and if one has woods and a rookery, has not the other the winding Nith through its borders? One cannot have the best of everything, even upon an English estate; neither can one life have the best possible of everything,

"For every blade o' grass keps its ain drap o' dew."

Let us, then, be thankful for our special mercies, and may all our ducks be swans, as friend Edward says mine are.

Have you never had your friend praise his wife to you in moments of confidence, when you have been fishing for a week together? You wonder for a few moments, as you recall the Betsey or Susan he extols; for, if the truth is to be spoken, you have, as it were, shed tears for him when you thought of his yoke. Well, that is the true way: let him make her a swan, even if she is not much of a duck.

We stopped at Rowsley for Miss F., who was to come there by rail from Elmhurst Hall. She brought the London *Times*, which gave us the first news of the terrible catastrophe in Washington. We would not believe that the shot was to prove fatal. It did not seem possible that President Garfield's career was to end in such a way; but, do what we could, the great fear would not down, and we reached Chatsworth much depressed. Our Fourth of July was a sad one, and the intended celebration was given up. Fortunately, the news became more encouraging day after day, so much so that the coaching party ventured to telegraph its congratulations through Secretary Blaine, and it was not until we reached New York that we knew that a relapse had occurred. The cloud which came over us, therefore, had its silver lining in the promise of recovery and a return to greater usefulness than ever.

We stopped to visit Haddon Hall upon our way to Chatsworth, but here we come upon tourists' ground. Every one does the sights of the neighborhood, and readers are therefore respectfully referred to the guide-books. We had our first dusty ride to-day, for we are upon limestone roads, but the discomfort was only trifling; the weather, however, was really warm, and our umbrellas were brought into use as sunshades.

Haddon Hall is a fine specimen of the old hall, and Chatsworth of the new, except that the latter partakes far too much of the show feature. It is no doubt amazing to the crowds of Manchester and Birmingham workers who flock here for a holiday and who have seen nothing finer, but to us who have seen the older gems of England, Chatsworth seems much too modern, for our fastidious tastes. I speak only of the interior, of course, for the house itself and its surroundings are grand; so is the statuary in the noble hall set apart for it—really the best feature in the house.

* * * * *

EDENSOR, July 4.

Edensor.

Edensor is the model village which the Duke of Devonshire has built adjoining the park—a very appropriate and pretty name, for it is perhaps the finest made-to-order village in England. Every cottage is surrounded by pretty grounds and is built with an eye to picturesqueness. It is entered by a handsome lodge from the park, and the road at its upper end is also closed by gates. The church, erected in 1870 from designs of Gilbert Scott, occupies the site of an older one. Opening from the south side of the chancel is a mortuary chapel containing monuments of the Cavendish family. In the churchyard is the monument of Sir Joseph Paxton, builder of the Crystal Palace, who was formerly head gardener at Chatsworth.

One or two epitaphs in the churchyard are worth noting. The following is dated 1787:

> "I was like grass, cut down in haste,
> For fear too long should grow;
> I hope made fit in heaven to sit,
> So why should I not go!"

To be sure, why not? But is there not a little ambiguity in the "too long should grow?"

The next one, dated 1818, seems to commemorate the decease of a plough-boy who was rash enough to leave his proper vocation for another—a sad illustration of *ne sutor ultra crepidam.*

> "When he that day with th' waggon went,
> He little thought his glass was spent;
> But had he kept his Plough in Hand,
> He might have longer till'd the Land."

A Modern Phaethon.

One could not expect that the moral inculcated here would find favor with our Americans. How could the Mighty Republic ever have been brought to its present height and embraced the majority of all English-speaking people in the world, if her sons had not been ambitious and changed from one occupation to another? "Stick to your last" is only fit for monarchical countries, where people believe in classes. This young man was of the right sort and should have a verse of praise on his tombstone instead of this one which reflects upon him. One of the party declared that the man must have been the best workman on the place, and that in America he would soon have owned the acres he ploughed instead of ploughing here for some landlord who spent the resources of the land in London or on the continent. The poetess of the party was commissioned to provide a substitute for the obnoxious verse which should applaud the act of this modern Phaethon who *would* try to drive the wagon, after he had learned all he could about ploughing. We were driving homeward, and as the discussion ended in the manner aforesaid, a sweet voice broke forth:

> "I winna hae the laddie that drives the cart and ploo,
> Although he may be tender, although he may be true;
> But I'll hae the laddie that has my heart betrayed,

The bonnie shepherd laddie that wears the crook and plaid."

The Charioteers gave it the swelling chorus:

"For he's aye true to his lassie,
Aye true to his lassie.
Aye true to me."

Who knows but the refusal of some rural beauty like her of the song to have the laddie that "ca'd the ploo" may have stirred our unfortunate youth to a change of occupation? The "sex" is at the bottom of most of man's misfortunes (and blessings too, let it be noted) and why not of this lamentable end of the would-be wagoner!

The day was so warm, and our next stage to Buxton being not very long (twenty-six miles), we decided to spend the day at Edensor and take an evening drive. We met here, enjoying their honeymoon, a bride and groom who were well known to our Wolverhampton delegation, and how do you suppose they were travelling? Not in the ordinary mode, I assure you. I mention this incident that some of my charming young lady friends, who give me so much pleasure riding with me, may make a note of it. They were doing beautiful Derbyshire on horseback! It was delightful to see them start off in this way. I became interested in the bride, who must be no ordinary woman to think of this plan; she told me it was proving a wonderful success; and the happy young fellow intimated to me, in a kind of confidential way, that her novel idea was the finest one he had ever been a party to. I asked him if he could honestly recommend it, and he boldly said he could. We must think over this.

The evening ride was one of our pleasantest experiences. How entrancing England is after a warm day, when everything seems to rejoice in the hours of peace, succeeding the sunshine which forces growth!

"When the heart-sick earth
Turns her broad back upon the gaudy sun,
And stoops her weary forehead to the night
To struggle with her sorrow all alone,
The moon, that patient sufferer, pale with pain,
Presses her cold lips on her sister's brow
Till she is calm."

Buxton.

It is thus the earth appeared to me as we drove along; it was resting after its labors of the sunny day. The night was spent at Buxton, that famous spa, which has been the resort of health-seekers for more than a thousand years, for it was well known to the Romans and probably to their predecessors. We saw many invalids there drinking the waters, which are chiefly chalybeate; but I take it, as is usual with such places, the change of air and scene, of thought and effort, and, with most, change of diet and freedom from excess, count for ninety-nine points, and the waters, may be, for one. But it is of no consequence what does it, so it is done, therefore Buxton continues to flourish.

How wise a physician was he who cured the Great Mogul when all other remedies had failed! The miraculous Tree of Life was upon a mountain five miles from the palace, and had to be visited daily, in the early morning, by the sufferer, who was required to repeat an incantation under its boughs. The words literally translated were no doubt something like this: "Pray away, you old fool! but it's the walk that does it." You need not laugh. This put into such Latin as the schools delight in might be made to sound frightful to the Mogul "and scare him good," as the negro exhorters deem to be essential for spiritual recovery.

Our hotel was a magnificent "limited company" affair. The start next morning was a sight, in the first real downpour in dead earnest we had experienced. The sky was dark—not one tiny ray of light to give us the slightest hope of change; the barometer low and still falling. Just such a morning as might have begun the flood. Clearly we were in for it; nevertheless, at the appointed hour the Gay Charioteers, arrayed in their waterproofs, with the good hats and bonnets all inside the coach, passed through the crowds of guests who lined the hall, wondering at these mad Americans, and took their accustomed seats with an alacrity that showed they considered the weather "perfectly lovely."

There are two miles of steep ascent as we leave the town, and a few of us decided to walk, two of the ladies among the number. Those who started upon the coach were all right; the pedestrians, however, found themselves far from dry when the top was reached—feet and knees were wet. By noon the rain had ceased, and we stopped at a little inn, where fires were made, our "reserve" clothing brought into use, and our wet clothes dried, and we were as happy as larks when we sat down to luncheon. Is not that a wise test which Thackeray puts into the mouth of one of his waiters: "Oh, I knew he was a gentleman, he was so easily pleased!" Well, our host and hostess at that little inn, who were taken so by surprise when a four-in-hand stopped at the door, said something like this about the American ladies and gentlemen as they left. Why not? Nothing comes amiss to the Gay Charioteers, and so on we go to Manchester, getting once more into the grim, smoky regions of manufacturing enterprise.

* * * * *

MANCHESTER, July 6.

Manchester.

Mine host of The Queen's takes the prize for the one best "swell" dinner enjoyed by the party; but then the rain and the moderate luncheon at the little inn, so different from the picnics on flowery banks, may have given it a relish. The Queen's was evidently determined that its American guests should leave with a favorable impression, and so they did.

There was time to visit the Town Hall and walk the principal streets, but all felt an invincible repugnance to large towns. It was not these we had come to see. Let us get away as soon as possible, and out once more to the green fields; we have cotton-mills and warehouses and dirty, smoky manufactories enough and to spare at home. The morning was cloudy, but the rain held off, and we left the hotel amid a great crowd. The police had at last to step in front of the coach and clear the way. The newspapers had announced our arrival and intended departure, and this brought the crowd upon us. Getting into and out of large cities is the most difficult part of our driving, for the Ordnance map is useless there—frequent stoppages and inquiries must be made; but so far we have been fortunate, and our horn keeps opposing vehicles out of our way in narrow streets and in turning corners. We were bound for Anderton Hall, to spend the night with our friend Mr. B——. Luncheon was taken in a queer, old-fashioned inn, where we ate from bare deal tables, and drank home-brewed ale while we sang:

> "Let gentlemen fine sit down to their wine,
> But we will stick to our beer, we will,
> For we will stick to our beer."

The number and variety of temperance drinks advertised in England is incredible. Non-alcoholic beverages meet us in flaming advertisements at every step—from nervous tonics, phosphated, down to the most startling of all, which, according to the London *Echo* of June 2d, the Bishop of Exeter advertised when he opened a coffee-house, saying:

> "It looks like beer,
> It smells like beer,
> It tastes like beer,
> Yet it is not beer."

Better if it had been, your reverence, for your new beverage was probably a villanous compound, certain to work more injury than genuine beer. In this country we also try to cheat the devil. I mean our unco good people try it; but we call it "bitters," and the worse the whiskey the better the bitters.

* * * * *

CHORLEY, July 7.

Anderton Hall.

As we approached Anderton Hall the English and American flags were seen floating from the archway, earnest of cordial welcome. We were quite at home immediately. Mr. and Mrs. B—— had their family and friends ready to greet us. The dining-hall was decorated with the flags of the old and the new lands, gracefully intertwined, symbolizing the close and warm friendship which exists between them—never, we hope, to be again disturbed. We had a long walk about the place and on the banks of the famous Rivington Reservoir, which supplies Manchester with water. In the evening, after dinner, came speeches. The evening passed delightfully. Next day we were sorely tempted. Mr. M—— was to have the school-children at his house to be entertained, and an opportunity to see a novel celebration was afforded us. Our host and hostess were pressing in their invitation for us to stay, but one night of fourteen guests, two servants, and four horses, was surely enough; so we blew our horn, and, with three ringing cheers for Anderton

Hall and all within it, drove out of its hospitable gates. We stopped and paid our respects to Mr. and Mrs. M— — as we passed their place, and left them all with very sincere regret. How pleasant it would be to linger! but Inverness lies far in the north. We are scarcely one-third of our way thither and the time-table stares us in the face. We do not quite "fold our tents like the Arabs and silently steal away," but at the thrilling call of the horn we mount, and with cheers and God-speeds take our departure for other scenes, but many a long day shall it be ere the faces of the kind people we leave behind fade from our memory.

Chorley has been one of the seats of the cotton manufacture in England for more than two hundred years, the business having been begun there about the time of the Restoration. During the American Revolution it was visited, like other places in Lancashire, by mobs who broke up the spinning machines because they feared that they would deprive the poor of labor. Similar mobs once destroyed sewing-machines in France. What a commentary upon such short-sightedness has been the success of the spinning-jenny and the sewing-machine, and the revolution they have made in the manufacturing industry of the world!

* * * * *

PRESTON, July 8.

Strolling Players.

Preston, sixteen miles away, is our destination, permitting a late start to be made. Our route is still through a manufacturing district; for Manchester reaches her arms far out in every direction. We pass now and then a company of show-people with their vans. Sometimes we find the caravan at rest, the old, weary-looking horses nibbling the road-side grass, for the irregularity of the hedges in England gives fine little plots of grass along the hedge-rows, and nice offsets, as it were, in the road, where these strolling players, and gypsies, pedlers, and itinerant venders of all sorts of queer things, can call a halt and enjoy themselves. Every van appears to be invested with an air of mystery, for was not our Shakespeare,

"Th' applause, delight, the wonder of our stage,"

a strolling player, playing his part in barns and outhouses to wondering rustics? There are such possibilities in every van that I greet the sweet little child as if she were a princess in disguise, and the dark-eyed, foreign-looking boy as if he might have within him the soul of Buddha. I do not believe that any other form of life has the attractions of this nomadic existence. To make it perfect one should put away enough in the funds as a reserve to be drawn upon when he could not make the pittance necessary to feed and clothe him and buy a few old copies of good books as he passed through a village. The rule might be, only when hungry shall this pocket-book be opened. I should have one other contingency in order to be perfectly happy — when I wanted to help a companion in distress. Elia was truly not very far from it when he said that if he were not the independent gentleman he was he would be a beggar. So, if I were not the independent gentleman I am, I would be a member of a strolling band, such as we often pass in this crowded land, and boast that Shakespeare was of our profession. What are the Charioteers, after all, in their happiest dream, but aristocratic gypsies? That is the reason we are so enraptured with the life.

But in Preston there is no scope for idealism. It is a city where cotton is king. No town can be much less attractive; but, mark you, a few steps toward the river and you overlook one of the prettiest parks in the world. The Ribble runs at the foot of the sloping hill upon which the city stands, and its banks have been converted into the pleasure-ground I speak of, in which the toilers sport in thousands and gaze upon the sweet fields of living green beyond far into the country. It is not so bad when the entire district is not given over to manufactures, as in Birmingham and Manchester. There is the cloud, but there is the silver lining also.

If ever the people of England and America are estranged in some future day, which God forbid, I could wish that every American were duly informed of the conduct of the people of Lancashire during the rebellion, and, indeed, of England, Ireland, and Scotland as well, but more particularly of such as were directly dependent upon the supply of cotton for work, as was the case here. The troops of Pennsylvania did not more truly fight the battle of the Union at Gettysburg, than did the thousands of men and women here under the lead of Bright and Cobden, Potter, Forster, Storey, and others, who held the enemies of Republicanism in check. The sacrifices they bore could never have been borne except for a cause which they felt to be their own and held as sacred. The ruling classes of the land were naturally against the Republic. This we must always expect till the day comes in Britain (and it is coming) when all forms of hereditary privilege are swept away and the people are equal politically one with another. Nothing could possibly please the aristocracy of Britain, or any aristocracy, more than the failure of a nation which ignores aristocracy altogether. That is obvious. Human nature would not be what it is were this not so, and they are not blamable for it, but, resisting every temptation, the working men of Britain—those to whom a Republic promises so much, for it gives all men political equality—these stood firm from first to last, the staunch and unflinching friends of the Republic. Some day, perhaps, it may be in the power of America to show that where the interests of the masses of Britain are concerned, she has not forgotten the deep debt she owes to them; no matter what the provocation, the people of America must remember it is their turn to forbear for the sake, not of the ruling classes, but for the sake of the masses of Britain who were and are her devoted friends.

Preston.

Preston, that is, Priest's Town, for it received its name from the many ecclesiastics resident there as early as the eighth century, was once the principal port of Lancashire; and when Charles I. collected ship-money it was assessed for nearly twice the amount of Liverpool.

This was the Charles of whom Lincoln knew so little. Mr. Blaine tells this good story among a hundred, for he is wonderful in this line: When Lincoln and Seward went to Fortress Monroe to meet Mr. Hunter, who represented the Confederate Government, the latter was exceedingly anxious to get the President to promise that if the rebels would lay down their arms no confiscation of property (slaves, of course, included) should follow, and that no man should be punished for taking part in the rebellion. Mr. Hunter concluded by saying that this would only be following the course pursued in England after the contest with King Charles. "Well, Mr. Hunter," said that sagacious and born leader of men, Father Abraham, "my friend Seward here is the historian of my Cabinet, but the only thing I remember about King Charles is *that Cromwell cut his head off!*" Lincoln did not know very much, you see, but then he knew the only part much worth knowing upon the subject, which is one of the differences between a great man and a learned one.

It was at this celebrated interview that Lincoln took up a blank sheet of writing-paper and said to the Confederates, let me write *Emancipation* here at the top and you can fill the rest of the page with your conditions.

Lincoln seized the key of a political position as Napoleon did of a military one, and never relaxed his grasp. He would tell stories all night and make his auditors shout with laughter, but whenever the real business was touched upon, he made his opponents feel that the natural division was that the buzzard should fall to them while his long bony fingers were already fast upon the turkey. He could afford to joke and be patient, for he saw the end from the beginning, and had faith in the Republic.

Richelieu and Cromwell.

See what the whirligig of time brings round. Near Preston, in the valley of the Ribble, was fought in 1648 the battle of Preston or Ribblesdale, in which Cromwell defeated the Scotch army under the Duke of Hamilton, and the English army under Sir Marmaduke Langdale. The Royalists were driven at the point of the bayonet through the streets of Preston, and, though they made a stand at Uttoxeter, were finally overthrown and both generals and many thousand men made prisoners. It was a notable struggle, for the Royalists had more than twice as many men as the Parliamentarians; but then the latter had the great Oliver, who knew how and when to strike a blow.

Booth may not be great in anything, as some think, but I do not know his equal in "Richelieu;" and in one scene in particular he has always seemed to me at his very best. The king sits with his new minister, Baradas, in attendance at his side. Richelieu reclines upon a sofa exhausted while his secretaries "deliver up the papers of a realm." A secretary is on his knee presenting papers. He says:

> "The affairs of England, Sire, most urgent. Charles
> The First has lost a battle that decides
> One half his realm—craves moneys, Sire, and succor.
> KING. He shall have both. Eh, Baradas?
> BARADAS.Yes, Sire.
> RICHELIEU. (*Feebly, but with great distinctness.*) My liege—
> Forgive me—Charles's cause is lost. A man,
> Named Cromwell, risen—*a great man—*"

That is enough, a great man *settles* things; a small one nibbles away at petty reforms, although he knows nothing is settled thereby, and that the question is only pushed ahead for the time to break out again directly. English politicians are mostly nibblers, though Gladstone can take a good bite when put to it.

Will you lay "violent hands upon the Lord's anointed?" "I'll anoint ye!" says Cromwell, and then, I take it, was settled for the future the "divine right of kings" theory; for since that time these curious appendages of a free state have been kept for show, and we hear nothing more of the "divinity which doth hedge a king." Some one of the party remarked that we had not seen a statue or even a picture of England's great Protector. I told them a wise man once said that the reason Cromwell's statue was not put among those of the other rulers of England at Westminster was because he would dwarf them. But his day is coming. We shall have him there in his proper place by and by, and how small hereditary rulers will seem beside him!

Cromwell at Drury Lane.

We noticed in the *Pall Mall Gazette* a curious proof of Cromwell's place in the hearts of the people of England. The pantomime at Drury Lane had a scene in which all the Kings and Queens of England marched across the stage in gorgeous procession. Each was greeted with cheers or hisses or with more or less cordial greeting as the audience thought deserved. When Cromwell appeared in the line a few hisses were answered by round after round of cheering, and the Lord Protector nightly received a popular ovation far beyond that accorded to any other ruler. That the manager of the leading theatre in London should have thought it admissible to introduce the Republican among the Kings is a straw which shows a healthy breeze blowing in the political currents of English life.

He was truly a host in himself; besides, his men were fighting for something better than had been, the others only for maintaining what had before existed. It is this which drives Conservatives to the wall when radicalism moves in earnest upon them. The aspirations of the race for further and higher development nerve the arm which strikes down the barriers of an ignorant past. Who could battle enthusiastically only for such incomplete and unsatisfactory development as we have already reached and pronounce it good! The prize is not worth it. What the race is capable of achieving in the broad future is the mainspring of our assault upon every abuse or privilege, the heritage of the past which disgraces the present.

At Preston many of us received letters from home. Harry's funny one from his little daughter Emma (a namesake of our Emma of the Charioteers) gave us a good laugh. I remember there was one announcement particularly noteworthy: "Ninety dollars gone to smash, papa. The pony's dead." There is your future special correspondent for you.

At eleven o'clock this evening the party received a notable addition—Andrew M., my old schoolfellow and "the Maester's son," arrived from Dunfermline. He was received at the station by a committee especially appointed for the purpose, and shortly thereafter duly initiated into all the rites and mysteries of the Gay Charioteers. He was required, late as it was, to sing two Scotch songs to determine

"Stay where you are, you rogue." Confound the fellow! I did not expect to be picked up in that manner.

Ah Cum was severely let alone after that upon the subject of his conversion. I have no hope of him until we agree among ourselves exactly what we wish the heathen to accept. It is in vain we preach one God and five different religions; there must be only one true religion as well. Ah Cum's defence of the worship of ancestors was clever. It ran thus: All religions acknowledge the Creator of life as the true object of worship. Taking hold of his watch chain he began at the first link and said: "I worshipee my parents (passing one link), my parents worshipee their parents" (passing another link, and so on till he had passed quite a number); "by by come to firstee, lifee Goddee. You jump up sky all oncee, miss him, may be."

He thought he had a sure thing passing up link by link to the end. We need clever missionaries to hold their own with these Celestials.

* * * * *

LANCASTER, July 9, 10.

Lancaster.

We had done our twenty-nine miles from Preston and reached Lancaster in good season. There we had a treat. The High Sheriff for the county had just been elected and made his entry into town according to immemorial custom. He represents royalty in the county during his term of office, which I believe is only two years. It costs the recipient of the honor a large sum to maintain the dignities of the office, for its emoluments are nil. The sheriff was staying at our hotel, a very fine one, The County. He is wakened every morning by two heralds richly dressed in the olden style and bearing halberds. They stand in front of the hotel and sound their bugles to call His Highness forth. It is the Lord Mayor's procession on a small scale. Nobody laughs outright at the curious mixture of feudal customs with this age's requirements, however much everybody may laugh in his sleeve; but England will have lost some picturesque features when all the shams are gone. If mankind were not greatly influenced by forms, I could wish that just enough of the "good old times"—which were very bad times indeed—could be preserved, if only to prove how far we have outgrown them; but every form and every sham, from royalty downward, carries its good or evil with it. That not only the substance should be right, but that the form should correspond truly to it, is important if we are to be honest; so I reconcile myself to the passing away of all forms which no longer honestly represent what they imply.

Lancaster is a beautiful place and noted for its admirable charitable institutions. The lunatic asylum and an orphanage attracted our special attention. These and kindred institutions abound in England, and are ably conducted. Rich Englishmen do not leave their fortunes for uses of this kind as often as Americans do. The ambition to found a family, and the maintenance of an aristocratic class by means of primogeniture and entail, tend to divert fortunes from this nobler path into the meaner end of elevating a name in the social scale; but the general public in Britain is most generous, and immense sums in the aggregate are annually collected for charitable institutions. It is common for a class to support its own unfortunates. The commercial travellers, for instance, have an extensive home near London for children of their fellows and for members in their old age, and there is scarcely a branch of industry which does not follow this example.

A Noble Charity.

One cannot travel far without seeing that the British are a people most mindful of the unfortunate. These pretty homes of refuge and of rest we see scattered everywhere over the land, nor are they the least glorious of the many monuments of England's true worth.

A Mr. Ripley, of Lancaster, left his fortune for an orphanage, open to all orphan children born within fifteen miles of Lancaster. Three hundred are now provided for, but so rapidly has the fund grown that it has been found practicable to extend the boundaries of its beneficence, and children from distant Liverpool are now admitted. Bravo! Mr. Ripley. What is an earldom for your eldest son to this! His father's name will carry him farther with the best, and he should be prouder of it. Show me the earl who has done as much for his neighborhood!

Lancaster Castle is a noble one. Here John o' Gaunt hundreds of years ago put his finger upon the dire root of England's woes, as far as the land goes:

> "This dear, dear land,
> Dear for her reputation through the world,
> Is now *leas'd* out."

There you have it—this England is leased out. The soil is not worked by its owners, and never, till England changes its practice and can boast a peasant proprietary working its own acres in small farms, untrammelled by vicious laws, will she know what miracles can be wrought by those who call each little spot their own—their home. Englishmen are slow to change, but the day is not far distant when ownership of land will depend upon residence on it and its proper cultivation. Denmark's example will be followed. Cumulative taxes will be levied upon each number of acres beyond a minimum number, and large proprietors taxed out of existence as they have been in Denmark, to the country's good and nobody's injury. We tax a man who keeps racing-horses or who sports armorial bearings. It is the same principle: we can tax a man who keeps a larger amount of land than he can work to the State's advantage. The rights of property are all very well in their place, but the rights of man and the good of the commonwealth are far beyond them. I wish England would just let me arrange that little land matter for her. It would save her a generation of agitation.

Lancaster was an ancient Roman station, as is shown by its name—Lune or Lone Castrum, the castle or camp on the Lune or Lone, the little river which washes its plain. For what saith Spencer in the Faery Queen:

> "——After came the strong shallow Lone
> That to old Lancaster its name doth lend."

The memory of man goeth not back to the time when the first castle was built. Indeed it is of little consequence now, for it was almost entirely razed by the Scots in the fourteenth century.

Lancaster Castle.

The present noble structure, or rather the older part of it, is the work of John O'Gaunt, that son of a king who was almost a king himself, and who became the father of kings. To him is due the magnificent Gateway Tower, flanked by two octagonal turrets sixty-six feet high, surrounded by watch-towers. Around the towers and across the curtain, perforated by the gate, which connects them, are overhanging battlements with vertical openings for pouring down molten metal or hot water on the heads of assailants. In a niche in front is a full-length statue of John O'Gaunt in the costume of his day, placed there in 1822. The sole remaining turret of the Lungess Tower, eighty-eight feet high, is called John O'Gaunt's Chair. It commands a view of great extent, comprising the hills of Cumberland and Westmoreland and nearly the whole extent of the valley of the Lune, with the Irish Sea in the distance.

Some moralists, who believe that men and times are degenerate, may lament that this grand old castle—the ancient residence of nobles—should now be the abode of criminals; but, while equally desirous that its architectural wonders may be preserved, I am not inclined to admit that the thieves and cutthroats who now have their homes within its walls through the puissance of the law are any worse morally than were many of the noble barons who robbed and ravished in the good old times when the question of might versus right was always settled in favor of the plaintiff. Some of them indeed more richly merited a halter than the comfortable seclusion from the outer world accorded to their modern representatives. Even good old John O'Gaunt himself was not so virtuous that he could shy moral stones at his neighbors.

Bicycles.

Sunday was spent in Lancaster, and much enjoyed. The service in church was fine and the afternoon's excursion to the country delightful. Here Miss A. B. and Mr. D. left us after receiving the blessing of the party. Miss G. and Miss D., who were to join us here, failed us, but we fortunately found them waiting at Kendall. We started for that town, twenty-two miles distant, on Monday morning. It is the entrance to the celebrated Lake District. Messrs. T. and M., whom we had met at Anderton Hall, passed us on Saturday, before we reached Lancaster, on bicycles. They were out for a run of a hundred and five miles that day, to visit friends beyond that city. We meet such travellers often. Their club now numbers seven thousand members. For an annual payment of half a crown (62 cents), a member has lists of routes and hotels sent him for any desired district, with the advantage of reduced charges. It is nothing to do a hundred miles per day; many have ridden from London to Bath, two hundred miles, within the twenty-four hours.

The country swarms with these fellows. I saw fifteen hundred in Bushy Park one day at a meet. I think seventy-five clubs were there, each in a different uniform.

Bicycles are also growing in use for practical purposes, and many post-routes in the country are served by men who use these machines. But it takes roads like the English, and a level country, to do much with them.

Our evening was spent in visiting the ruined castle and admiring a pretty Japanese kind of garden, so much in so little space, which attracted our attention as we passed. The owner, Mr. T., a solicitor, kindly invited us in, and afterward showed us his house. We are always receiving kindnesses from all sorts and conditions of men.

Next day, July 12th, our objective point was Grassmere, eighteen miles away. Such a lovely morning! but, indeed, we are favored beyond measure with superb weather all the time. This stage in our progress introduced us to the scenery of the lakes, and we all felt that it deserved its Wordsworth; but were we ever to let loose and enter the descriptive, where would it lead? This is the rock upon which many a fair venture in story-telling has suffered shipwreck. Great mountains always carry one upward, but those of the Lake District are not great, nor is there anything great in the region. All is very sweet and pleasing and has its own peculiar charm, like the school of Lake Poets.

At Bowness, about midway of the lake, we left the coach for the first time for any other kind of conveyance. After enjoying a rare treat in a sail up and down the lake in the pretty steamer, we rejoined the coach at Ambleside, where we had ordered it to await us.

Passing Storr's Hall, the mind wandered back to the meeting there of Wordsworth, Southey, Coleridge, Christopher North, and greater than all, our own Walter Scott; and surely not in all the earth could a fitter spot than this have been found for their gathering. How much the world of to-day owes to the few names who spent days together here! Not often can you say of one little house, "Here had we our country's honor roofed" to so great an extent as it would be quite allowable to say in this instance. But behold the vanity of human aspirations! If there was one wish dearer than another to the greatest of these men, it was that Abbotsford should remain from generation to generation the home of his race. This very hour, while sailing on the lake, a newspaper was handed to me, and my eye caught the advertisement, "Abbotsford to let," followed by the stereotyped description, so many reception-rooms, nursery, outbuildings, and offices, suitable for a gentleman's establishment. Shade of the mighty Wizard of the North, has it come to this! Oh, the pity of it! the pity of it! Well for your fame that you built for mankind other than this stately home of your pride. It will crumble and pass utterly away long before the humble cot of Jeannie Deans shall fade from the memory of man. The time will come when the largest son of time, who wandering sang to a listening world, shall be as much forgot

> "As the canoe that crossed a lonely lake
> A thousand years ago."

Abbotsford to Let!

But even the New Zealander who stands on the ruins of London Bridge will know something of Walter Scott if he knows much worth knowing. "Abbotsford to let!" This to come to us just as we were passing one of the haunts of Scott, than whom no greater Scot ever lived save one. Fortunately no such blow is possible for the memory of Burns.

> "After life's fitful fever, he sleeps well;
> Treason has done his worst: nor steel, nor poison,
> Malice domestic, ... nothing,
> Can touch him further!"

For this let us be thankful. We visited Wordsworth's grave reverently in the twilight. Fresh, very fresh flowers lay upon it. God bless the hand that strewed them there this day! I think the following the one very great thing he gave the world; it contains "the golden guess which ever is the morning star to the full round of truth." The thought of the age—whether right or wrong we need not discuss—is hitherward:

> "For I have learned
> To look on Nature, not as in the hour
> Of thoughtless youth; but hearing oftentimes
> The still, sad music of humanity,
> Not harsh nor grating, though of ample power
> To chasten and subdue. And I have felt
> A presence that disturbs me with the joy
> Of elevated thoughts: a sense sublime
> Of something far more deeply interfused,
> Whose dwelling is the light of setting suns,
> And the round ocean, and the living air,
> And the blue sky, and in the mind of man
> A motion and a spirit that impels
> All thinking things, all objects of all thought,
> And rolls through all things."

There's a platform upon which this sceptical age may eventually stand. It is not materialistic and it is not dogmatic; perhaps it is the golden mean between extremes. I commend its teachings to both sides of all the cock-sure disputants, one of whom knows it is just so, and the other as presumptuously knows there is nothing to know. Let them shake hands and await patiently the coming of clearer light, and get together in solid work here. Surely there is enough to keep them busy. We still "see through a glass darkly."

We spent our night at Grassmere, and had a fine row upon the lake; and can anything be finer than music upon the waters, the dip of the oar, the cadence of the song which seems to float upon the glassy lake? It came to us again lulling us to sleep—the sweetest lullaby, sure precursor of happy dreams.

＊ ＊ ＊ ＊ ＊

GRASSMERE, July 13.

Carnegie Weather.

"Right, Perry!" Off for Keswick, only twelve miles distant; but who wants to hurry away from scenes like these? It rained heavily through the night, but this morning is grand for us. The mist was on the mountains though, and the clouds passed slowly over them, wrapping the tops in their mantle. The numerous rills dashing down the bare mountains were the themes of much praise. They reminded me of two fine verses from the "Light of Asia" upon "Being's ceaseless tide,"

> "Which, ever-changing, runs, linked like a river
> By ripples following ripples, fast or slow —
> The same, yet not the same — from far-off fountains
> To where its waters flow
> Into the seas. These steaming to the sun,
> Give the lost wavelets back in cloudy fleece
> To trickle down the hills, and glide again;
> Knowing no pause or peace."

We seem to be miraculously protected from rain. Many times it has poured during the night, and yet the days have been perfect. "Carnegie weather" begins to be talked about, and we are all disposed to accept the inference that the fair goddess Fortune has fallen deep in love with us, since Prosperity seems to be our page during this journey.

The influence of America and of American ideas upon England is seen in various ways. We meet frequently one who has visited the Republic, whose advanced ideas, in consequence of the knowledge derived from actual contact with American affairs, are very decidedly proclaimed.

While on the train to-day we met a rattler of this kind, who gave many instances of the non-receptivity of his countrymen. I remember one of his complaints was in regard to a pea-sheller which he had seen at work in one of our monster hotels. He was so pleased that he bought one and took it in triumph to his innkeeper at home: "Blessed if the servants would work it, sir; no, sir, wouldn't shell a pea with it, sir. Look where we are in the race of new inventions, sir. *We're not in it.* Lord bless you, sir, *England isn't in it.*"

This man, like converts in general to new ideas, went much too far. Any one who thinks that England is not in the race, and pretty well placed too, has not looked very deep. We did what we could to give him a juster conception of his country's position than he apparently entertained. "What on earth," I said to him, "has a small English hotel to do with a pea-sheller? I have never heard of this Yankee notion, but I doubt not that one pea-sheller would shell all the peas required by all the guests of all the hotels in town, if they fed the inmates on nothing but pea soup!" But he would not be convinced. It was just the same with any other improvement, he said, and he got out at a station, muttering as he went: "No, sir, she isn't in it, I tell you; she *isn't in it.*" All right, you constitutional grumbler, have it your own way. If this man were upon our side, he would not live twenty-four hours without finding fault with something. He is one of those who carry their pea-sheller with them, or find it at every turn. He belongs to the class of grumblers—those who cannot enjoy the bright genial rays of the sun for thinking of the spots upon it—just such another as he who found that even in Paradise "the halo did not fit his head exactly."

American Presidents and Royalty.

The coaches in the Lake District have now the English and the American flags upon their sides, and we often see the Stars and Stripes displayed at hotels. Our present hostelry has a flaming advertisement ending with: "Patrons—Royalty and American Presidents." There must be slender grounds for both claims, I fancy General Grant, however, may have been there. As the elected of the largest division of the English-speaking race, he no doubt outranked all other patrons, and the proper way to put it would be "American Presidents and Royalty."

At luncheon to-day it was found that our drinkables had better be cooled in the brook—an unusual performance this for England; but how vividly this little incident brings to mind the happy scene—the row of bottles (contents mostly harmless) in the stream, sticking up their tiny heads as if resentful at the extraordinary bath! Do not imagine that our party were worse to water than to corn; sixteen hungry people need a good many bottles of various kinds, for we had many tastes to gratify. We were all temperance people, however; a few of us even total abstinence, who required special attention, for their milk and lemonade were often more difficult to procure than all the other fluids. The guest who gives least trouble in England, in the drinkable department, is he who takes beer.

At Keswick we wandered round the principal square and laughed at the curious names of the inns there. In this region inns abound. Almost every house in that square offered entertainment for man and beast. Here is a true copy of names of inns noted in a few squares in the village: "Fighting Cocks," "Packhorse," "Red Lion," "Dog and Duck," "Black Lion," "Deerhound," "White Hart," "Green Lion," "Pig and Whistle," "White Lion," "Black Bull," "Elephant and Castle," "Lamb and Lark," "The Fish." If the whole village were scanned there would be beasts enough commemorated in its inns to make a respectable menagerie. Indeed, for that one "Green Lion" Barnum might safely pay more than for Jumbo.

Freedom and Equality.

The names of English inns we have seen elsewhere are equally odd; let me note a few: "Hen and Chickens," "Dog and Doublet," "King and Crown," "Hole in the Wall," "Struggling Man," "Jonah and the Ark," "Angel and Woolsack," "Adam and Eve," "Rose and Crown," "Crown and Cushion." We laughed at one with an old-fashioned swinging sign, upon which a groom was scrubbing away at a naked black man (you could almost hear his pruss, pruss, pruss). The name of the house was "Labor in Vain Inn"—a perfect illustration, no doubt, in one sense; in the higher sense, not so. Under the purifying influences of equality, found only in republican institutions, America has taught the world she can soon make white men out of black. Her effort to change the slave into a freeman has been anything but labor in vain; what is under the skin can be made white enough always, if we go at it with the right brush. None genuine unless stamped with the well-known brand "Republic." "All men are born free and *equal*" is warranted to cure the most desperate cases when all other panaceas fail, from a mild monarchy up to a German despotism; and is especially adapted for Irishmen. To be well shaken, however, before taken, and applied internally, externally, and eternally, like Colonel Sellers' eye-wash.

Harry and I were absent part of this day, having run down to Workington to see our friend Mr. G., at the Steel Rail Mills. Pardon us!—this was our only taste of business during the trip; never had the affairs of this world been so completely banished from our thoughts. To get back to blast-furnaces and rolling mills was distressing; but we could not well pass our friend's door, so to speak. We have nothing to say about manufacturing, for it is just with that as with their political institutions: England keeps about a generation behind, and yet deludes herself with the idea that she is the leader among nations. The truth is, she is often not even a good follower where others lead, but exceptions must be noted here: a few of her ablest men are not behind America in manufacturing, for there are one or perhaps two establishments in England which lead America. A great race is the British when they do go to work and get rid of their antiquated prejudices. Visitors to America like Messrs. Howard, Lothian Bell, Windsor Richards, Martin, and others, have no prejudices which stick. But let Uncle Sam look out. If he thinks John Bull will remain behind in the industrial or the political race either, I do not; and I believe when he sets to work in earnest he cannot be beaten. The Republic of England, when it comes, will excel all other republics as much as the English monarchy has excelled all other monarchies, or as much as Windsor Richards' steel practice and plant excel any we can boast of here at present. It is our turn now to take a step forward, unless we are content to be beaten. This is all right. Long may the two branches of the family stimulate each other to further triumphs, the elder encouraging us to hold fast that which is good, the younger pointing the way upward and onward—a race in which neither can lose, but in which both must win! Clear the course! Fair play and victory to both!

Democracy in England.

The report of the annual public debate of University College, London, attracted our notice to-day before leaving Kendal. The subject debated was: "That the advance of Democracy in England will tend to strengthen the Foundations of Society."

Lord Rosebery presided, and it is his speech at the close which possesses political significance as coming from one who wears his rank

> "For the sake of liberal uses
> And of great things to be done,"

and of whom almost any destiny may be predicted if he hold the true course. He said:

"As regards government, there seemed to be great advantage in democracy. With an oligarchy the responsibility was too great and the penalty for failure too high. He did not share the asperity manifested by one of the speakers against

American institutions, and, having visited the country on several occasions, he felt the greatest warmth for America and the American people. Persons who elected by free choice a moderate intellect to represent them were better off than those who had a leviathan intellect placed over them against their will, and this free choice the people of the United States possessed. It had been said by the opponents of democracy that the best men in America devoted themselves to money-getting; but this was a strong argument in its favor, as showing that democracy was not correctly represented as a kind of grabbing at the property of others."

Never were truer words spoken than these, my lord. What a pity you were not allowed the privilege of starting "at scratch" in life's race, like Gladstone or Disraeli! From any success achieved there must be made the just deduction for so many yards allowed *Lord* Rosebery. Receive the sincere condolences of him who welcomed you to honorary membership of the Burns Club of New York, not because of these unfortunate, unfair disadvantages, for he would not have welcomed a prince for his rank, but for your merits as a man.

* * * * *

PENRITH, July 14.

We reached Penrith, July 14th, after a delightful day's drive. Never were the Gay Charioteers happier, for the hilly ground gave us many opportunities for grand walks. When these come it is a red-letter day. The pleasure of walking should rank as one of the seven distinct pleasures of existence, and yet I have some friends who know nothing of it; they are not coaching through England, however.

I have omitted to chronicle the change that came over the Queen Dowager shortly after we started from Wolverhampton; till then she had kept the seat of honor next to Perry, inviting one after another as a special honor to sit in front with her. She soon discovered that a good deal of the fun going on was missed; besides, she had not all of us under her eye. Her seat was exchanged for the middle of the back form, where she was supported by one on each side, while four others had their faces turned to hers, giving an audience of no less than six for her stories and old ballads. Her tongue went from morning till night, if I do say it, and her end of the coach was always in for its share of any frolic stirring. She was "in a gale" all day to-day, and kept us all roaring.

On the Borders.

Our next stage would take us to Carlisle, the border-town behind which lay the sacred soil, "Scotia dear." Mr. B. and his son joined us here and went on with us the last day upon English soil, waving adieu, as it were, as we plunged into Scotland. Mr. and Mrs. K. left us for Paisley to see the children, and what a loss I here record no one but the members can possibly understand. Aaleck and Aggie gone! If anything could long dampen the joyous spirits of the party, this separation surely would have done it; but we were to meet again in Edinburgh, where the reconstruction of the Charioteers was to take place. At Carlisle, too, the Parisians were to be welcomed back again—plenty to look forward to, you see. We started for Carlisle July 15th, the day superb as usual.

We had left the Lake District, with its hills and flowing streams, to pass through a tamer land; but our luncheon to-day, in a field near "Hesketh in the Forest," was not unromantic. The members from Anderton Hall caught the fever, as was usual with neophytes, and regretted that their return was imperatively required. One day gave them a taste of the true gypsy life. Hesketh was "in the Forest," no doubt, but this was many long years ago. To-day there is nothing to justify its name. Smiling green fields, roads as perfect as they can be made, pretty houses, trim hedge-rows and gardens, and all so intensely civilized as to bring vividly before you the never ceasing change which the surface of the earth undergoes to fit it for the sustenance of dense masses of men.

* * * * *

CARLISLE, July 15.

Here is reconstruction for you with a vengeance! First, let us mourn the unhappy departures: Mr. and Mrs. K. went yesterday and Miss R., Miss G., the Misses B., Miss D. and Mr. B. and son go to-day. Cousin Maggie, who had become absorbed in this kind of life, so dazed with happiness, her turn has come too, even she must go; Andrew M., with his fine Scotch aroma and his songs, must report to his superior officer at the encampment, for is he not a gallant volunteer and an officer under Her Majesty, "sworn never to desert his home except in case of invasion!" Well, we cannot help these miserable changes in this world, nor the "sawt, sawt tears" of the young ladies as they kiss each other, swearing eternal friendship, and sob good-byes.

But if farewell ever sighs, welcome comes in smiling. Look! Cousin E. in my arms and a warm kiss of welcome! That is the very best of consolation. Clever, artistic Miss R., too, from Edinburgh; and then are we not to have our four originals back again, after two long weeks' absence! It was fortunate that our sad farewells were so promptly followed by smiling welcomes.

Do any people love their country as passionately as the Scotch? I mean the earth of it, the very atoms of which its hills and glens are composed. I doubt it. Now here is Maggie, a douse, quiet, sensible girl. I tried to say something cheery to her to-day as we were approaching Carlisle, where we were to part, reminding her jokingly that she had received five weeks' coaching while her poor sister Eliza would have only two. "Ah! but she has Scotland, Naig!" "Do you really mean to tell me that you would rather have two weeks in your own country than five weeks seeing a new land, and that land England, with London and Brighton, and the lakes and all?" I just wish you could have seen and heard how the "Of course" came in reply. The Scotch always have Scotland first in their hearts, and some of them, I really believe, will get into trouble criticising Paradise if it be found to differ materially from Scotland.

Farewell to England.

To-morrow we are to enter that land of lands. Fair England, farewell! How graciously kind has been the reception accorded by you to the wanderers! How beautiful you are! how tenderly dear you have become to all of us! Not one of us but can close his eyes and revel in such quiet beauty as never before was his.

> "Not a grand nature . . .
> On English ground
> You understand the letter . . . ere the fall
> How Adam lived in a garden. All the fields
> Are tied up fast with hedges, nosegay like;
> The hills are crumpled plains—the plains pastures,
> And if you seek for any wilderness
> You find at best a park. A nature
> Tamed and grown domestic . . .
> A sweet familiar nature, stealing in
> As a dog might, or child, to touch your hand,
> Or pluck your gown, and humbly mind you so
> Of presence and affection."

"There is no farewell to scenes like thine." From the depths of every heart in our company comes the trembling "God bless you, England!"

SCOTLAND.

"Away, ye gay landscapes, ye gardens of roses!
In you let the minions of luxury rove;
Restore me the rocks where the snowflake reposes,
Though still they are sacred to freedom and love:
Yet, Caledonia, beloved are thy mountains,
Round their white summits though elements war;
Though cataracts foam 'stead of smooth flowing fountains,
I sigh for the valley of dark Loch na Garr."

It was on Saturday, July 16th, that we went over the border. The bridge across the boundary line was soon reached. When midway over a halt was called, and vent given to our enthusiasm. With three cheers for the land of the heather, shouts of "Scotland forever," and the waving of hats and handkerchiefs, we dashed across the border. O Scotland, my own, my native land, your exiled son returns with love for you as ardent as ever warmed the heart of man for his country. It's a God's mercy I was born a Scotchman, for I do not see how I could ever have been contented to be anything else. The little plucky dour deevil, set in her own ways and getting them too, level-headed and shrewd, with an eye to the main chance always and yet so lovingly weak, so fond, so led away by song or story, so easily touched to fine issues, so leal, so true! And you suit me, Scotia, and proud am I that I am your son.

We stopped at Gretna Green, of course, and walked to the site of the famous blacksmith-shop where so many romantic pairs have been duly joined in the holy bonds of wedlock. A wee laddie acted as guide, and from him we had our first real broad Scotch. His dialect was perfect. He brought "wee Davie" to mind at once. I offered him a shilling if he could "screed me aff effectual calling." He knew his catechism, but he could not understand it. Never mind that, Davie, that is another matter. Older heads than yours have bothered over that doctrine and never got to the bottom of it. Besides there will be a "revised edition" of that before you are a man. Just you let it alone; it is the understanding of that and some other dogmas of poor ignorant man's invention that thin the churches of men who think and "make of sweet religion a rhapsody of words." "But do you ken Burns?" "Aye," said Davie, "I ken 'A man's a man for a' that,' and 'Auld Lang Syne.'" "Good for you, Davie, there's another shilling. Good-bye! But I say, Davie, if you can't possibly remember all three of these pieces, don't let it be 'A man's a man for a' that' that you forget, for Scotchmen will need to remember that one of these days when we begin to set things to rights in earnest and demand the same privileges for prince, peer, and peasant. Don't let it be 'Auld Lang Syne,' either, for there is more of 'Peace and Good-will upon Earth,' the essence of true religion, in that grand song than in your effectual calling, Davie, my wee mannie. At least there is one who thinks so." Davie got my address, and said may be he would come to America when he grew to be a man. I promised to give him a chance if he had not forgotten Burns, which is all we can do in the Republic, where merit is the only road to success. We may make a Republican out of him yet, and have him return to his fellows to preach the equality of man, the sermon Scotland needs.

Lunch at Annan.

We lunched at Annan. It was at first decided that we had better be satisfied with hotel accommodations, as the day though fine was cool, with that little nip in the air which gives it the bracing quality; but after we had entered the hotel the sun burst forth, and the longing for the green fields could not be overcome. We walked through the village across the river, and found a pretty spot in a grove upon high ground commanding extensive views up and down the stream, and there we gave our new members their first luncheon. It would have been a great pity had we missed this picnic, for it was in every respect up to the standard. I laugh as I recall the difficulties encountered in selecting the fine site. The committee had fixed upon a tolerably good location in a field near the river, but this knoll was in sight, and we were tempted to go to it. We had gone so far from the hotel where the coach was, that Perry and Joe had to get a truck to bring the hampers. I remember seeing them pushing it across the bridge and up against the wall over which most of us had clambered. When the Queen Dowager's turn came the wall was found to be rather too much for her, but our managers were versatile. The truck was brought into requisition, and she was safely drawn from its platform over the wall. I stood back and could do nothing for laughter, but the Dowager, who was not to be daunted, went over amid the cheers of the party. It was resolved, however, to be a little more circumspect in future; wall-climbing at seventy-one has its limits.

Here is the bridge built by that worthy man and excellent representative of what is best in Scottish character in lowly life, James Carlyle—an honest brig destined to stand and never shame the builder. I remember how proudly Carlyle speaks of his father's work. No sham about either the man or his work, as little as there was in his more famous son. I wish I could quote something from "Adam Bede" I think it is—where Garth the stone-mason thinks good work in his masonry the best prayer he had to stand upon.

Carlyle and Black.

Many have expressed surprise at "Carlyle's Reminiscences," at the gnarled, twisted oak they show, prejudiced here, ill-tempered there. What did such people expect, I wonder? A poor, reserved, proud Scotch lad, who had to fight his way against the grim devils of poverty and neglect, of course he is twisted and "thrawn"; but a grand, tough oak for all that, as sound, stanch timber as ever grew, and Scotch to the core. Did any one take you, Thomas Carlyle, for a fine, symmetrical sycamore, or a graceful clinging vine? I think the "Reminiscences," upon the whole, a valuable contribution to literature. Nor has Carlyle suffered in my estimation from knowing so much of what one might have expected. But will these critics of a grand individuality be kind enough to tell us when we shall look upon his like again, or where another Jenny Carlyle is to come from? She is splendid! The little tot who "bluided a laddie's nose" with her closed fist and conquered "the bubbley jock." This was in her early childhood's days, and look at her woman's work for Carlyle if you want a pattern for wives, my young lady friends, at least as a bachelor pictures wifehood at its best. The story told of Mr. Black's meeting with Carlyle should be true, if it be not. "Oh, Mr. Black," exclaimed Carlyle, "I'm glad to see ye, man. I've read some of yer books; they're vera amusin'; ye ken Scotch scenery well; but when are yer goin' to do some *wark*, man?" Great work did the old man do in his day, no doubt; but they also work who plant the roses, Thomas, else were we little better than the beasts of the field. Carlyle did not see this. Black is doing his appointed work and doing it well too, and Scotland is proud of her gifted son.

* * * * *

Dumfries, July 16-17.

Dumfries.

We were at Dumfries for Sunday. We had just got housed at the hotel and sat down to dinner when we heard a vehicle stop, and running to the window saw our anxiously expected Parisians at the door. Hurrah! welcome! welcome! Once more united, never to part again till New York be reached! It was a happy meeting, and there was much to tell upon both sides, but the coachers evidently had the better of it. The extreme heat encountered in France had proved very trying. The Prima Donna was tired out. She vividly expressed her feelings thus, when asked how she had enjoyed life since she left the Ark: "*Left* the Ark! I felt as if I had been poked out of it like the dove to find out about the weather, and had found it rough. When I lose sight of the coach again, just let me know it!" We, on our part, were very glad to get our pretty little dove back, and promised that she should never be sent forth from among us again.

One becomes confused at Dumfries, there is so much to learn. We are upon historic ground in the fullest sense, and so crowded too with notable men and events. Bruce slew the Red Comyn here in the church of the Minorite Friars, now no longer existing. The monastery, of which it formed a part, the foundation of the mother of John Baliol, King of Scotland, stood on an eminence, the base of which is washed on the north and west by the waters of the Nith. It is said to have been deserted after the pollution of its high altar with the blood of the Comyns, and about two centuries afterward the Maxwells built a splendid castle out of its ruins and almost on its site; but the fortune of war and old Father Time levelled its massive walls in turn, and now no vestige remains of either monastery or castle. The castle of the Comyns, too, which occupied a romantic site a little way south of the town, at a place still called Castledykes, has left but slight memorials of its olden grandeur.

Among the noted men of the world whom Dumfries numbers among her children are the Admirable Crichton, Paul Jones, Allan Cunningham, Carlyle, Neilson of the hot blast, Patterson, the founder of the Bank of England, and Miller of the steamship. Still another, a Scotch minister, was the founder of savings-banks. While not forgetting to urge his flock to lay up treasures in the next world, he did not fail to impress upon them a like necessity of putting by a competence for this one, sensible man! How many ministers leave behind them as powerful an agency for the improvement of the masses as this Dumfries man, the Rev. Mr. Duncan, has in savings-banks? All the speculative opinions about the other world which man can indulge in are as nothing to the acquisition of those good, sober, steady habits which render possible upon the part of the wage-receiving class a good deposit in that minister's savings-bank. The Rev. Mr. Duncan is my kind of minister, one who works much and preaches little. There is room for more of his kind.

It is to Dumfries we are also indebted for the steamship, as far as Britain's share in that crowning triumph is concerned, for, upon Dalwinston Lake, Miller used the first paddles turned by steam. The great magician also has waved his wand over this district. Ellangowan Castle, Dirk Hatteraick's Cave, and even Old Mortality himself are all of Dumfries; and as for Burns, there is more of his best work there than anywhere else, and there he lies at rest with the thistle waving over him, fit mourner for Scotland's greatest son, and of all others the one he would have chosen. How he loved it! Think of his lines about the emblem dear, written while still a boy.

Home of Burns.

I wanted to stay a week in Dumfries, and I deemed myself fortunate to be able to spend Sunday there. Two Dunfermline gentlemen now resident there, Messrs. R. and A., were kind enough to call upon us and offer their services. This was thoughtful and pleased me much. Accordingly on Sunday morning we started with Mr. R. and did the town, Maxwelton Braes, Burns's house, and last his grave. None of us had ever been there before, and we were glad to make the pilgrimage. Horace Greeley (how he did worship Burns!) has truly said that of the thousands who yearly visit Shakespeare's birthplace, most are content to engrave their names with a diamond upon the glass, but few indeed leave the resting-place of the ploughman without dropping a tear upon the grave; for of all men he it was who nestled closest to the bosom of humanity. It is true that of all the children of men Burns is the best beloved. Carlyle knew him well, for he said Burns was the Æolian harp of nature against which the rude winds of adversity blew, only to be transmitted in their passage into heavenly music.

I think these are the two finest things that have been said about our idol, or about any idol, and I believe them to be deserved. So did Carlyle and Greeley, for they were not flatterers. Of what other human being could these two things be truly said? I know of none.

Our friends, Mr. and Mrs. N., are the fortunate owners of Friars Carse estate. They called upon us Sunday noon, and invited us to dine with them that evening. A delegation from the party accepted, and were much pleased with their visit. Friars Carse is a lovely spot. The winding Nith is seen at its best from the lawn.

As we drove past on Monday we stopped and enjoyed a morning visit to our friends, who were exceedingly kind. Mr. N. has earned the grateful remembrance of every true lover of Burns by restoring the heritage and guarding with jealous care every vestige of one of the half dozen geniuses which the world will reverence more and more as the years roll by. He has wisely taken out the window upon the panes of which Burns wrote with a diamond, "Thou whom chance may hither lead," one of my favorites. This is now preserved, to be handed down as an heirloom in the family, finally, we hope, to find its place in some public collection. While we were in the mansion a granddaughter of Annie Laurie actually came in. I know of no young lady whose grandmother is so widely and favorably known. We were all startled to be brought so near to the ideal Annie Laurie of our dreams. It only shows that the course of true love never runs smooth when we hear that she did not marry the poetic lover. Well, may be she was happier with a dull country squire. Poets are not proverbially model husbands; the better poet, the worse husband, and the writer of Annie Laurie had the poetic temperament pretty well developed.

Drumlanrig Castle.

"Right, Perry!" We are off for Sanquhar, twenty-eight miles away; the day superb, with a freshness unknown in the more genial South we are rapidly leaving behind. What a pretty sight it was to see Miss N—— bounding along upon her horse in the distance, an avant courier leading us to a warm welcome at her beautiful home! Would I had been beside her on Habeebah! We spent an hour or two there, and then with three enthusiastic cheers for "Friars Carse and a' within it," the Charioteers drove off; but long must fond recollections of that estate and of the faces seen there linger in our memories as among the most pleasing of our ever-memorable journey. A home upon the Nith near Dumfries has many attractions indeed. Our drive to-day lay along the Nith and through the Duke of Buccleugh's grounds to his noble seat, Drumlanrig Castle. Here we have a real castle at last; none of your imported English affairs, as tame as caged tigers. How poor and insignificant they all seem to such as this! You want the moors, the hills and glens, and all the flavor of feudal institutions to give a castle its dignity and impress you with the thoughts of by-gone days. Modern castles in England built to order are only playthings, toys; but in Scotland they are real and stir the chords. You cannot have in England a glen worthy of the name, with its dark amber-brown, foaming, rushing torrent dashing through it. We begin to feel the exhilarating influences of the North as we drive on, and to understand its charm. Byron says truly:

> "England! thy beauties are tame and domestic
> To one who has roamed on the mountains afar.
> Oh, for the crags that are wild and majestic!
> The steep frowning glories of dark Loch na Garr."

This was the feeling upon the coach to-day. My eyes watered now and then and my heart beat faster as the grandeur of the scenery and the influences around came into play. This was my land, England only a far-off connection, not one of the family. "And what do you think of Scotland noo?" was often repeated. "The grandest day yet!" was said more than once as we drove through the glen; but this has been said so often during this wonderful expedition, and has so often been succeeded by a day which appeared to excel its famous predecessor, that we are careful now to emphasize the yet; for indeed we feel that there is no predicting what glories Scotland may have in store for us beyond.

Our luncheon to-day was taken upon the banks of the Nith; an exquisitely beautiful spot. There was no repressing our jubilant spirits, and sitting there on the green sward the party burst into song, and one Scotch song followed another. There was a strange stirring of the blood, an exaltation of soul unknown before. The pretty had been left behind, the sublime was upon us. There was a nip in the air unfelt in the more genial climate of the South. The land over which brooded peace and quiet content had been left behind, that of the "mountain and the flood" was here, whispering of its power, swaying us to and fro and bending us to its mysterious will. In the sough of the wind comes the call of the genii to mount to higher heights, that we may exult in the mysteries of the mountain and the glen,

"The steep frowning glories of dark Loch na Garr."

Even our songs had the wail of the minor key suggesting the shadows of human life, eras of storm and strife, of heroic endurance and of noble sacrifice; the struggle of an overmatched people contending for generations against fearful odds and maintaining through all vicissitudes a distinctively national life. That is what makes a Scotchman proud of this peculiar little piece of earth, and stirs his blood and fills his eyes as he returns to her bosom.

The Cameronians.

We rested over Monday night, July 18th, at Sanquhar, a long one-main-street village, whose little inn could not accommodate us all, but the people were kind, and the gentlemen of the party had no cause to complain of their quarters. It was here that the minister absolved the Cameronians from allegiance to "the ungodly king"—a great step. Those sturdy Cameronians probably knew little of Shakespeare, but I fancy the speech of that rebel minister could not have been better ended, or begun either, than with the outburst of Laertes to another wicked king:

"I'll not be juggled with:
To hell, allegiance!"

Bravo! They would not be juggled with King Charles, neither will their descendants be, if any king hereafter is ever rash enough to try his "imperial" notions upon them. That day is past, thanks to that good minister and his Cameronians. I gazed upon the monument erected to these worthies, and gratefully remembered what the world owes to them.

We stepped into a stationer's shop there and met a character. One side of the shop was filled with the publications of the Bible Society, the other with drugs. "A strange combination this," I remarked.

"Weel, man, no sae bad. Pheseek for the body an pheseek for the soul. Castor oil and Bibles no sae bad."

Harry and I laughed.

"Have you the revised edition here yet?" I inquired.

"Na, na, the auld thing here. Nane of yer new-fangled editions of the Scripture for us. But I hear they've shortened the Lord's Prayer. Noo, that's na a bad thing for them as hae to get up early in the mornin's."

He was an original, and we left his shop smiling at his way of putting things. Scotland is the land of odd characters.

* * * * *

Sanquhar, July 18.

We are off for old Cumnock, the entire village apparently out to see the start. Sanquhar on the moors does not seem to have many attractions, but last evening we had one of our pleasantest walks. There is a fine deep glen hid away between the hills, with a torrent rushing through it, over which bridges have been thrown. We were tempted to go far up the glen. The long gloaming faded away into darkness and we had a weird stroll home. It was after ten o'clock when we reached the hotel. This may be taken as a specimen of our evenings; there is always the long walk in the gloaming after dinner, which may be noted as one of the rare pleasures of the day.

School Children.

Our luncheon to-day could not be excelled, and in some features it was unique. The banks of Douglas Water was the site chosen. The stream divides, and a green island looked so enchanting that the committee set about planning means to cross to it. The steps of the coach formed a temporary bridge over which the ladies were safely conducted, but not without some danger of a spill. As many as thirty school children, then enjoying their summer vacation, followed, and after a while ventured to fraternize with us. Such a group of rosy, happy little ones it would be difficult to meet with out of Scotland. Children seem to flourish without care in this climate. The difference between the children of America and Britain is infinitely greater than that between the adults of the two countries. Scotch children learn to pronounce as the English do in the schools, but in their play the ancient Doric comes out in full force. It is all broad Scotch yet in conversation. This will no doubt change in time, but it seemed to us that so far they have lost very few of the Scotch words and none of the accent. We asked the group to appoint one of their number to receive some money to buy "sweeties" for the party. Jeannie Morrison was the lassie proposed and unanimously chosen. Jeannie was in the sixth standard. In answer to an inquiry, it was at first said that no one else of the party was so far advanced, but a moment's consultation resulted in a prompt correction, and then came: "Aye, Aggie McDonald is too." But not one of the laddies was beyond the fifth. Well, the women of Scotland always were superior to the men. If a working-man in Scotland does not get a clever managing wife (they are helpmeets there), he never amounts to much, and many a stupid man pulls up well through the efforts of his wife. It is much the same in France, or, indeed, in any country where the struggle for existence is hard and expenditure has to be kept down to the lowest point—so much depends upon the woman in this department.

The shyness of these children surprised our Americans much. They could scarcely be induced to partake of cakes and jelly, which must be rare delicacies with them. I created a laugh by insisting that even after I had been in America several years I was as shy as any of these children. My friends were apparently indisposed to accept such an assertion entirely, but an appeal to Davie satisfied them of my modesty in early youth. "Ah, *then!*" said Miss M. But this was cruel.

We left some rare morsels for these children. When they had done cheering us at our departure, I warrant they "were nae blate." The dear little innocent, happy things! I wish I could get among them again. What would not one give to get a fresh start, to be put back a child again, that he might make such a record as seems possible when looking backward! How many things he would do that he did not do, how many things he would not do that he did do! I sympathize with Faust, the offer was too tempting to be successfully withstood. One point worth noting occurs to me. In looking back you never feel that upon any occasion you have acted too generously, but you often regret that you did not give enough, and sometimes that you did not give at all. The moral seems to be—always give the higher sum or do the most when in doubt. It seems to me that parents and others having charge of children might do more than is done to teach them the only means of making life worth living, and to point out to them the rocks and eddies from which they themselves have suffered damage in life's passage.

A Pleasant Meeting.

With the cheers of the children ringing in our ears we started on our way. While stopping at the inn to return what had been lent us in the way of baskets, pitchers, etc., a lady drove up in a stylish phaeton, and, excusing herself for intruding, said that a coach was so rarely seen in those parts she could not resist asking who we were and whither bound. I gave her all desired information, and asked her to please gratify our ladies by telling in return who she was. "Lady Stuart M." was the reply. She was of the M.'s of Closeburn Castle, as we learned from Mr. Murray, our landlord at Cumnock. The estate will go at her death to a nephew who is farming in America. We thought there must be some good reason why he did not return and manage for his aunt, who indeed seems well qualified to manage for herself. The young exiled heir had our sympathy, but long may it be ere he enters upon Closeburn, for we were all heartily in favor of a long and happy reign to the present ruler of that beautiful estate. Lady M. assured us that we would be well taken care of at the Dumfries Arms, and she was right. Mr. Murray and his handsome sisters will long be remembered as model hotel-keepers. They made our stay most agreeable. Mr. Murray took us to the Bowling Green in the evening, and many of our party saw the game for the first time. Great excitement prevails when the sides are evenly matched. It is, like the curling pond, a perfect republic. There is no rank upon the ice or upon the green in Scotland. The postman will berate the provost for bad play at bowls, but touch his hat respectfully to him on the pavement. A man may be even a provost and yet not up to giving them a "Yankee" when called for. We were curious to know what a "Yankee" shot was, for we heard it called for by the captains every now and then. We were told that this was a shot which "knocked all before it, and played the very deevil." That is not bad.

While a few of us who had recently seen the land of Burns remained at Cumnock, the remainder of the party drove to Ayr and saw all the sights there and returned in the evening. Our walks about Cumnock were delightful, and we left Mr. Murray's care with sincere regret.

* * * * *

OLD CUMNOCK, July 19.

Our Photograph.

Passing out of the town this morning, we stopped at the prettiest little photographic establishment we had ever seen, and the artist succeeded in taking excellent views of the coach and party, as the reader may see by a glance at the frontispiece, where the original negative is reproduced by the artotype process. It was done in an instant; we were taken ere we were aware. A great thing, that instantaneous photography; one has not time to look his very worst, as sitters usually contrive to do, ladies especially. It is so hard to be artificial and yet look pretty.

"Right, Perry!" and off we drove through the crowd for Douglas. The General Manager soon confided to me that for the first time he was dubious about our resting-place for the night. A telegram had been received by him from the landlord at Douglas just before starting, stating that the inn was full to overflowing with officers of the volunteer regiment encamped there, and that it was impossible for him to provide for our party. What was to be done? It was decided to inform that important personage, mine host, that we were moving upon him, and that if he gave no quarters we should give none either. He must billet us somewhere; if not, then

> "A night in greenwood spent
> Were but to-morrow's merriment."

But we felt quite sure that the town of Douglas would in council assembled extend a warm welcome to the Americans and see us safely housed, even if there were not a hotel in the place. So on we went. While passing through Lugar, a pretty young miss ran out of the telegraph office, and holding up both hands, called: "Stop! It's no aff yet! it's no aff yet!" A message was coming for the coaching party. It proved to be from our Douglas landlord, saying, All right! he would do the best he could for us. When the party was informed how much we had been trusting in Providence for the past few hours, such was their enthusiasm that some disappointment was expressed at the reassuring character of the telegram. Not to know where we were going to be all night—may be to have to lie in and on the coach—would have been such fun! But "Behind yon hill where Lugar flows," sung by Eliza, sounded none the less sweet when we knew we were not likely to have to camp out upon its pretty banks. It is essential for successful happy coaching with ladies that every comfort should be provided. I am satisfied it would never do to risk the weaker sex coaching in any other land. The extreme comfort of everything here alone keeps them well and able to stand the gypsy life.

We travelled most of the day among the ore lands and blast furnaces of the Scotch pig-iron kings, the Bairds. To reach Edinburgh we had to drive diagonally eastward across the country, for we had gone to the westward that Dumfries and the Land of Burns might not be missed. This route took us through less frequented localities, off the main lines of travel, but our experience justified us in feeling that this had proved a great advantage, for we saw more of Scotland than we should have done otherwise.

Our luncheon to-day was a novel one in some respects. No inn was to be reached upon the moors, and feed for the horses had to be taken with us from Cumnock; but we found the prettiest little wimpling burn, across which a passage was made by throwing in big stones, for the shady dell was upon the far side. The horses were unhitched and allowed to nibble the wayside grass beside our big coach, which loomed up on the moor as if it were double its true size.

Scotch Weather.

The thistle and the harebell begin to deck our grassy tables at noon, and fine fields of peas and beans scent the air. All is Scotch; and oh, that bracing breeze, which cools deliciously the sun's bright rays, confirms us in the opinion that no weather is like Scotch weather, when it is good; when it is not I have no doubt the same opinion is equally correct, but we have no means of judging. Scotland smiles upon her guests, and we love her with true devotion in return. "What do you think of Scotland noo?" came often to-day; but words cannot express what we do think of her. In the language of one of our young ladies, "She is just lovely!"

The question came up to-day at luncheon, would one ever tire of this gypsy life? and it was unanimously voted never! At least no one could venture to name a time when he would be ready to return to the prosy routine of ordinary existence while blessed with such weather and such company. Indeed, this nomadic life must be the hardest of all to exchange for city life. It is so diametrically opposed to it in every phase. "If I were not the independent gentleman I am," says Lamb, "I should choose to be a beggar." "Chapsey me a gypsy," gentle Elia, you could not have known of that life, or perhaps you considered it and the beggar's life identical. But, mark you, there is a difference which is much more than a distinction. A gypsy cannot beg, but he or she tells fortunes, tinkers a little and deals in horses. Even if he steals a little now and then, I take it he is still within the lines of the profession; while your beggar who does anything in the way of work, or who steals, is no true man. His license is for begging only. The gypsy obviously has the wider range, and I say again, therefore, "Chapsey me a gypsy," gentle Elia.

Davie and I walked over to the railway line after luncheon to have a talk with the surfacemen we saw at work. They were strong, stalwart men, and possessed of that shrewd, solid sense which is invariably found in Scotch workmen. Their pay seemed very small to us; the foreman got only twenty shillings per week ($5), while the ordinary surfaceman got fourteen shillings ($3.50). Although this was only a single-track branch line, it was almost as well laid as the Pennsylvania Railroad. None of the men had ever been in America, but several had relatives there who were doing well, and they looked forward to trying the new land some day.

We reached pretty Douglas in the evening, and sounded our horn longer than usual to apprize mine host that the host was upon him. We were greatly pleased to see him and his good wife standing in the door of the inn with pleasant, smiling faces to greet us. They had arranged everything for our comfort. Many thanks to those gentlemanly officers who had so kindly given up their rooms to accommodate their American cousins. Quarters for the gentlemen had been found in the village, and Joe and Perry and the horses were all well taken care of. Thus we successfully passed through the only occasion where there seemed to be the slightest difficulty about our resting-place for the night.

Home Castle.

Douglas, the ancient seat of that family so noted in Scotland's history, is really worth a visit. Home Castle, their residence, is a commanding pile seen for many miles up the valley as we approach the town. Our visit to it was greatly enjoyed, we had such a pretty walk in the evening, and a rest on the slope of the hill overlooking the castle. We lay there in the grass and enjoyed the quiet Scotch gloaming which was gathering round us, and so silently, so slowly shutting in the scene. The castle upon the left below us, the Douglas water so placidly gliding through the valley at our feet, the old church where lay mouldering generations of the Douglases, and the dark woods beyond, formed a picture which kept us long upon the hill.

In their day, what bustling men were these doughty Douglases—full of sturt and strife—the very ideal representatives of the warrior bold, who made their way and held their own by the strength of their good right arms.

> "A steede, a steede of matchless speede,
> A sword of metal keene,
> All else to noble minds is dross,
> All else on earth is meane;
> And O the thundering press of knights,
> When loud their war cries swell,
> Might serve to call a saint from heaven
> Or rouse a fiend from helle."

This was their ideal—the very reverse, thank God, of the ideal of to-day—but note how peacefully they lie now in the little antiquated church in this obscure valley. What shadows we are! What shadows we pursue! This vein once started in the Scotch gloaming upon the hills, where the coloring of the scene is so sombre as to be not only seen but felt, must be indulged in sparingly, or some of the Charioteers might soon have to record a new experience—a fit of the blues. But this was prevented by comparing the advance made by the race upon this question of war within the past century. The "profession of arms" is very soon to be rated as it deserves. The apology for it will be the same as for any other of the butchering trades—it is necessary. Granted for the present, but what of the nature which selects such a profession!

Epitaphs.

The inscriptions upon the tombs of the Douglases recalled other epitaphs; some one said of all the inscriptions yet seen, he thought that upon the tomb of the Duke of Devonshire gave us the best lesson.

It runs thus:

> "Who lyeth heare?
> Ye gude Yearle of Devenshere—
> What he had is gone,
> What he kept is lost,
> What he gave—*that* he hath."

We were on the verge of moralizing. Some one scenting the danger, said he thought an equally suggestive epitaph headed one of the chapters of "David Elginbrod":

> "Here lies David Elginbrod,
> Hae mercy on his soul, oh God!
> As he'd a-had, had he been God,
> An ye'd been David Elginbrod."

Yes, there is food for thought here too. David must have been a queer one.

The sky grew darker, and the far-off woods faded into a cloud upon the horizon; the party rose, and in so doing regained their usual hilarity—forgot all about tombs and were off for a run hand-in-hand down the gentle slope to the valley, shouting and laughing in great glee—and so on over the pretty bridge to their delightful inn.

* * * * *

Douglas, July 20.

Edinburgh, Scotia's darling seat, only forty-four miles distant. All aboard, this pretty morning, for Edinburgh! "Right, Perry!" and off we went quite early through Douglas, for the capital. Our path was through woods for several miles, and we listened to the birds and saw and heard many of the incidents of morn so prettily described by Beattie:

> "The wild brook babbling down the mountain-side,
> The lowing herd; the sheep-fold's simple bell;
> The hum of bees, and linnet's lay of love,
> And the full choir that wakes the universal grove."

It was to be a long day's drive, but an easy one; only one hill, and then a gradual descent all the way to Edinburgh. So it might have been by the other road, but the mile-stones which told us so many miles to Edinburgh should also have said: "Take the new road; this is the old one, over the hills and far away." But they did not, and we could not be wrong, for this was a way, if not *the* way, to "Auld Reekie." After all, it was one of the richest of our experiences as we look back upon it now. So many hills to walk up and so many to walk down; so many moors with not a house to be seen, nothing but sheep around us and the lights and shadows of a Scotch sky overhead. But it was grand, and recalled some of Black's wonderful pen pictures. And then we enjoyed the heather which we found in its beauty, though scarcely yet tinted with its richest glow of color. This was our introduction to it. The heathery moor was new to most of the party and many were the exclamations produced by its beauty. There's "meat and drink" to a Scotchman in the scent of the heather.

About luncheon time we began to look longingly for the expected inn, but there was no habitation to be seen, and we became suspicious that, notwithstanding the mile-stones, which stood up and told us the lie which was half the truth (ever the blacker lie), we were not upon the right road to Edinburgh. At this juncture we met a shepherd with his collies, and learnt from him that we were still twelve miles from an inn. It was a cool, breezy day; the air had the "nip" in it which Maggie missed so in England, and we were famishing. There was nothing else to do but to stop where we were, at the pretty burn, and tarry there for entertainment for man and beast.

As proof of our temperance, please note that the flasks filled with sherry, whiskey, and brandy, at Brighton, I believe, as reserve forces for emergencies, still had plenty in them when called for to-day; and rarely has a glass of spirits done greater good, the ladies as well as we of the stronger sex feeling that a glass was necessary to keep off a chill. We were "o'er the moors among the heather" in good earnest to-day, but how soon we were all set to rights and laughing over our frolic! The shepherd and his dogs lunched with us, and many a glint of Scottish shepherd life did we get from his conversation. He was a happy, contented man, and ever so grateful that he was not condemned to live in a city. He thought such a cramped-up life would soon kill him.

Sheep and Collies.

Good-bye, my gentle shepherd and "Tweed" and "Rab," your faithful, sagacious companions. Your life leads to contentment, and where will you find that jewel when you leave mother earth and her products, her heather and her burns, your doggies and your sheep?

Davie, in Andrew M——'s absence, sang us that song whose prettiest verse, though all are fine, is this:

> "See yonder paukie shepherd
> Wha lingers on the hill,
> His ewes are in the fauld
> And his sheep are lying still."

Softly, softly, pianissimo, my boy! These lines must be sung so, not loudly like the other verses. Andrew knows the touch.

> "But he downa gang to rest,
> For his heart is in a flame

> To meet his bonnie lassie,
> When the kye come hame."

And so we parted from our shepherd, the chorus of our song reaching him over the moors till he faded out of sight. I am sure we wish him weel. Happiness is not all in the higher walks of life; and surely in virtue's paths the cottage leaves the palace far behind.

Another song followed, which I thought equally appropriate, for it tells us that "Ilka blade o' grass keps its ain drap o' dew." Ah, the shepherd's drops of the dew of life are often what princes vainly sigh for.

Arthur's Seat.

After many miles up and down, we finally reached the top of the hill from which we saw lying before us, fourteen miles away, the modern Athens. There was no mistaking Arthur's Seat, the lion crouching there. "Stop, Perry!" Three times three for the "Queen of the Unconquered North!" "What do you think of Scotland noo?" Match that city who can! Not on this planet will you do it, search where you may.

It was only a few miles from where we now stood that Fitz Eustace, enraptured with the scene,

> "And making demi-volte in air,
> Cried, Where's the coward that would not dare
> To fight for such a land!"

Fight for it? I guess so, to the death! Scotland forever!

We were about completing one stage of our journey, for Edinburgh had been looked forward to as one of the principal points we had to reach, and we were to rest there a few days before marching upon the more ancient metropolis, Dunfermline. Most of us had been steadily at work since we left Brighton, and the prospect of a few days' respite was an agreeable one; but after all it was surprising how fresh even the ladies were. Still, steady coaching is pretty hard work; none of us gained weight during the journey, but we all felt as if in condition just fit to do our very best in the way of athletic exercise.

Miss R——, a native of Edinburgh, was here called to the front, alongside of Perry, to act as guide into and through the city to our hotel in Prince's Street. The enthusiasm grew more and more intense as we came nearer and fresh views were obtained. There remained one more toll-gate, one of the few which have not yet been abolished. Joe had as usual gone forward to pay the toll, but the keeper declared she did not know the charge, as never since she kept toll had anything like that—pointing to the coach—passed there. Was it any wonder that we attracted attention during our progress northward?

From one hill-top I caught sight of the sparkling Forth, beyond which lay "the dearest spot on earth to me." The town could not be seen, but when I was able to cry, "Dunfermline lies there," three rousing cheers were given for the "Auld gray Toon," my native city.

* * * * *

EDINBURGH, July 21-26.

Edinburgh.

Our route lay through Newington, that we might leave the young artist at home. We tried to do it quietly, but our friend Mrs. H. was out and shaking hands with us ere we could drive off. Mr. MacGregor, of the Royal, had been mindful of us; a grand sitting room fronting on Prince's Street and overlooking the gardens gave us the best possible view, the very choice spot of all this choice city. The night was beautiful, and the lights from the towering houses of the old town made an illumination, as it were, in honor of our arrival. That the travellers were delighted with Edinburgh, that it more than fulfilled all expectations, is to say but little; and those who saw it for the first time felt it to be beyond all that they had imagined. Those of us who knew its picturesque charms were more than ever impressed with its superiority over all other cities. Take my word for it, my readers, there is no habitation of human beings in this world as fine in its way, and its way itself is fine, as this, the capital of Scotland.

The surprise and delight of my friends gave me much pleasure. Scotland had already won all hearts. They had admired England, but Scotland they loved. Ah, how could they help it! I loved her too, more deeply than ever.

It is best to disband a large party when in a city possessed of many and varied attractions, allowing each little group to see the sights in its own way; assembling, however, at breakfast and dinner, and spending the evenings together, recounting the day's adventures. This was the general order issued for Edinburgh.

The new docks at Leith were opened with much ceremony during our stay, and I took a party of our Edinburgh friends upon the coach to witness the opening. It was not a clear day, meteorologically considered, but nevertheless it was a happy one for the coaching party. Upon our return, a stop at Mr. N.'s magnificent residence was specially agreeable. He and his daughters were most kind to us while in Edinburgh. Mr. N. gave us a rare treat by showing us through their immense printing establishment, where such exquisite things are done, such Easter and Christmas cards, such friendship tokens, and a thousand other lovely forms we had never seen before, in their various stages of manufacture.

Valuable Importations.

I asked Mr. N. what he had to say in reply to the admissions of the leading art authorities of the superiority of American work in black and white, such as our magazines excel in. He said this could not be questioned; there was nothing done in British publications that equalled the American. The reason he gave furnishes food for thought. I pray you, fellow countrymen, take note of it. Two principal American illustrated magazines, *Harper's* and the *Century*, print each more than one hundred thousand copies, while no British magazine prints half that number. The American publisher can consequently afford to pay twice as much as the British publisher for his illustrations. If this be the true reason of America's superiority in this respect, and I am sure Mr. N. knows what he is stating, then as its population increases more rapidly than the British the difference between their respective publications must increase, and finally drive the home article into a very restricted position. Pursuing this fact to its logical conclusion, Britain may soon receive from her giant child all that is best in any department of art which depends upon general support for success. This seems to me to betoken a revolution, not as implying the inherent superiority of the American, but simply flowing from the fact that fifty-five millions of English-speaking and reading people can afford to spend more for any certain article than thirty-five millions can. That Colonel Mapleson now brings over Her Majesty's Opera Company for the New York season as regularly as he opens his London season, and especially that he makes far more profit out of the former than out of the latter, is another significant fact. That leading actors find a wider field here than at home is still another, and even ministers are finding that the call of the Lord to higher labors and higher salaries often comes from the far side of the Atlantic. Drs. McCosh, Hall, Ormiston, and Taylor, our leading divines, get treble salaries in the Republic, and are said to be valuable importations. As Mr. Evarts said one night in a post-prandial effort: "They are about the only specimens of 'the cloth' admitted duty free." As long as America sent Britain only pork and cheese and provisions, and such products of the soil, it was all well enough, but if she is beginning to send the highest things of life, the art treasures, which give sweetness and light to human existence, it is somewhat alarming. For my part, I do not like to think that these Americans are to send Britain every good thing, and that the once proud country that led the world is to stand receiving as it were the crumbs from this rich land's table. In one department America can be kept second for as long a term as we need worry about—she has nothing to compare with the leading English reviews. Our generation will see no close rival to the *Fortnightly* or the *Nineteenth Century*, to *Blackwood* or *Chambers' Journal*, or to the *Edinburgh* or *Westminster Review*; although the *North American* and the *International* show that even in this race America enters two not indifferent steeds.

I must not forget to mention that the birds in the *Century* magazine which the *Athenæum* pronounced so far superior to any British work were designed by a young lady and engraved by her sister. The work of two American young ladies excelled the best of England; and then did not Miss Rosina Emmet send a Christmas greeting of her own composition to friends in England which took the second prize at the London Exhibition, although not intended for anything more than a private token of friendship. Let a note be made of all this, with three loving cheers for the young lady artists of the Republic. Instead of losing the charms of women by giving public expression to their love of the beautiful in all its forms, they but add one more indescribable charm which their less fortunate sisters can never hope to attain. How a man does reverence a woman who does fine things in art, literature, or music, or in any line whatever!

On a Yacht.

The Charioteers gave leave of absence to the Scribe and General Manager to spend Sunday with my friends Mr. and Mrs. G., at Strathairly House, on the banks of the Forth. It was a most delightful visit. The Commodore of the Forth Yachting Squadron (for such Mr. G. is) had the Ranee ready to take us back to Edinburgh Monday morning. We enjoyed the sail down the Forth very much. That we could not accept the Commodore's invitation to change the Gay Charioteers into Bold Mariners for a day and visit St. Andrews in the Ranee gave rise to deep regret, when the other members of the party were informed of the treat proposed; but we cannot glean every field upon our march. Some other time, Commodore, the recently elected member of the squadron will report for duty on the flagship and splice the main brace with you and your jolly crew. There is a craze for yachting in Britain, which is also showing its symptoms on this side. I am not at home in vessels much smaller than an Atlantic steamer. The Charioteers resolved unanimously that their yacht should have four wheels and four horses, and should run on land.

Upon our return to Edinburgh Monday morning, the first rumbling of the distant thunder from Dunfermline was heard, and it dawned upon us that serious work was at hand. Our friend Mr. D., of the Council, had called upon us and intimated that something of a demonstration might be made upon our arrival in my native town; but when I found a telegram from Mr. Simpson, the clerk, asking us to postpone our coming for a day, I knew there was an end to play. Things looked serious, but I was not going to be the sole sufferer. At dinner I laid it down as the law from which there could be no appeal, that if any public speaking were to be done, Messrs. P., McC., K., the General Manager, and V., were in for it. It is surprising how much it mitigates one's own troubles to see his dearest friends more frightened than himself. I grew bolder as I encouraged these victims. Their speeches were bound to be hits—no speeches have so often created sensations as maiden efforts. The last two offered great inducements to the ladies if they would vote that they should be excused. As for the others, I made it a question of ministerial confidence, and the administration was sustained. If you read their speeches I am sure you will see the wisdom of my selections.

I was glad to see Sir Noel Paton, Dunfermline's most distinguished son, able to be at his sister's that evening. The recent narrow and heroic escape from drowning of himself, Lady Paton, and his son Victor, gave us all renewed interest in grasping his hand again. Thrown from a small sail-boat into the sea, at least two hundred yards from shore, with ropes and sail tangled about them, the three rallied to each other's support (for all could swim), and bore each other up until finally Lady Paton got between her husband and son, with one hand on the shoulder of each, and thus they struggled grandly to shore. Where is another trio that could do that, think you? I tell you, who don't know Dunfermline, that these Patons were always a marked family, and have had genius hovering about their pretty home for generations, and now and then touching the heads and hearts of father, sons, and daughters with its creative wand. There is a great deal in blood, no doubt, but the blood from an honest weaver or shoemaker is, as a rule, a much better article, something to be much prouder of, than you find from nobles whose rise came from such conduct as should make their descendants ashamed to talk of descent.

It's a God's mercy we are all from honest weavers; let us pity those who haven't ancestors of whom they can be proud, dukes or duchesses though they be.

* * * * *

DUNFERMLINE, July 27-28.

Dunfermline.

Put all the fifty days of our journey together, and we would have exchanged them all for rainy ones if we could have been assured a bright day for this occasion. It came, a magnificent day. The sun shone forth as if glad to shine upon this the most memorable day of my mother's life or of mine, as far as days can be rendered memorable by the actions of our fellow-men. We left Edinburgh and reached Queensferry in time for the noon boat. Here was the scene so finely given in "Marmion," which I tried, however, in vain to recall as I gazed upon it. If Dunfermline and its thunders had not been in the distance, I think I could have given it after a fashion, but I failed altogether that morning.

> "But northward far, with purer blaze,
> On Ochil mountains fell the rays,
> And as each heathy top they kissed,
> It gleamed a purple amethyst.
> Yonder the shores of Fife you saw,
> Here Preston Bay, and Berwick Law;
> And broad between them rolled,
> The gallant Firth the eye might note.
> Whose islands on its bosom float,
> Like emeralds chased in gold."

And truly it was a morning in which nature's jewels sparkled at their best. Upon reaching the north shore we were warmly greeted by Uncle and Aunt, and Maggie and Annie. It was decided better not to risk luncheon in the ruins of Rosythe Castle, as we had intended, the grass being reported damp from recent rains. We accordingly drove to the inn, but we were met at the door by the good landlady, who, with uplifted hands, exclaimed: "I'm a' alane! There's naebody in the house! They're a' awa' to Dunfermline! There'll be great goings on there the day."

A hotel without one servant. The good woman, however, assured us we might come in and help ourselves to anything in the house; so we managed to enjoy our luncheon, though some of us only after a fashion. There were three gentlemen, a wife, and a cousin, who for the first time did not care much for anything in the form of luncheon. Speeches, speeches, these are what troubled Harry, Davie and me; and I had cause for grave alarm, of which they could form little idea, for I felt that if Dunfermline had been touched and her people had determined to give us a public reception, there was no saying to what lengths they might go.

A Trying Ordeal.

If I could decently have stolen away and gone round by some circuitous route, sending my fellow townsmen an apology, and telling them that I really felt myself unable to undergo the ordeal, I should have been tempted to do so. I was also afraid that the Queen Dowager would break down, for if ever her big black eyes get wet it's all over with her. How fortunate it was that Mrs. H. was with her to keep her right! It was wisely resolved that she should take her inside of the coach and watch over her. I bit my lip, told the Charioteers they were in for it and must go through without flinching, that now the crisis had come I was just bound to stand anything. I was past stage-fright, and I assured myself that they could do their worst—I was callous and would not be moved—but to play the part of a popular hero even for a day, wondering all the time what you have done to deserve the outburst, is fearful work. When I did get time to think of it, my tower of strength lay in the knowledge that the spark which had set fire to their hearts was the Queen Dowager's return and her share in the day's proceedings. Grand woman, she has deserved all that was done in her honor even on that day.

A man stopped us at the junction of the roads to inform us that we were expected to pass through the ancient borough of Innerkeithing; but I forgot myself there. It seemed a fair chance to escape part of the excitement (we had not yet begun the campaign as it were); at all events I dodged to escape the first fire, as raw troops are always said to do, and so we took the direct road. When the top of the Ferry Hills was reached we saw the town, all as dead as if the holy Sabbath lay upon it, without one evidence of life. How beautiful is Dunfermline seen from the Ferry Hills, its grand old abbey towering over all, seeming to hallow the city and to lend a charm and dignity to the lowliest tenement. Nor is there in all broad Scotland, nor in many places elsewhere, that I know of, a more varied and delightful view than that obtained from the park upon a fine day. What Benares is to the Hindoo, Mecca to the Mohammedan, Jerusalem to the Christian, all that Dunfermline is to me.

But here I must stop. If you want to learn how impulsive and enthusiastic the Scotch are when once aroused, how dark and stern and true is the North, and yet how fervid and overwhelming in its love when the blood is up, I do not know where you will find a better evidence of it than in what followed. See how a small spark kindled so great a flame. The Queen Dowager and I are still somewhat shamefaced about it, but somehow or other we managed to go through with our parts without breaking down.

The Free Library.

The Queen Dowager had been chosen to lay the Memorial Stone of the Free Library, and the enthusiasm of the people was aroused by her approach. There was something of the fairy tale in the fact that she had left her native town, poor, thirty odd years before, with her loved ones, to found a new home in the great Republic, and was to-day returning in her coach, to be allowed the privilege of linking her name with the annals of her beloved native town in one of the most enduring forms possible; for whatever agencies for good may rise or fall in the future, it seems certain that the Free Library is destined to stand and become a never-ceasing foundation of good to all the inhabitants. Well, the future historian of that ancient town will record that on this day, under bright sunshine, and amidst the plaudits of assembled thousands, the Queen Dowager laid the Memorial Stone of the building, an honor, compared with which, I was charged to tell the citizens, in the Queen Dowager's estimation, Queen Victoria has nothing in her power to bestow. So say also the sons of the Queen Dowager. The ceremonies passed off triumphantly. The procession, workingmen and address, banquet, and all the rest of it may be summed up in the remark of the Dunfermline press: "The demonstration may be said to be unparalleled in the history of Dunfermline."

I will not be tempted to say anything further about this unexpected upheaval except this: after we had stopped and saluted the Stars and Stripes, displayed upon the Abbey Tower in graceful compliment to my American friends (no foreign flag ever floated there before, said our friend, Mr. R— —, keeper of the ruins), we passed through the archway to the Bartizan, and at this moment came the shock of all that day to me. I was standing on the front seat of the coach with Provost Walls when I heard the first toll of the abbey bell. My knees sank from under me, the tears came rushing before I knew it, and I turned round to tell the Provost that I must give in. For a moment I felt as if I were about to faint. Fortunately I saw that there was no crowd before us for a little distance. I had time to regain control, and biting my lips till they actually bled, I murmured to myself, "No matter, keep cool, you must go on;" but never can there come to my ears on earth, nor enter so deep into my soul, a sound that shall haunt and subdue me with its sweet, gracious, melting power like that.

The Abbey Bell.

By that curfew bell I had been laid in my little couch to sleep the sleep of childish innocence. Father and mother, sometimes the one, sometimes the other, had told me, as they bent lovingly over me night after night, what that bell said as it tolled. Many good words has that bell spoken to me through their translations. No wrong thing did I do through the day which that voice from all I knew of heaven and the great Father there did not tell me kindly about ere I sank to sleep, speaking the very words so plainly that I knew that the power that moved it had seen all and was not angry, never angry, never, but so very, *very* sorry. Nor is that bell dumb to me to-day when I hear its voice. It still has its message, and now it sounded to welcome back the exiled mother and son under its precious care again.

The world has not within its power to devise, much less to bestow upon us, such a reward as that which the abbey bell gave when it tolled in our honor. But my brother Tom should have been there also; this was the thought that came. He, too, was beginning to know the wonders of that bell ere we were away to the newer land.

Rousseau wished to die to the strains of sweet music. Could I choose my accompaniment, I could wish to pass into the dim beyond with the tolling of the abbey bell sounding in my ears, telling me of the race that had been run, and calling me, as it had called the little white-haired child, for the last time—*to sleep*.

We spent two days in Dunfermline. The tourist who runs over from Edinburgh will find the Abbey and the Palace ruins well worthy a visit. Take a day and see them, is my advice. Queen Margaret, King Robert the Bruce, and many other Kings and Queens are interred in the Abbey, for this was the capital of Scotland long ere Edinburgh rose to importance. Who does not remember the famous ballad of Sir Patrick Spens:

> "The King sits in Dunfermline toon,
> Drinking the bluid red wine;
> Oh where will I get a skelly skipper
> To sail this ship of mine."

Dunfermline is now the principal seat of the damask manufacture. Americans will be interested in knowing that at least two-thirds of all the table linen made in the eleven factories here are for republican use. While we were there the rage was for designs showing the American race-horse Iroquois leading all the fleet steeds of England; now it is said to be for "Jumbo" patterns.

The New Kings.

A visit to one of the leading factories cannot fail to be interesting to the sight-seer, and to such as may go I suggest that a good look be taken at the stalwart lassies and good-looking young women who work there. Several thousand of them marched in the procession formed to greet us at the city line, and their comely appearance and the good taste shown in their dress surprised the coaching party very agreeably. Indeed, our Poetaster improvised a verse which illustrates the change which has come over the ancient capital since the days of Sir Patrick Spens, and gave it to us as we rolled along:

> "The old Kings sat in Dunfermline town,
> Drinking the blood red wine;
> The new Kings are at better work,
> Weaving the damask fine."

Quite correct, Davie. Does not Holy Writ declare that the diligent man shall stand *before* Kings? And is it not time that the bibulous King should give place to the useful citizen—the world over!

Friday was a cloudy day, but some of our friends, who spent the early morning with us and saw us off, unanimously predicted that it would clear. They proved true weather prophets, for it did turn out to be a bright day. Passing the residence of Colonel Myers, the American Consul, we drove in and gave that representative of the great Republic and his wife three farewell cheers.

* * * * *

KINROSS, Friday, July 28.

Kinross was the lunching-place. Mother was for the first and last time compelled to seek the inside for a few hours after leaving Dunfermline. These farewells from those near and dear to you are among the cruelest ordeals one has to undergo in life. One of the most desirable arrangements held out to us in all that is said of heaven is to my mind that there shall be no parting there. Hell might be invested with a new horror by having them daily.

We had time while at Kinross to walk along Loch Leven and see the ruined castle upon the island, from which Douglas rescued Queen Mary. What a question this of Mary Queen of Scots is in Scotland! To intimate a doubt that she was not purity itself suffices to stir up a warm discussion. Long after a "point of divinity" ceases to be the best bone to snarl over, this Queen Mary question will probably still serve the purpose. What matters it what she was? It is now a case of beauty in distress, and we cannot help sympathizing with a gentle, refined woman (even if her refinement was French veneering), surrounded by rude, coarse men. What is the use of "argie bargieing" about it? Still, I suppose, we must have a bone of some kind, and this is certainly a more sensible one than the "point of divinity," which happily is going somewhat out of fashion.

To-day's talk on the coach was all of the demonstration at Dunfermline, and one after another incident was recalled. Bailie W— — was determined we should learn what real Scotch gooseberries are, and had put on the coach an immense basketful of them. "We never can dispose of so many," was the verdict at Kinross; at Perth it was modified, and ere Pitlochrie was reached the verdict was reversed and more wished for. Our American friends had never known gooseberries before, friend Bailie, so they said.

The Carse of Gowrie.

Fair Perth was to be our resting-place, but before arriving there the pedestrians of the party had one of their grandest excursions, walking through beautiful Glen Farg. They were overpowered at every turn by its loveliness, and declared that there is nothing like it out of Scotland. The ferns and the wild flowers, in all their dewy freshness after the rains, made us all young again, and the glen echoed our laughter and our songs. The outlet from the glen into the rich Carse of Gowrie gave us another surprise worthy of record. There is nothing, I think, either in Britain or America, that is equal in cultivation to the famous Carse of Gowrie. They will be clever agriculturists who teach the farmers of the Carse how to increase very greatly the harvest of that portion of our good mother earth. Davie began to see how it is that Scotland grows crops that England cannot rival. Perthshire is a very beautiful county, neither Highland nor Lowland, but occupying, as it were, the golden mean between, and possessed of many of the advantages of both.

* * * * *

Perth, Saturday, July 29.

Fair Perth.

The view from the hill-top overlooking Perth is superb. "Fair Perth indeed!" we all exclaim. The winding Tay, with one large sail-boat gliding on its waters, the fertile plains beyond, and the bold crag at the base of which the river sweeps down, arrested the attention of our happy pedestrians and kept them long upon the hill. I had never seen Perth before, and it was a surprise to me to find its situation so very fine; but then we are all more and more surprised at what Scotland has to show when thoroughly examined. The finer view from the hill of Kinnoul should be seen, if one would know of what Scotland has to boast.

Antiquaries refer the foundation of Perth to the Roman Agricola, who saw in its hills another Rome, and in its river another Tiber.

> "'Behold the Tiber!' the vain Roman cried,
> Viewing the ample Tay from Baiglie's side;
> But where's the Scot that would the vaunt repay,
> And hail the puny Tiber for the Tay?"

But Agricola, poor fellow, was probably homesick, and felt much like the expatriated Scot who tries to imagine himself on his native heath when eating his annual haggis at St. Andrew's dinner in New York.

From the days of Kenneth McAlpine down to the times of James I., Perth was the capital of Scotland, and witnessed the coronation of all her kings. Every Scot knows the story of James I.—how he hid from the assassins in the Dominican Convent, how fair Catherine Douglas thrust her arm through the socket of the bolt and held the door against them until her bones were brutally crushed, and how the fugitive was finally dragged from his place of concealment by

> "Robert Grahame
> That slew our king,
> God give him shame!"

The old Abbey of Scone, the place of coronation, is about two and a half miles from the town, but little remains of it now besides its name and its associations. The ancient mound is there, but the sacred stone on which the monarchs stood when crowned was carried away by Edward I., and is now in Westminster Abbey, an object of interest to all true Scotsmen. In those royal days—rude and rough days they were too, viewed through modern spectacles—Perth was the centre toward which most of the clansmen looked, and almost every available hill in its vicinity was crowned by a castle, the stronghold of some powerful chieftain. Of course these autocrats were often at feud with each other, and frequently even with the magistrates of the town. In the latter case, if not strong enough to beard the lion in his den, they would waylay provision trains or vessels carrying necessaries to the city, and then the citizens would rise in their wrath and sally forth with sword and buckler and burn a castle or two. But quarrels with the towns-people did not pay in the long run, and their brands were oftener turned against each other.

It is a sad commentary on the morals of the day that these neighborly feuds were rather fostered than checked by the authorities, who thought to win safety for themselves out of this brotherly throat-cutting. Sometimes the king set a score or two of them by the ears in the outskirts of the town for the court's amusement, just as bears and bandogs were pitted against each other in those godless days. Everybody has read in the "Fair Maid of Perth" the graphic account of one of these savage battles between thirty picked men of the Clan Quhele and as many of the

Clan Chattan, on the North Inch of the city—that beautiful meadow in which Agricola saw a striking resemblance to the Campus Martius. The story is historically true, the battle having actually taken place in the reign of Robert III., who had in vain tried to reduce the rivals to order. As a last resort it was suggested that each should select his champions and fight it out in the presence of the king, it being shrewdly hoped that the peace of the community would be secured through the slaughter of the best men of both sides. The place chosen was prepared by surrounding it with a trench and by erecting galleries for spectators, for the brutal combat was witnessed by the king and his court and by many English and French knights, attracted thither by the novelty of the spectacle. The contestants, armed with their native weapons—bows and arrows, swords and targets, short knives and battle axes—entered the lists, and at the royal signal butchered each other until victory declared in favor of Clan Chattan, the only survivor of its opponents having swam the river and escaped to the woods. The few left of the conquering party were so chopped and carved and lopped of limbs that they could be no longer regarded as either useful or ornamental members of society—and thus good king Robert's sagacity in pitting these turbulent fellows against each other was apparently justified.

Before starting to-day we had time to stroll along the Tay for an hour or two. We were especially attracted by a volunteer regiment under drill upon the green, and were gratified to see that the men looked remarkably well under close inspection, as indeed did all the militia and volunteers we saw. The nation cannot be wrong in accounting these forces most valuable auxiliaries in case of need. I have no doubt but in the course of one short campaign they would equal regular troops; at least such was the experience in the American war. The men we saw were certainly superior to regulars as men. It is in a war of defence, when one's own country is to be fought for, that bayonets which can think are wanted. With such a question at issue, these Scotchmen would rout any regular troops in the world who opposed them for pay. As for miserable skirmishes against poor half-armed savages, I hope these men would think enough to despise the bad use they were put to.

Villas on the Tay.

The villas we saw upon the opposite bank of the Tay looked very pretty—nice home-like places, with their gardens and boat-houses. We voted fair Perth very fair indeed. After luncheon, which was taken in the hotel at Dunkeld, we left our horses to rest and made an excursion of a few miles to the falls, to the place in the Vale of Athol where Millais made the sketch for his celebrated picture called "O'er the hills and far awa'." It is a grand view, and lighted as it then was by glimpses of sunshine through dark masses of cloud, giving many of the rainbow tints upon the heather, it is sure to remain long with us. For thirty miles stretch the vast possessions of the Duke of Athol; over mountain, strath, and glen he is monarch of all the eye can see—a noble heritage. A recent storm is said to have uprooted seventy thousand of his trees in a single night.

The scenery in the neighborhood of Dunkeld is very beautiful. The description of the poet Gray, who visited it in 1766, will do as well to-day. "The road came to the brow of a deep descent; and between two woods of oak we saw, far below us, the Tay come sweeping along at the bottom of a precipice at least a hundred and fifty feet deep, clear as glass, full to the brim, and very rapid in its course. It seemed to issue out of woods thick and tall that rose on either hand, and were overhung by broken rocky crags of vast height. Above them, to the west, the tops of higher mountains appeared, on which the evening clouds reposed. Down by the side of the river, under the thickest shades, is seated the town of Dunkeld. In the midst of it stands a ruined cathedral; the tower and shell of the building still entire. A little beyond it a large house of the Duke of Athole, with its offices and gardens, extends a mile beyond the town: and, as his grounds are intersected by the streets and roads, he has flung arches of communication across them, that add much to the scenery of the place."

Dunkeld Cathedral.

The cathedral, still a noble ruin, stands a little apart from the town, in a grove of fine old trees. It owes its destruction to the Puritans, who sacked it in the sixteenth century, though the order "to purge the kyrk of all kinds of monuments of idolatrye" was directed only against images and altars. But the zeal of men in those days of bigotry was hard to control, and the mob did not desist from its work while a door remained on its hinges or a window was unbroken. Since then tower, nave, and aisles have remained open to sun and storm; the choir alone has been refitted and is now used as the parish church. In the choir is still to be seen the tomb and recumbent statue of the famous Earl of Buchan, better known as the Wolf of Badenoch.

The coachman who drove us to-day interested us by his knowledge of men and things—such a character as could hardly grow except on the heather. He "did not think muckle o' one man owning thirty miles o' land who had done nothing for it." His reply to a question was given with such a pawkie expression that it remains fixed in the memory. "Why do not the people just meet and resolve that they will no longer have kings, princes, dukes or lords, and declare that all men are born equal, as we have done in America?"

"Aye, maan, it would hae to be a *strong* meeting that!"

That strong was so *very* strong; but there will be one strong enough some day, for all that. We cannot stand nonsense forever, patient as we are and slow.

Dunkeld is the gateway of the Highlands, and we enter it, singing as we pass upward:

> "There are hills beyond Pentland
> And streams beyond Forth;
> If there are lords in the south
> There are chiefs in the north."

We are among the real hills at last. Yonder towers Birnam, and here Dunsinane Hill. Mighty master, even here is your shade, and we dwell again in your shadow. The very air breathes of Macbeth, and the murdered Banquo still haunts the glen.

How perfectly Shakespeare flings into two words the slow gathering darkness of night in this northern latitude, among the deep green pines:

> "Ere the bat hath flown
> His cloister'd flight; ere, to black Hecate's summons,
> The shard-borne beetle, with his drowsy hum,
> Hath rung night's yawning peal, there shall be done
> A deed of dreadful note . . . .
> . . . . *Light thickens*; and the crow
> Makes wing to the rooky wood:
> Good things of day begin to droop and drowse;
> Whiles night's black agents to their prey do rouse."

That man shut his eyes and imagined more than other men could see with their eyes wide open even when among the scenes depicted. The light does "thicken," and the darkness creeps upon us and wraps us in its mantle unawares.

Birnam Wood.

Birnam, a wooded hill on the bank of the Tay, is about twelve miles from Dunsinane or Dunsinnane Hill, the traditional stronghold of Macbeth the Giant, as the usurper was known to the country people. According to the common story, when Macbeth heard from his spies of the coming of Malcolm Canmore's troops from Birnam with branches in their hands, he recalled the prophecy of the witches, and, despairing of holding the castle against them, deserted it and fled, pursued by Malcolm, up the opposite hill, where finding it impossible to escape, he threw himself from a precipice and was killed on the rocks below. His place of burial is still shown at a spot called Lang Man's Grave, not far from the road where Banquo is said to have been murdered.

Some Shakesperean scholars have thought that the great bard must have collected the materials for his tragedy upon the site. It is well known that Her Majesty's Players exhibited at Perth in 1589, and it is not impossible that Shakespeare may have been among them; but it is scarcely probable. The play follows very closely the history of Macbeth as narrated by Hollinshed, in which the usurper falls in single combat with Macduff, and there can be little doubt that Shakespeare derived his facts from the chronicle rather than from personal investigation.

It is very evident, however, that Dunsinane was anciently a strong military post. The hill, which rises about eight hundred feet above its base, is steep and difficult of access on all sides but one, where are traces of a winding road cut into the rock. Its flat summit was once defended by a strong rampart, which, judging from its remains, must have been of considerable height and thickness. The area enclosed by it is more than two hundred feet long.

* * * * *

PITLOCHRIE, July 30-31.

This is a great resort in the Highlands; and deservedly so, for excursions can be made in every direction to famous spots, embracing some of the finest scenery in Scotland. About three miles north of it rises Ben Vracky, and within easy distances are Glen Tilt, Bruar Water, the Pass of Killicrankie, Loch Tummel, the Falls of Tummel, and other places well worthy of a visit; but as the Gay Charioteers' time was limited they could pay their respects to only a few of them.

We visited the hydropathic establishment in the evening, and found something resembling an American hotel. Such establishments are numerous in England and Scotland. Few of the guests take the cold-water treatment, as I had supposed, but visit the hotels more for sake of a change, to make acquaintances, and to "have a good time," as we say. I have no doubt that a month of Pitlochrie air is highly beneficial for almost any one.

Falls of Tummel.

We walked to the falls of Tummel, and spent some happy hours there. Cousin Eliza is up in Scotch songs, and I start her every now and then. It has a charm of its own to sit on the banks of the very stream, with Athol near, and listen to the inquiry finely sung:

> "Cam ye by Athol,
> Lad wi' the philibeg,
> Down by the Tummel
> And banks of the Garry?"

Through these very glens the mountaineers came rushing,

> "And with the ocean's mighty swing
> When heaving to the tempest's wing
> They hurled them on the foe."

There is a new meaning to the song when Davie pours it forth in the glen itself:

> "Sweet the lavrock's note and lang,
> Lilting wildly up the glen,
> But aye to me it sings ae sang,
> Will ye no come back again?"

What a chorus we gave him! There are some days in which we live more than twenty-four hours; and these days in Scottish glens count for more than a week of ordinary life. We are in the region of gamekeepers and dogs. It is the last day of July, and the whole country is preparing for the annual massacre of the 12th of August. Is civilization so very far advanced when the titled and wealthiest portions of cultured society have still for their chief amusements—which are in many cases with them the principal business of life—the racing of horses one half of the year, and the murdering of poor half-domesticated birds or the chasing to death of poor foxes and hares the other half? Can civilized man find nothing better to furnish needful recreation after useful toil?

The prices paid for a deer forest in Scotland are incredible. Twenty-five to fifty thousand dollars per annum for the right to shoot over a few thousand acres of poorly timbered land, and a force of gamekeepers and other attendants to pay for besides.

For the present the British are what is called a sporting people, and the Highlands are their favorite hunting-grounds. Their ideas of sport are curious. General Sheridan told me that, when abroad, he was invited to try some of their sport, but when he saw the poor animals driven to him, and that all he had to do was to bang away, he returned the gun to the attendant. He really could not do this thing, and the General is not very squeamish either. As for hunting down a poor hare—that needs the deadening influence of custom—women ought to be ashamed of it now; men will be anon.

Pass of Killiecrankie.

The first of all our glens is the Pass of Killiecrankie, that famous defile which gave its name to the battle that proved so fatal to the Stuarts, for the victory won there by the adherents of the so-called James VII., was more than counterbalanced by the loss of Claverhouse. The pass is a narrow, ragged break through the mountains, giving a passage to the River Garry, and forming the only practicable entrance from the low country to the Highlands above. It is now accessible by a broad, smooth highway as well as by the railway, but at the time of the battle the only road through it was a rough path between the swirling river and the rocks, and so steep and narrow that but two men could march abreast. Along this path the royal forces under McKay slowly made their way; and though the pass is only about a mile and a half long it was afternoon before the little army of three thousand debouched into the plain at its extremity, and took position on the high ground beyond. Do you see that eminence a mile away yonder, on the north, whose sides slope down into the plain? It was from that height that the Highlanders—McLeans, McDonalds, Camerons, Lochiel, Dundee and all—came down like a torrent upon King William's men below. The red sun was just above the western hills. With fearful yells the tide of ragged, barefooted mountaineers (Macaulay says that Lochiel took off before the battle what was probably the only pair of shoes in the clans) swept on, undismayed by the volleys of musketry that decimated them as they ran. Plaids and haversacks were thrown away, and dropping their fusils as they fired them, they were upon the astonished Southrons before they had time to screw on their bayonets. The fight was over in a few minutes. More than a thousand men went down under the strokes of the dreaded claymores and Lochaber axes, and away went King William's men in a panic down the valley with the clans at their heels. The victory was a decisive one, but Claverhouse, who had insisted, against the remonstrances of Lochiel and others, upon leading in the charge, was fatally wounded by a bullet early in the action. Up yonder on the right is Urrard House, where he was carried to die. With this brave, unscrupulous leader, passed away the last hope of the Stuarts of winning their "own again." When King William heard of the defeat and of Dundee's death, he said, "Well, were it not so, Dundee would have been at my gates to tell it himself."

We walked through the pass on our way northward, and concluded that we had thus far seen nothing quite so wild. The cliffs rise precipitously on each side, clothed here and there with patches of oak and birch. The dark, amber-brown rushing torrent is superb, swirling among the rocks, down which it has poured through eons of time, wearing them into strange forms. The very streams are Scotch, with a character all their own, portraying the stern features of the race, torn and twisted by endless ages of struggle with the rocks which impeded their passage, triumphantly clearing their pathway to the sea at last by unceasing, persistent endeavor. The sides of Scotia's glens are a never-failing source of delight, the wild flowers and the ferns seem so much more delicately fine than they are anywhere else. One understands how they affected Burns.

Some of our ladies, the Queen Dowager always for one, will delay the coach any time to range the sides of the glen; and it is with great difficulty that we can get them together to mount once more. The horn sounds again and again, and still they linger and when they at last emerge from the copse, it is with handfuls or rather armfuls of Nature's smiles—lapfuls of wild flowers—each one rejoicing in her trophies, happy as the day is long, only it is not half long enough. Go the sun down never so late it sinks to its rest too soon.

* * * * *

DALWHINNIE, August 1.

Pitlochrie to Dalwhinnie.

Our drive from Pitlochrie to Dalwhinnie, thirty-two miles, was from beginning to end unsurpassed—mountain and moor, forest and glen. The celebrated falls of Bruar lay in our route, and we spent two hours walking up the glen to see them. Well were we repaid. This is decided to be the finest, most varied fall of all we have seen. The amber torrent works and squirms itself through caldrons there, and gorges here, and dashes over precipices yonder, revealing new beauties and giving us fresh delights at every step. No gentle kiss gives this Scotch fiend to every sedge it overtaketh in its pilgrimage, for in truth, dashing and splashing against the rocks, the surging, boiling water, with its crest of sparkling foam, seems a live spirit escaping from the glen and bounding to the sea, pursued by angry demons behind. Standing on the bridge across the Bruar, one need not be entirely off his balance to sympathize to some extent with the wild wish of my young lady friend, who thought if she had to be anything dead she would be a plunging, mad stream like this, dancing among the rocks, snatching to its breast, as it passed, the bluebell and the forget-me-not, the broom and the fox-glove, leaping over precipices and tossing its gay head in sparkling rainbow sprays forever and ever.

Bruar Water.

It was while gazing at this fall that Burns wrote the petition of Bruar Water. The shade asked for has been restored—"Clanalpine's pines, in battle brave," now fill the glen, and the falls of the Bruar sing their grateful thanks to the bard who loved them.

I have often reminded you, good readers, that the coaching party, with a few exceptions, hailed with delight every opportunity for a walk. Contrary to expectation, these came much less frequently in Scotland than in England. Far away up among the towering hills, where the roads necessarily follow the streams which have pushed themselves through the narrow defiles, we get miles and miles in the glens along the ever-changing streams; but it is too level for pedestrianism unless we reduce the pace of the coach and walk the horses. It is after a two hours' climb up the glen to see such a waterfall as the Bruar that we return to the coach, feeling, as we mount to our seats, that we have done our duty. We were many miles from our lunching site, and long ere it was reached we were overtaken by the mountain hunger. When we arrived at the house on the moors where entertainment had been promised us, it was to find that it had been rented for the season for a shooting-box by a party of English gentlemen, who were to arrive in a few days for their annual sport—the slaughter of the carefully preserved birds. The people, however, were very kind, and gave us the use of the house. Few midday halts gave rise to more gayety than this, but there is one item to be here recorded which is peculiar to this luncheon. For the first and only time the stewardess had to confess that her supplies were exhausted. Due allowance, she thought, had been made for the effects of Highland air, but the climb to Bruar, "or the brunt of the weather," had produced an unusual demand. The very last morsel was eaten, and there seemed a flavor of hesitancy in the assurance some of us gave her that we wished for nothing more. There was not even one bite left for the beautiful collies we saw there.

Has the amount and depth of affection which a woman can waste on a collie dog ever been justly fathomed? was a question raised to-day; but our ladies declined to entertain it at all unless "waste" was changed to "bestow." The amendment was accepted. Many stories were told of these wonderful pets, and what their mistresses had done for them. My story was a true one. Miss Nettie having to go abroad had to leave her collie in some one's care. Many eligible parties had been thoughtfully canvassed, when I suggested that, as I had given her the dog, it might be perfectly safe to leave him with me, or rather with John and the horses. A grave shake of the head, and then, "I have thought of that, but have given it up. It would never do. Trust requires *a woman's care.*" Not a smile, all as grave as if her pet had been a delicate child. "You are quite right," I replied; "no doubt he would have a dog's life of it at the stable." She said yes, mournfully, and never suspected a joke. In a stable in New York I once saw a doctor's card nailed up. Inquiry revealed that this gave the coachman the address of the physician who was to be called in case the lady's dog should be taken ill during her absence. If the ladies must go wild over some kind of a dog, let it be a collie. I like them myself a little.

In the Highlands.

It was gloaming ere we reached Loch Ericht, twelve hundred and fifty feet above the sea. What a wild, solitary country it is around us! The lake lies as it were in the lap of the mountains. It is easy to believe that this was a famous Highland stronghold in the olden time. Even Cromwell's Ironsides met with a rude check in its savage glens from the men of Athol. Do you see rugged Ben Alder yonder, the highest of the group that looks down into the still waters of the lake? In its recesses is the cave where Prince Charlie was hidden by Cluny Macpherson.

The gathering of the night shadows warn us that we must seek shelter, and in a few minutes we are housed in the queer little inn at Dalwhinnie. A bright fire was made, and we were as gay as larks at dinner. I am sure nothing could surprise Americans more than the dinners and meals generally which were given us even in such out-of-the-way stations as this. Everything is good, well-cooked, and nicely served. It is astonishing what a good dinner and a glass of genuine old claret does for a party after such a long day's drive and a climb.

Reassembling after dinner in our neat little parlor, the Stars and Stripes displayed as usual over the mantel, we were all as fresh and bright as if we had newly risen, and were in for a frolic. The incidents of the day gave us plenty to talk about—the falls, the glen, that mountain blue, the lake, and oh! that first dazzling glint of purple heather upon the high rock in the glen which drew forth such exclamations! A little patch it was which, having caught more of the sunshine there than that upon the moors, had burst before it into the purple, and given to the most of us for the first time ample proof of the rich, glorious beauty of that famous plant.

What says Annie's song?

> "I can calmly gaze o'er the flowery lea,
> I can tentless muse o'er the summer sea;
> But a nameless rapture my bosom fills
> As I gaze on the face of the heather hill."

Aye, Annie, the "nameless rapture" swells in the bosom of every Scotchman worthy of the name, when he treads the heather.

Andrew M.'s prize song, "The Emigrant's Lament," has the power of a flower to symbolize the things that tug hardest at the heart-strings very strongly drawn. By the way, let it here be recorded, this is a Dunfermline song, written by Mr. Gilfillan—three cheers for Dunfermline! (that always brings the thunder, aye, and something of the lightning too). The Scotchman who left the land where his forefathers sleep sings:

> "The palm-tree waveth high, and fair the myrtle springs,
> And to the Indian maid the bulbul sweetly sings;
> *But I dinna see the broom* wi' its tassels on the lea,
> Nor hear the linties sang o' my ain countrie."

There it is, neither palm-tree nor myrtle, poinsetta nor Victoria Regia, nor all that luscious nature has to boast in the dazzling lands of the south, all put together, will ever make good to that woe-begone, desolate, charred heart the lack of that wee yellow bush o' broom—never! Nor will all "the drowsy syrups of the East," quiet the ache of that sad breast which carries within it the doom of exile from the scenes and friends of youth. They cannot agree, in these days, where a man's soul is, much less where it is going; let search be made for it close, very close, to the roots of that ache. It is not far away from the centre which colors the stream of man's life.

Many times to-day, in the exhilaration of the moment, one or another enthusiastic member called out, "What do ye think o' Scotland noo?" and even Emma had to confess in a half-whisper that England was nothing to this. Perry and Joe had never been beyond the border before, and gave in their adhesion to the verdict— there is no place like Scotland. "Right, Perry!"

Scotland's Flowers.

We have never seen that paragon of grace, the Scottish bluebell, in its glory till now. It is not to be judged in gardens, for it is not in its element there; but steal upon it in the glen and see how it goes to your heart. Truly I think the Scotch are the best lovers of flowers, make the most of them, and draw more from them than any other people do. This is a good sign, and may be adduced as another proof that the race has a tender, weak spot in the heart to relieve the hard level head with which the world credits them.

Whew! Thermometer 53° during the night, the coldest weather experienced during our journey. But how invigorating! Ten years knocked off from the age of every one of us since we got among the hills, excepting from that of several of the ladies, who could hardly spare so much and still be as charming.

We were stirring early this morning, in for a walk across the moors, with the glorious hills surrounding us. A grand walk it was too, and the echoes of the horn from the coach overtaking us came all too soon upon us. Looking back down the valley of Loch Ericht, we had the ideal Highland view—mountains everywhere fading into blue in the distance, green to their tops except when capped with snow, and bare, not a tree nor a shrub to break their baldness, and the lake lying peacefully among them at the foot of the vale. These towering masses

"Seem to stand to sentinel Enchanted Land."

I am at a loss for any scenery elsewhere with which to compare that of the Highlands. The bluish tinge above, the rich purple tint below, the thick and thin marled, cloudy sky with its small rifts of clear blue, through which alone the sun glints to relieve the dark shadows by narrow dazzling lights—these give this scenery a weird and solemn grandeur unknown elsewhere; at least I have seen nothing like it. During my strolls at night amid such scenes, I have always felt nearer to the awful mysteries than ever before. The glowering bare masses of mountain, the deep still lake sleeping among them, the sough of the wind through the glen, not one trace of man to be seen, no wonder it makes one eerie, and you feel as if

"Nature had made a pause,
An awful pause, prophetic of its end."

Memory must have much to do with this eerie feeling upon such occasions, I take it, for every scrap of Scottish poetry and song bearing upon the Highlands comes rushing back to me. There are whispering sounds in the glen:

"Shades of the dead, have I not heard your voices
Rise on the night-rolling breath of the gale?
Surely the soul of the hero rejoices
And rides on the wind o'er his own Highland vale."

I hear the lament of Ossian in the sough of the passing wind.

Ruthven Castle.

We stopped at the inn at Kingussie, one of the centres of sporting interest, but drove on beyond to spread our luncheon upon the banks of the Spey, close to the remains of Ruthven Castle, a fine ruin in this beautiful valley. We walked to it after luncheon. It was here that the Highland clans assembled after the defeat at Culloden Field and resolved to disband, and the country was rid of the Stuarts forever. How far the world has travelled since those days! The best king or family of kings in the world is not worth one drop of an honest man's blood. If the House of Commons should decide to-day that the Prince of Wales is not a fit and proper figure-head and should vote that my Lord Tom Noddy is, there is not a sane man in the realm who would move a finger for the rightful heir; yet our forefathers thought it a religious duty to plunge their country into civil war to restore the Stuarts,

> "A coward race to honor lost;
> Who knew them best despised them most."

But I suppose they were about a fair average of royal races. "Life can be lived well even in a palace," sings Matthew Arnold, and the more credit to such as do live it well there, like Queen Victoria, but it is difficult work and needs a saint to begin with. It does one good to mark such progress. I will not believe that man goes round in a circle as the earth does; upon the king absurdity he has travelled a straight line. When we made kings by act of Parliament (as the Guelphs were made), another lesson was learned, that Parliament can unmake them too. That is one bloody circle we need never travel again. Not one drop of blood for all the royal families in Christendom. Carried, *nem. con.*

There was a discussion to-day upon the best mode of enjoying life. Sydney Smith's famous secret was mentioned. When asked why he was always so bright and cheerful, he replied: The secret is "I take short views of things." Somehow this is the Scriptural idea, "Sufficient unto the day is the evil thereof." A good story was told of an old man who had endured many of the ills of life in his long journey. His friends upon one occasion, more trying than usual, condoled with him, saying that he really had more troubles than other men. "Yes, my friends, that is too true. I have been surrounded by troubles all my life long, but there is a curious thing about them—*nine-tenths of them never happened.*"

That is a story with a moral for you. How many of our troubles ever happened! We dream of ten for every one that comes. One of the Charioteers was ready with a verse to enforce the moral:

> "When fortune with a smiling face
> Strews roses on our way,
> When shall we stop to pick them up?
> To-day, my love, to-day.
> But should she frown with face of care,
> And speak of coming sorrow,
> When shall we grieve, if grieve we must?
> To-morrow, love, to-morrow."

Honeysuckle and Roses.

This was received with evident approval, and just as it ended the huge beds of honeysuckle lying on the hedge-rows we were passing, and the wild roses rising above them on long graceful sprays, nodding their heads as if desirous of doing us obeisance, caused one of the ladies to cry out, "Oh, here are the roses on our way just now! Do let us stop and pluck them to-day, as the poet advises." "Stop, Perry!" "Right, sir!" "Steps, Joey!" "Right, sir!" — and down we are in a moment gathering the spoils. "Do let the coach drive on and wait for us at the top of the next hill." "But wait, ladies, let us all put our flowers inside and arrange them when we stop for luncheon."

It is a superb morning, the hedge-rows prettier than ever; the larks are rising; now and then a hare darts across the road in advance. The whirr of the partridge or pheasant stirs the sportsman's blood, and upon every tree some feathered song-ster pours forth his song. Faust need not have sold himself to the devil for youth, after all. We find it here in this glorious gypsy life.

Upon remounting the coach after an hour's frolic in the lane, some one wanted the reciter to repeat the verse which had caused the stop, but he said there was a second verse which also had its moral, and, if permitted, he would give this instead. Agreed to, provided he would give the ladies a copy of both verses for their books—one copy for the lot, and this each would copy for herself. His terms, however, were that he should repeat it alone to Miss — — and teach it to her (sly dog), and she could make the copies. He then gave us the second verse:

> "If those who've wronged us own their faults
> And kindly pity pray,
> When shall we listen and forgive?
> To-day, my love, to-day.
> But if stern justice urge rebuke
> And warmth from memory borrow,
> When shall we chide, if chide we must?
> To-morrow, love, to-morrow."

This was voted a fit companion for the first verse, so the Charioteers to-day had two moral lessons.

Good Philosophy.

The student said it was also good philosophy, and taught by no less an author-ity than Herbert Spencer himself, who had exposed the folly of postponing present enjoyments in the hope that they will be better if enjoyed at a later date. Here are the words of the sage:

"Hence has resulted the belief that, irrespective of their kinds, the pleasures of the present must be sacrificed to the pleasures of the future. So ignorant is this belief, that it is wrong to seek immediate enjoyments and right to seek remote ones only, that you may hear from a busy man who has been on a pleasure excursion a kind of apology for his conduct. He deprecates the unfavorable judgments of his friends by explaining that the state of his health had compelled him to take a holiday, nevertheless if you sound him with respect to his future, you will find out his ambition is by and by to retire and devote himself wholly to the relaxation which he is now somewhat ashamed of taking. The current conception further errs by implying that a gratification which forms a proper aim if it is remote, forms an improper aim if it is proximate."

And this from the "Data of Ethics." So that the poet and the philosopher are as one.

"Does Herbert Spencer write so clearly and simply as that upon such subjects?" asked one of the young ladies. "I thought he was so fearfully deep. His books sound so very learned and abstruse, I have only read his work on 'Education'; that was splendid, and I understood it all, every word. If that book you just quoted from had an easy name I'd go to work at it—but 'Data of Ethics' frightens me. I don't know exactly what Data means, and I'm mixed on Ethics."

The voice of the Coach was clear upon "Education," however, and I recall just now the remark of my little nephew to his mother, when Mr. Spencer did us the honor of visiting us: "Mamma, I want to see the man who wrote in a book that there is no use studying grammar." Amid the thousands of very grateful ones who feel what they owe to Herbert Spencer, may be safely classed that young scion of our family. His gratitude is profound, and with good reason.

Boat o' Garten was to be our refuge, a small, lovely inn on the moors, the landlady of which had telegraphed us in a rather equivocal way in response to our request for shelter. There was no other house for many miles, so we pushed on, trusting to our star. We were all right. The house was to be filled on the morrow with sportsmen, and we could be entertained "for this night only." Such is luck. Even as it was, the family rooms had to be given up to us; but then, dear souls, there is nothing they would not do for the Americans. As for the coach, there was no building on the moors high enough to take in the huge vehicle; but as showing the extreme care taken of property in this country, I note that heavy tarpaulins were obtained, and it was nicely covered for the night. What a monster it seemed standing out in the darkness!

After dinner we received packages of the Dunfermline papers containing the full account of the demonstration there and of the speeches. It goes without saying that there was great anxiety to read the account of that extraordinary ovation. Those who had made speeches and said they were not very sure what, were seen to retire to quiet corners and bury themselves in their copies. Ah, gentlemen, it is of no use! Read your orations twenty times over, you are just as far as ever from being able to gauge your wonderful performances; besides the speech made is nothing compared to any of half a dozen you have since made to yourself on the same subject. Ah! the Dunfermline people should have heard these. So sorry! One can tell all about the speeches of his colleagues, however, and we made each other happy by very liberal laudations, while we each felt once more the generous rounds of applause with which we had been greeted.

Last Night on the Moors.

After mailing copies of the newspapers to numerous friends, there came a serious cloud over all. This was to be our last night on the moors; the end of our wayward life had come. One more merry start at the horn's call, and to-morrow's setting sun would see the end of our happy dream. Arcadia would be no more; the Charioteers' occupation would be gone. It was resolved that something should be done to celebrate the night to distinguish it from others. We would conform to the manners and customs of the country and drink to our noble selves in whiskey toddy with Highland honors. This proved a success. Songs were sung; Aaleek was in his most admirable fooling; "your health and song" went round, and we parted in tolerably good spirits.

There was an unusual tenderness in the grasp of the hand, and mayhap something of a tremor in the kind "Good-night, happy dreams," with which it was the custom of the members to separate for the night, and we went to bed wondering what we had done to deserve so much happiness.

* * * * *

BOAT O' GARTEN, August 2.

Inverness at last! But most of us were up and away in advance of the coach, for who would miss the caller air and the joy of the moors these blessed mornings when it seems joy enough simply to breathe? But did not we catch it this morning! No use trying to march against this blow; the wind fairly beat us, and we were all glad to take refuge in the school-house till the coach came; and glad were we that we had done so. Was it not a sight to see the throng of sturdy boys and girls gathered together from who knows where! For miles and miles there are seen but a few low huts upon the moors; but as some one has said, "Education is a passion" in Scotland, and much of the admitted success of the race has its root in this truth. The poorest crofter in Scotland will see that his child gets to school.

Note this in the fine old song:

> "When Aaleck, Jock, and Jeanettie
> *Are up and got their lair,*
> They'll serve to gar the boatie row
> And lichten a' our care."

Advantages of Poverty.

Heavy is the load of care that the Scotch father and mother take upon themselves and struggle with all the years of their prime that the bairns "may get their lair." To the credit of the bairns let it be said that the hope expressed in the verse just quoted is not often disappointed. They do grow up to be a comfort to their parents in old age when worn out with sacrifices made for them. Our great men come from the cradles of poverty. I think he was a very wise man who found out that the advantage of poverty was a great prize which a rich man could never give his son. But we should not condemn the Marquises of Huntley, the Dukes of Hamilton, and the rest of them; they never had a fair chance to become useful men. It is the system that is at fault, and for that we the people are responsible. The privileged classes might turn out quite respectably if they had justice done them and were permitted to start in life as other men are. For my part, I wonder that they generally turn out as well as they do. The kite mounts only against the wind.

Coaching brings us close to Nature's sweetest charms, and the good universal mother is always so gracious to her children; the cawing of the rook or the crowing of the cock awakens us; the green things and the pretty flowers about the inn, which greet the eyes as we pull up the blinds, and the sniff of fresh morning air which a short stroll before breakfast gives us, make a splendid start for the day, so different from the usual beginning of city life. The whole day is spent in the open air, walking or driving, or lolling upon sunny braes at luncheon, amid brooks and wild flowers, and the hum of bees, the songs of birds, and the grateful scent of new-mown hay. And when night comes we fall asleep, with the sense of dropping softly upon banks of flowers without a thorn. Tell me if such a life for a few weeks now and then is not the best cure for most of the serious ills of this high-pressure age! Every man who can afford it should give it a trial. If overworked, he should go to find the cure—if well, he should certainly go in order to keep so.

We all need to learn what the poet says:

> "Better that man and nature were familiar friends;
> That part of man is worst which touches this base life;
> For though the ocean in its inmost depths be pure,
> Yet the salt fringe which daily licks the shore
> Is foul with sand."

I think the last line worthy of Shakespeare, even if it be the product of a poor young Glasgow poet. In this coaching life we touch the base every-day life of care and struggle at very few points indeed and hence our joy. We are deep in love with Nature, and true worshippers at her shrine have few sorrows.

Scotland's School Houses.

While revelling in the exquisite beauty of England—such quiet and peaceful beauty as we had never seen before—the thought often came to me that I should be compelled to assume the apologetic strain for my beloved Scotland. It could not possibly have such attractions to show as the more genial South, but so far from this being so, as I have already said, there was scarcely a morning or afternoon during which the triumphant inquiry was not made, "What do you think of Scotland noo?" Of all that earned for Scotland the first place in our hearts I mention the pretty stone school-houses, with teacher's residence and garden attached, which were seen in almost every village; and if I had no other foundation than this upon which to predict the continued intellectual ascendency of Scotland and an uninterrupted growth of its people in every department of human achievement, I should unhesitatingly rest it upon these school-houses. A people which passes through the parish school in its youth cannot lose its grasp, or fall far behind in the race. Indeed, compared with the thorough education of the masses, the lives and quarrels of politicians seem petty in the extreme. It is with education as with righteousness, seek it first and all political blessings must be added unto you. It is the only sure foundation upon which to rear the superstructure of a great State, and how happy I am to boast that Scotland is not going to yield the palm in this most important of all work! No, not even to the Republic. From what I saw of the new schools, I'll back their scholars against any lot of American children to-day; but I admit one great lack: the former would strike you as somewhat too deferential, disposed to bow too much to their superiors in station, while American boys are said to be born repeating the Declaration of Independence. No more valuable lesson can be taught a lad than this: that he is born the equal of the prince, and what privileges the prince has are unjustly denied him. It would do Scotch boys good to hear my young American nephews upon the doctrine that one man "is as good as another and a good deal better." Of the sights which cause me to lose temper, one is to see a splendid young Briton, a real manly fellow, standing mum like a duffer when he is asked why the son of a Guelph or of any other family should have a privilege denied to him. Are you less a man? Have not you had as honest parents and a better grandfather? Why do you stand this injustice? And then he has nothing to say. Well, I have sometimes thought I have noticed the cheek a little redder. That is always a consolation. Thank God! we have nothing like this in America. Our young men carry in their knapsacks a President's seal, and no one is born to any rank or position above them. Under the starry flag there are equal rights for all. It will be so in Scotland perhaps ere I die (D. V.). If I had the schooling of young Scotland I would make every class repeat in the morning before lessons:

> "If thou hast said I am not peer
> To any lord in Scotland here,
> Highland or lowland, far or near,
> Lord Angus, thou hast lied."

I would teach them the new meaning of that stirring verse, and tell them that the lad who did not believe himself the peer of any man born and entitled to every privilege "might do for an Austrian, a Russian, a Prussian, or an Italian," but never would be much of a Scotchman—never.

Popular Amusements.

I do not think I have spoken of the announcements of amusements seen everywhere during the trip throughout the rural districts: band competitions, cricket matches, flower shows, wrestling matches, concerts, theatricals, holiday excursions, races, games, rowing matches, football contests, and sports of all kinds. We are surprised at their number, which gives incontestable evidence of the fact that the British people work far less and play far more than their American cousins do. No toilers, rich or poor, like the Americans! The band competitions are unknown here, but no doubt we shall soon follow so good an example and try them. The bands of a district meet and compete for prizes, which stirs up wholesome rivalry and leads to excellence. We saw eight gathered for competition in one little town which we passed, and the interest excited by the meet was so great as to put the town *en fête*. I do not know any feature of British life which would strike an American more forcibly than these contests. We should try one here, and, by and by, why not an international contest—the Dunfermline band playing the "Star-Spangled

Banner," and the Pittsburgh performers "Rule Britannia." Yes, that's right; I insist upon "Rule Britannia"—that is the nation's song; I am growing tired of "God Save the Queen"—even such a model as the present one—for the strain is only personal, after all. I wish Her Majesty well, but I love my country more. "Rule Britannia" is the national song.

I hope Americans will find some day more time for play, like their wiser brethren upon the other side.

We came to the crossing of the Spey to-day to find that the long high bridge was undergoing extensive repairs and closed to travel. In America it would never have occurred to us that a bridge could be closed while being rebuilt, but in the science of bridge-building British engineers are a generation behind us, because they have not had to build so many. However, there was nothing for it but to follow down the stream until another bridge was found. When we did find it, we saw a notice prohibiting loads beyond two tons from crossing. It was a light iron structure (perhaps a Tay blunder upon a small scale). The wind was whistling like a fiend about our ears as it came roaring down the glen; all pleasant while we were in the woods skirting the river with our backs to it, but when we turned to cross it seemed as if we should be blown bodily from the top of the coach. Everything was taken off the top, and we all dismounted. Perry and Joe drove over, while we all walked, some of us on the lee side of the coach for shelter, and in a few minutes we were so sheltered in the glen again as scarcely to know there was a breath of air stirring; but these "Highland homes where tempests blow" know what gales are. We have had great blows now and then at some high points crossing the moors, for the hills you rarely cross; these you have to avoid, but to-day was the only time we were compelled to dismount.

The Last Luncheon.

We had not far to drive before we reached the pretty little burn which falls into the Findhorn, the spot selected for the last luncheon.

This spot seemed made to order; the burn, the fire, the mossy grass, the wild river, the moor and glen, all here. Down sat the Charioteers for the last happy luncheon together. We were all so dangerously near the brink of sad regret that a bold effort was necessary to steer clear of thoughts which pressed upon us. We had to laugh for fear we might cry, the smile ever lies so near the tear. It *had* to be a lively luncheon, that was all there was about it; and when duty calls it doesn't take much to start our boys to frolic. A few empty bags which we had used for horse-feed in emergencies suggested a sack-race. Such roars of laughter when one or the other of the too ambitious contestants went to grass! This was a capital diversion. Any one looking down upon us (but in these lonely glens no eye is there to see) would never have imagined that this sport was started only as a means to prevent the travellers becoming mournful enough for a funeral. A little management is a great thing; it pulled us through the last luncheon with only tears of laughter.

"In, Joe! Right, Perry! Sound the horn! All aboard for Inverness!" There was something in the thought, "We have done it," which kept us from regret, although the rebuke came sharply from the ladies, as one pointed out another milestone, "Oh, don't, please!" With every white stone passed there was a mile less of Arcadia to enjoy. Over moor and dale lies the way, a beautiful drive, gradually descending for many miles, from about twelve hundred and fifty feet above the sea level at Dalwhinnie to a few hundred only near Inverness.

At last the call is made, "Stop, Perry! Capital of the Highlands, all hail! Three rousing cheers for bonnie Inverness!" There she lies so prettily upon the Moray Frith, surrounded by fields of emerald green, an unusually grand situation and a remarkably beautiful town. We stopped long upon the hill-top to enjoy the picture spread out below. The Charioteers will forget much ere their entrance into Inverness fades from the memory. A telegram from friend G., conveyed to us the congratulations of our Wolverhampton connection upon the triumphant success of our expedition, to which something like this was sent: "Thanks! We arrived at the end of this earthly paradise at six o'clock this evening. When shall we look upon its like again?"

* * * * *

INVERNESS, August 3.

Inverness.

It was Saturday, 6 P.M., August 3d, exactly seven weeks and a day after leaving Brighton, when we entered Inverness and sat down in our parlor at the Caledonian Hotel. Up went the flags as usual; dinner was ordered; then came mutual congratulations upon the success of the journey just finished. Not one of the thirty-two persons who had at various times travelled with us ever missed a meal, or had been indisposed from fatigue or exposure. Even Ben had been improved by the journey. Nor had the coach ever to wait five minutes for any one; we had breakfasted, lunched, and dined together, and not one had ever inconvenienced the company by failing to be in time.

How shall I render the unanimous verdict of the company upon the life we had led?

"I never was so happy in my life. No, Aaleck, not even upon my wedding journey." That is the verdict of one devoted young wife, given in presence of her husband.

"I haven't been so happy since my father took me fishing, and I wasn't as happy then," was Aaleck's statement.

"Oh, Andrew, I have been a young girl again!" We all know who said that, Miss Velvety.

"I can't help it, but I don't want to speak of it just now. It's too sad." Prima Donna, this was a slightly perilous line to follow, for the heart was evidently near the mouth there.

"To think of it, Naig, I have to go home to-morrow." That was Eliza.

"Jerusalem the golden! it would make a wooden Indian jump, this life would." No need of putting a name to that, Bennie, my lad.

"Andrew, I've just been in a dream of happiness all the time." That was oor Davie.

"I never expect to be as happy for seven weeks again," met with a chorus of supporters.

The Queen Dowager, however, put us all in a more gleeful mood by her verdict: "Well, I expect to have another coaching trip yet. You'll see! He can't help doing more of this, and I'll be there. He can't keep *me* at home!" And her hearty laugh and a clap of her hands above her head brought us all merrily to dinner. She is very often a true prophet. We shall see, we shall see!

After dinner we strolled about the city and admired its many beauties, especially the pretty Ness, which flows through the town to the sea. Its banks and islands constitute one of the finest of pleasure-grounds for the people, and many a lover's tale, I trow, has been told in the shady walks beside it. I felt quite sentimental myself, sauntering along between the gloaming and the mirk with one of the young ladies. The long, long gloaming of the north adds immensely to the charms of such a journey as this we have just taken. These are the sweetly precious hours of the day.

Macbeth's Castle.

At Inverness we are again on classic ground; for Macbeth had a castle there, which good King Duncan visited, and of which he said:

> "This castle hath a pleasant seat: the air
> Nimbly and sweetly recommends itself
> Unto our gentle senses."

It was razed by Malcolm III. or Canmore, Duncan's son, who built a new castle not far from its site. This latter fortress existed until about the middle of the last century, when it was blown up by the troops of Charles Edward Stuart. Portions of its walls may still be seen. Culloden field, too, is hard by, and all the country round is rich in ruined keeps and towers.

On reassembling in our parlor an ominous lack of hilarity prevailed. We did manage, however, to get the choir up to the point of giving this appropriate song with a slight variation:

> "Happy we've been a' thegither,
> Happy we've been in ane and a',
> Blyther folk ne'er coached thegither,
> Sad are we to gang awa'."

(Chorus).

It wasn't much of a success. We were not in tune, nor in time either. Joe and Perry were to come at ten to say good-by. Here the serious business of life pressed upon us, escape being impossible. We had to meet it at last. They came and received the thanks and adieux of all. I handed them notes certifying to all coming coaching parties that fortunate indeed would be their lot were Perry and Joe to take them in charge. Joey responded in a speech which so riveted our attention during delivery that not one of us could recall a sentence when he ceased. This is one of the sincere regrets of the travellers, for assuredly a copy of that great effort would have given the record inestimable value. It was a gem. I have tried to catch it, but only one sentence comes to me: "And has for the 'osses, sir, they are better than when we started, sir; then they 'ad flabby flesh, sir; now they're neat an' 'ardy." So are we all of us, Joey, just like the 'osses; "neat an' 'ardy," fit for walk, run, or climb, and bang-up to everything.

We had all next day to enjoy Inverness. What a fine climate it has as compared with the Highlands south of it! Vegetation is luxuriant here and the land fertile. One would naturally expect all to be bleak and bare so far north, but that Gulf Stream which America sends over to save the precious tight little isle from being a region of ice makes it delightful in summer and not extremely cold even in winter. We are assured that the climate of Inverness is more genial than that of Edinburgh, which is not saying very much for the capital of the North surely, but still it is something.

* * * * *

CALEDONIAN HOTEL,
INVERNESS, August 5, evening.

Farewell to the Coach.

General Manager, at dinner.

To waiter: "What time do we start in the morning?"

Waiter: "The *omnibus* starts at seven, sir."

Shakespearean Student—"Ah! There was the weight which pulled us down. The omnibus! Farewell the neighing steeds, the spirit-stirring horn, whose sweet throat awakened the echoes o'er mountain and glen. Farewell, the Republican banner, and all the pride, pomp, and circumstance of glorious coaching, farewell! The Charioteers' occupation's gone."

First Miltonic Reciter—

> "From morn till noon,
> From noon till dewy eve,
> A summer's day we fell."

Our fall from our own four-in-hand to a public omnibus—oh, what a fall was there, my countrymen!—involved the loss of many a long summer's day to us, for long as they had been the sun ever set too soon.

It was all up after this. Perry and Joe, the coach and the horses, were speeding away by rail to their homes; we were no longer *the* coaching party, but only ordinary tourists buying our tickets like other people instead of travelling as it were in style upon annual passes. But fate was merciful to us even in this extremity; we were kept from the very lowest stage of human misery by finding ourselves alone and all together in the omnibus; our party just filled it. If it was only a hotel omnibus, as one of the young ladies said, it was all our own yet, as was the MacLean boat at the flood, and the ladies, dear souls, managed to draw some consolation from that.

We returned from Inverness by the usual tourist route: canal and boat to Oban, where we rested over night, thence next day to Glasgow. Under any other circumstances I think this part of the journey would have been delightful. The scene indelibly impressed upon our minds is that we saw at night near Ballachulish. I remember a party of us agreed that what we then saw could never be forgotten. But Black alone could paint it. It is saying much for any combination of the elements when not one nor two, but more of a party like ours stand and whisper at rare intervals of the sublime and awful grandeur which fascinates them into silence; never am I lifted up apparently so close to the Infinite as when amid such weird, uncanny scenes as these. We had an hour of this that night, fitting close to our life in the Highlands of Scotland.

The First Separation.

The first separation came at Greenock. The Queen Dowager, and Mr. and Mrs. K. disembarked there for Paisley. The others continued by boat to Glasgow and enjoyed the sail up the Clyde very much. It was Saturday, a holiday for the workers. The miles of shipyards were still, "no sound of hammers clanking rivets up," that fine sunny day, but as we passed close to them we saw the iron frames of the future monsters of the deep, the Servia, Alaska, and others destined to bear the palm for a short time, and then to give place to others still greater, till the voyage between England and America will be only a five-day pleasure excursion, and there will be "two nations, but one people." God speed the day! But the old land must come after a time up to Republicanism! I make a personal matter of that, Lafayette, my boy, as Mulberry Sellers says. No monarchy need apply. We draw the line at this. All men were created free and *equal*. Brother Jonathan takes very little "stock" in a people who do not believe that fundamental principle.

We landed at the Broomielaw, whither father and mother and Tom and I sailed thirty odd years ago, on the 800-ton ship Wiscasset, and began our seven weeks' voyage to the land of promise, poor emigrants in quest of fortune; but, mark you, not without thoughts in the radical breasts of our parents that it was advisable to leave a land which tolerated class distinctions for the government of the people, by the people and for the people, which welcomed them to its fold and insured for their sons, as far as laws can give it, equality with the highest and a fair and free field for the exercise of their powers.

My father saw through not only the sham but the injustice of rank, from king to knight, and loved America because she knows no difference in her sons. He was a Republican, aye, every inch, and his sons glory in that and follow where he led.

I remember well that our friends stood on the quay and waved farewell. Had their adieu been translated it would have read:

> "Now may the fair goddess Fortune
> Fall deep in love with thee,
> Prosperity be thy page."

Thanks to the generous Republic which stood with open arms to receive us, as she stands to-day to welcome the poor of the world to share with her own sons upon equal terms the glorious heritage with which she is endowed—thanks to it, prosperity has indeed been our page.

At St. Enoch's Station Hotel, Glasgow, another separation of the party took place. A delegation of five of our members were sent to investigate the Irish question and report at Queenstown. Miss E. L. returned to Dunfermline. Miss F. and Mr. and Mrs. K. were visiting the Queen Dowager at Paisley. Harry and I ran down to see friend Richards at his basic process at Eston, stopping over night at York and Durham, however, to enjoy once more the famous cathedrals and hear the exquisite music.

* * * * *

LIVERPOOL, August 13.

Embarkation for Home.

We sailed to-day in the Algeria, the great Servia having been delayed. Many were there to see us off, including four or five Charioteers. The English are, as Davie said, "a kindly people," a warm-hearted, affectionate race, and as true as steel. When you once have them you have them forever. There was far more than the usual amount of tears and kisses among the ladies. One would have thought our American and English women were not cousins, but sisters. The men were, as befitting their colder natures, much less demonstrative. There seems never to be a final good-by on shipboard; at every ringing of the bell another tender embrace and another solemn promise to write soon are given. But at last all our friends are upon the tug, the huge vessel moves, one rope after another is cast off, handkerchiefs wave, kisses are thrown, write soons exchanged, and the tug is off in one direction and we in another. Some one broke the momentary silence and brought the last round of cheers with the talismanic call "Skid, Joe! Right, Perry!" That touched all hearts with remembrance of the happy, happy days, the happiest of our lives. So parted the two branches of the Gay Charioteers.

At Queenstown we received the Irish contingent, who had enjoyed their week in the Emerald Isle. Very nice indeed was the report, but with this quite unnecessary addenda, "But, of course, nothing to coaching." That goes without saying in our ranks.

The Algeria was a great ship in her day; now she is sold to a freight line. But when she does not give a good account of herself in a hurricane do not pin your faith in any iron ship. You may still, however, believe that one of steel like the Servia will stand anything. She has at least double the strength of any iron steamer afloat. When she does not outride the tempest, you may give up in earnest and decide, like Mrs. Partington at sea, "never to trust yourself so far out of the reach of Providence again."

On Wednesday morning, August 24th, the party reached New York again, and were finally disbanded. Two or three of the most miserable hours I ever spent were those at the St. Nicholas Hotel, where the Queen Dowager, Ben, and I lunched alone before starting for Cresson. Even Ben had to take an earlier train for Pittsburgh, and I exclaimed: "All our family gone! I feel so lonely, so deserted; not one remains." But the Queen was equal to the emergency. "Oh, you don't count me, then! You have still one that sticks to you." Oh, yes, indeed, sure of that, old lady.

> "The good book tells of one
> Who sticks closer than a brother;
> But who will dare to say there's one
> Sticks closer than a mother!"

(Original poetry for the occasion.)

Final Farewells.

These horrid partings again; but whatever the future has in store for those who made the excursion recorded here, I think I can safely say that they could not wish their dearest friend a happier life than that led from June 1st to August 24th by the Gay Charioteers.

Those who have mounted the coach become, as it were, by virtue of that act members of an inner circle; a band of union knits them closely together. To a hundred dear, kind friends in the Beautiful Land we send thanks and greeting. Their kindness to us can never be forgotten, for they soon taught us to feel that it was not a foreign land which we had visited after all, but the dear old home of our fathers.

Forever and ever may the parent land and the child land grow fonder and fonder of each other, and their people mingle more and more till they become as one and the same. All good educated Americans love England, for they know that she alone among the nations of the world

> "On with toil of heart and knees and hand
> Through the long gorge to the far light hath won
> Her path upward and prevailed."

She it was who pointed out to America what to plant, and how, and where. The people of England should love America, for she has taught them in return that all the equal rights and privileges of man they are laboring for at home are bearing goodly fruit in the freer atmosphere of the West. May the two peoples, therefore, grow in love for each other, and with this fond wish, and many a sad farewell, the Gay Charioteers disband, forever afterward in life to rally round each other in case of need at the mystic call of "Skid, Joe," "Right, Perry;" and certain of this, that whatever else fades from the memory, the recollection of our coaching trip from Brighton to Inverness remains a sacred possession forever.

THE RECORD.

MILES.

Date	Place	Miles
June 17	BRIGHTON (The Grand Hotel)	
June 17	GUILDFORD (The White Lion)	42
June 18 and 19	WINDSOR (The Castle)	32
June 20	READING (The Queen's)	27
June 21	OXFORD (The Clarendon)	34
June 22	BANBURY (The White Lion)	23
June 23	STRATFORD-ON-AVON (The Red Horse)	18
June 24	COVENTRY (The Queen's)	22
June 25 to 30	WOLVERHAMPTON (English Homes, best of all)	33
July 1	LICHFIELD (The Swan)	20
July 2 and 3	DOVEDALE (The Izaak Walton)	26
July 4	CHATSWORTH (The Edensor)	24
July 5	BUXTON (The Palace)	26
July 6	MANCHESTER (The Queen's)	23
July 7	CHORLEY (Anderton Hall)	14
July 8	PRESTON (The Victoria)	16
July 9 and 10	LANCASTER (The County)	29
July 11	KENDAL (King's Arms)	22
July 12	GRASSMERE (Prince of Wales)	18
July 13	KESWICK (The Keswick)	12
July 14	PENRITH (The Crown)	16
July 15	CARLISLE (The County and Station)	16
July 16 and 17	DUMFRIES (The Commercial)	32
July 18	SANQUHAR (The Queensberry)	28
July 19	OLD CUMNOCK (Dumfries Arms)	29
July 20	DOUGLAS (Douglas Arms)	28
July 21 to 26	EDINBURGH (The Royal)	44

July 27 and 28	DUNFERMLINE (The City Arms)	16
July 29	PERTH (The Royal George)	32
July 30 and 31	PITLOCHRIE (Fisher's Hotel)	33
August 1	DALWHINNIE (The Loch Ericht)	32
August 2	BOAT O' GARTEN (The Boat o' Garten)	35
August 3	INVERNESS (The Caledonian)	29
	TOTAL MILES,	831

Lector House believes that a society develops through a two-fold approach of continuous learning and adaptation, which is derived from the study of classic literary works spread across the historic timeline of literature records. Therefore, we aim at reviving, repairing and redeveloping all those inaccessible or damaged but historically as well as culturally important literature across subjects so that the future generations may have an opportunity to study and learn from past works to embark upon a journey of creating a better future.

This book is a result of an effort made by Lector House towards making a contribution to the preservation and repair of original ancient works which might hold historical significance to the approach of continuous learning across subjects.

HAPPY READING & LEARNING!

LECTOR HOUSE LLP
E-MAIL: lectorpublishing@gmail.com